MAKE ME A MAN!

Masculinity, Hinduism,
and Nationalism in India

SIKATA BANERJEE

STATE UNIVERSITY OF NEW YORK PRESS

Published by
STATE UNIVERSITY OF NEW YORK PRESS
ALBANY

© 2005 State University of New York

All rights reserved

Printed in the United States of America

For information, address
State University of New York Press
194 Washington Avenue, Suite 305, Albany, NY 12210-2365

Production, Laurie Searl
Marketing, Michael Campochiaro

Library of Congress Cataloging-in-Publication Data

Banerjee, Sikata.
   Make me a man! : masculinity, Hinduism, and nationalism in India / Sikata Banerjee.
   p. cm. — (SUNY series in religious studies)
   Includes bibliographical references and index.
   ISBN 0-7914-6367-2 (hardcover) — ISBN 0-7914-6368-0 (pbk.)
   1. Nationalism—Religious aspects—Hinduism. 2. Masculinity—Religious aspects—Hinduism. 3. Hinduism and state—India. 4. Nationalism and feminism—India—Religious aspects. I. Title. II. Series.
BL1215.S83B36 2005
155.3'32'0954—dc22

                                                                                    2004006922

10   9   8   7   6   5   4   3   2   1

Make Me a Man!

SUNY SERIES IN RELIGIOUS STUDIES

Harold Coward, editor

O Thou, Mother of the Universe, vouchsafe manliness unto me!

O Thou, Mother of Strength, take away my weakness,

Take away my unmanliness and make me a Man!

—Swami Vivekananda, Nineteenth-Century Indian Nationalist

Contents

Acknowledgments

A grant from the Social Science and Humanities Research Council of Canada made research for this book possible. I am also grateful to all the women and men in India who were incredibly hospitable and took the time to answer my endless questions. The Rockefeller Foundation enabled me to spend a month as a resident scholar at the Villa Serbelloni in Bellagio, Italy, where I finished up this manuscript among luxurious surroundings. Conversations with my fellow residents clarified my thoughts and stimulated my writing. Thank you, February Group! Thanks are also due to Christine St. Peter, Annalee Lepp, and Helen Rezanowich, my colleagues at the University of Victoria, who made the Bellagio trip possible by cheerfully covering my responsibilities as Chair. I would also like to thank Harold Coward for his encouragement and support. Finally, this project could not have been completed without my husband, Dan, who listened, edited, provided support during periods of doubt, and patiently put up with the chaos of an ongoing book project. Thank you.

ONE

Introduction

Constructs of Nation and Gender

[F]or the creation of men and women with muscles of iron and nerves of steel to fulfill their duties in the great up-hill battle of nation-building that await us today . . . is the paramount duty of all national-minded children of India.
—Anthony Elenjimittam, *Philosophy and Action of the R.S.S. for the Hind Swaraj*

You will understand the *Gita* better with your biceps, your muscles a little stronger. . . . You will understand the *Upanishads* better and the glory of Atman, when your body stands upon your feet, and you feel yourselves as men.
—Swami Vivekananda, nineteenth-century Indian nationalist

Characteristics associated with "manliness," such as toughness, courage, power, independence, and even physical strength, have, throughout history, been those most valued in the conduct of politics, particularly international politics. Frequently, manliness has also been associated with violence and the use of force, a type of behavior that, when conducted in the international arena, has been valorized.
—J. Ann Tickner, *Gender in International Relations: Feminist Perspectives on Achieving Global Security*

A GROUP OF YOUNG, tough Hindu men follow my American husband, who is white, and myself along the River Ganges in the holy city of Varanasi. They call out to me, tauntingly, "What does he have that we don't have?" This male behavior in conjunction with two powerful images—a young Hindu man holding a staff, face distorted in anger, on the cover of an Indian news magazine reporting on Hindu-Muslim riots, and the presence of saffron-robed

Hindu *sadhvis* (celibate women who have renounced worldly pleasures) stridently calling for aggressive action against (perceived) Islamic betrayers of the Hindu nation—captures a provocative nationalist narrative currently at work in modern India. A particular interpretation of manhood—armed masculinity—informs them. When armed masculinity intersects with the idea of nation, it disseminates an ideology centered on enacting aggressive, sometimes violent defense of the national community.

The youthful male figure on the cover of the Indian magazine is representative of an ideology, one linking armed masculinity and nation, that is disseminated by a network of powerful Indian organizations. The *sadhvis* have erased outer markers of their womanhood—jewelry, makeup, and feminine dress—to enter the realm of this discourse. The young men who followed my husband and myself had signaled their distress at seeing me, an Indian woman, with a white man; obviously, their anxiety stemmed from perceived slights to Indian male honor. This incident was by no means an isolated event but one of several similar encounters. In another example, a muscular young man in Mumbai stepped up to my husband and claimed, "First you rule us, then you steal our land, and now you take our women." These experiences raise serious questions: If an Indian woman chooses a white man over an Indian man, is she denigrating an Indian man's virility and strength, that is, markers of his manliness? In the Indian context, does this anxiety draw on memories of colonialism and British critiques of Indian manhood? And what does this manhood have to do with nation? Male and female bodies as well as societal ideas defining cultural interpretations of masculinities and femininities are potent metaphors for expressing nation.

In this book, I examine a particular intersection of armed masculinity and nation: Hindu nationalism (Hindutva). I argue that two dominant models of masculine Hinduism—the Hindu soldier and the warrior-monk—have mediated a visible and powerful interpretation of Hindu nationalism in India. These images emerged out of the interaction between the British and Indian colonial elite in nineteenth- and early twentieth-century India. The British had categorized Indian men as the "effeminate other" by using a gender hierarchy rooted in a specific Anglo-Protestant interpretation of manhood—Christian manliness—defined by values of martial prowess, muscular strength, rationality, and individualism. Some Indian elite resisted this categorization by forging an oppositional masculine identity that I term masculine Hinduism. Masculine Hinduism has had considerable impact on the modern interpretation of Hindu nationalism evoked by powerful Hindu organizations—the Rashtriya Swayamsevak Sangh (RSS) and Vishwa Hindu Parishad (VHP)—and political parties, the Shiv Sena and the Bharatiya Janata Party (BJP), leader of the last ruling coalition in the Indian Parliament. It is important to acknowledge that although these organizations may not represent the entire spectrum of Hindu nationalist activism in India, currently they are the most visible and powerful.

This masculinization of nationalism carries important implications for women's activism. Do women get written out of this masculine narrative? I argue that they do not. Women in visible Hindu nationalist groups such as the Rashtriya Sevika Samiti (Samiti) and Sadhvi Shakti Parishad (Parishad), affiliated with the RSS and VHP respectively, draw on images of women as heroic mother, chaste wife, and celibate masculinized warrior to negotiate their way into this landscape. Careful negotiation within this masculinist landscape, however, has created tension with ideas of feminism in Indian society. For example, if certain Indian feminists argue that domestic violence or women's limited access to power is tied to women's roles as wife and mother in the family, then can we contend that Hindu organizations such as the Samiti and the Parishad are antifeminist? I will argue that any analysis of this issue cannot be contained within the binary opposition feminism/antifeminism. Rather, analysis needs to be rooted in a more complex and nuanced idea of feminism and "woman" in the Indian context. Notions of female virtue and chastity inherent in Hindutva interpretations of female identity form the point of departure for exploring the relationship between Hindu nationalist women and feminism.

The nationalism defined by masculine Hinduism is a unique cultural manifestation that fits into the schema of a more general narrative. For example, consider two seemingly disparate images: a young Israeli woman dressed in army fatigues, eyes hidden behind mirrored sunglasses, patrolling Jerusalem and the catastrophic sight of the Twin Towers of the World Trade Center crashing to the ground on September 11. The young Israeli soldier, like the sadhvi, also has shed all explicit expression of her femininity (clothing, cosmetics, and jewelry). The tension between certain Arab elite and the United States as the "other" of an amorphous pan-Arabic nation plays out in the language and action of martial prowess, militarism, and violence. Osama bin Laden poses with a machine gun among his followers (all men), attacks symbols of American capitalism and military might (to prove his masculinity?), and interprets the massive destruction in New York City as a symbol of American weakness, rooted in moral corruption. President George Bush, the second, in the meantime, with his vocal advisor Donald Rumsfeld, Secretary of Defense, vows to assert American strength, martial prowess, and military might in response.

The gendered story of nationalism nested within masculine Hinduism as well as in the images described above begins with a dominant political doctrine defined by the idea of a nation or a people. It usually locates an "other" that is used to reinforce communal unity. In other words, a coherent community exists because "we" are ethnically, linguistically, religiously, and/or ideologically distinct from "them." It has become a truism to acknowledge that nationalism, in the oft-quoted words of Benedict Anderson (1991), is imagined. The theoretical rooting of the process of nation-building in imagination denies malicious intent to deceive or falsify; rather, it highlights the creative attempts on the part of communities to build an intersubjective identity marked by common cultural myths, symbols, heroes, and heroines.

Identity draws on the grammar of everyday life. In other words, daily communication takes place because ordinary people have a shared cultural context that forms the basis for why they feel an affinity toward a certain identity and with other members who share it. Identities are fluid and multiple. They are fluid in that over time new interpretations of identity may emerge. For example, the relational meaning of the American and Indian nations has been renegotiated over the course of the past hundred years within a context of changing demographic patterns and emerging identity politics. Identities are multiple in that during one particular period in a specific nation-state various interpretations of identity contesting for dominance may exist, or even new readings of an identity may emerge to challenge a dominant interpretation. For example, currently, the communities of America and India are open to multiple interpretations as minority groups resist official, mainstream views of nation within these states. Thus, the process of imagining a nation is contested as well as being historically, socially, and politically constituted. One of the more important dichotomies that has shaped the debate on nationalism is that of civic versus cultural nationalism.

In Bosnia, the nation is defined by religion (Christianity versus Islam) and ethnicity (Serbian versus Croatian); in Northern Ireland the marker of the national community is religion (Protestant versus Catholicism) as it is in Algeria, Egypt, and Iran (Islam versus non-Islamic infidels). In Germany, France, and England, certain groups like the National Front of France and the British National Party have used race (white versus non-white) to imagine a nation, and members of the French community in Canada have used both language and religion to distinguish themselves from the so-called English nation. These constructions of nation are seen by some scholars (e.g., Greenfeld, 1992; Ignatieff, 1994) as examples of "cultural nationalism," that is, a view of nation defined by markers rooted in religion, language, or ethnicity. The idea of "we the people" may vary over time in one cultural context or historical period, with competing views of cultural nationalism even occurring within one society. Finally, internationally, interpretations of cultural nationalism will also differ. In other words, most probably the idea of a Serbian or Egyptian or Quebecois nation has changed over time or within a particular historical era. Multiple ways may exist in which Serbians or Quebecois interpret cultural nationalism. Serbians or Egyptians or the Irish obviously construct the nation dissimilarly. Some scholars view cultural nationalism with suspicion, believing that volatile emotions arising from an inflexible loyalty to a certain cultural category are exclusionary and circumvent possibilities of compromise, and, as a result, may provide the basis for conflict.

In contrast, civic nationalism purports to define nationhood by rejecting cultural markers and emphasizing allegiance to an ideology (e.g., democracy) and legal rights (e.g., a constitution guaranteeing individual freedoms and rights). Supposedly, such markers transcend religion or linguistic or ethnic affiliation to create a nationalism perceived to be more open to negotiation and, consequently, less prone to violent conflict.

The tension between cultural and civic nationalism is played out in the Indian context. "Communalism" or cultural nationalism in India refers to prejudices dividing and defining communities (usually Hindus and Muslims). The term sometimes is used to describe the politics of Hindutva because many believe that parties espousing this viewpoint do not support religious pluralism and hence can construct policies that may violate minority rights or in some cases justify outright aggression against minorities. Communalism or cultural nationalism is seen in opposition to secularism or civic nationalism.

Civic nationalism is silent about the notion of "us and them," claims to be inclusionary (as opposed to the potentially exclusionary implications of cultural nationalism), and hence assumes that the issue of "us versus them" by definition will disappear. In reality, of course, this rarely happens, and the boundaries between cultural and civic nationalism become blurred. According to Anderson (1991) this slippage occurs because abstract formulations (democracy, socialism)—empty of the building blocks of life (religion, ethnicity, language)—address human fears about day-to-day struggle with impatient silence and may not be adequate to attract human loyalty. Resolute, nonemotional levels of thinking can neither elicit nor sustain the degrees of loyalty necessary for a nation to survive and, if need be, to persuade its citizens to die for its sake. Put another way, historical evidence seems to indicate that passionate human loyalty reaches unprecedented heights when the nation, imagined as a monolithic community, faces another undifferentiated community constructed as the enemy. (For example, we saw the outpouring of American patriotism in the wake of the September 11 attacks.) As elites and masses draw on nationalism to support sovereignty and independence, even those nationalisms that are firmly civic can easily slip into the realm of cultural nationalism. For example, when Americans feel pride at the sight of their flag, are they responding to the abstract rights enshrined in their nation's Constitution or resonating to an imagined community peopled with English-speaking, white Christian descendants of the players of the American revolution? There is no way to disentangle the two; certainly, Martin Luther King, Jr., and Malcolm X, protesting cultural constructs of intolerance, perceived that America contained both cultural and civic nationalism.

In the interests of social order, some individuals, both elite and mass, try to control the slippage, while others perceive benefits in encouraging it, even to the extent of supporting violence in the name of nationalism. The implicit condemnation of cultural nationalism or the Indian interpretation, communalism, found in many works is based on fears that if passionate appeals based on intolerance and exclusion enter politics, they may easily be (mis)used to support ideas leading to violence. This complicated relationship between civic and cultural nationalism will form the implicit background of this study's gendered analysis of Hindu nationalism. The salient dichotomy shaping the construction of this national identity valorizes "we the people" as manly (strong, aggressive, brave in battle) while it denigrates an effeminized "other" as weak, passive, and cowardly.

Not until the emergence of feminist analysis has the gendered nature of imagined political identities been uncovered and deconstructed (e.g., Blom, Hall, and Hagemann, 2000; Enloe, 1989, 2000; Mayer, 2000; McClintock, Mufti, and Shohat, 1997; McClintock, 1995; Yuval-Davis and Anthias, 1989). But how precisely does gender play itself out within forms of nationalisms? Usually, a nationalism is gendered in that it draws on socially constructed ideas of masculinity and femininity to shape female and male participation in nation-building as well as the manner in which the nation is embodied in the imagination of self-professed nationalists.

The values defining manhood, manliness, masculinity—perceived to be a collection of features necessary for being and becoming an adult male in specific cultural and historical contexts—will be illustrated in the narrative of nationalism considered in this book. Using masculinity as a point of departure, this book goes on to explore the location of women, womanhood, and femininity in the Hindu nation. If sex refers to the physical attributes signaling biological male and female bodies, then gender is the collection of cultural traits deemed socially necessary for acting as adult men and women in specific moments of history within a single culture. There is no biological link between sex and gender per se; men can take on "feminine" traits and women can take on "masculine" ones. However, such crossover may impose social costs, such as ostracism, ridicule, and even bodily harm on both men and women.

In the slightly paraphrased words of Simone de Beauvoir, one is not "born a man" but becomes one. Moreover, cultural understanding of this process of becoming a man has implications for female participation in all social spaces including nationalist politics. As Anne McClintock (1993) points out, no nation has been equitable in its distribution of resources to men and women. Enloe (1989) describes nation as a masculinized space springing from masculine hopes. In other words, masculinized imaginations construct the dominant view of nation; indeed, it may be feasible to envision the nation as a male fantasy. Thus, women can enter this male fantasy according to the terms of masculine rules or overthrow it to create an equally powerful female fantasy or choose to renegotiate a completely different vision by transcending the binary dichotomies of gender. But whatever path is chosen, the terms of masculinity and its historical evolution need to be examined. Susan Faludi's book *Stiffed* (1999) and Gardiner's edited collection *Masculinity Studies and Feminist Theory* (2002) are two of many contemporary works that signify a feminist interest in the construction of masculinity. Further, in the passage below taken from her study of gender and nationalism, Tamar Mayer (2000) also calls for a focus on masculinity:

> Much of this scholarship has focused on women's marginality *vis à vis* the construction of nation and as a result these discussions have, for the most part, neglected to analyze *men* as an equally constructed category. This imbalance has arisen, I believe, from Women's Studies' tendency until recently to concentrate on recovering women's experience, without necessarily positioning it in the larger context of gender construction, and from the unmarked status of masculinity within the nation and in nationalist discourse. (p. 5)

My study will address this imbalance by focusing on masculinity within a specific construct of nation, that is, Hindutva, in India. It is one that offers a unique cultural configuration of a more general gendered narrative set within a dominant view of nationalism, wherein "the ideal of the glorified male warrior has been projected onto the behavior of states" (Hooper, 2001, p. 2). For the purposes of this book, the word "nation" will be substituted for "state." Existing gendered studies of nationalism in various cultural contexts buttress the idea of a connection between masculinity and nationalism.

Patriarchy and male dominance have meant that masculinity has been seen as immutable and natural. The dominant discourse, because it sets the terms for societal debate, does not have to examine or justify itself. It is there. It exists. But in reality, like other forms of identity, masculinity is historically, politically, and culturally constituted. As a result, in twenty-first-century United States or Canada or Britain or India there may be various competing forms of masculine identity. However, as Nagel (1998) claims, one form always becomes dominant:

> Whatever the historical or comparative limit of these various definitions and depictions of masculinity, scholars argue that at any time, in any place, there is an identifiable "normative" or "hegemonic" masculinity that sets the standards for male demeanour, thinking and action. (p. 247)

In the nineteenth, twentieth, and early twenty-first centuries, militarism formed and forms an important component of Anglo-American hegemonic masculinity (hereafter, hegemonic masculinity): "Soldiering is characterized as a manly activity requiring the 'masculine' traits of physical strength, action, toughness, capacity for violence. . . . It has historically been an important practice constitutive of masculinity" (Hooper, 2001, p. 47). Hooper (2001) identifies four ideal types of hegemonic masculinity: (1) the Greek citizen-warrior, wherein the manly citizen is characterized by a rational militarism; (2) the more domesticated, patriarchal Judeo-Christian model, rooted in the idea of paternal authority in the family; (3) the aristocratic ideal defined by male camaraderie, risk-taking, and military heroism; and finally (4) the Protestant bourgeois-rationalist model, emphasizing competition, individualism, reason, self-control, and self-denial (p. 65). To the list of these values, I would add the zero-sum notion of strength. Put another way, any attempt to negotiate or compromise is interpreted by all involved in this discourse of masculinity as weakness or a retreat from a position of power. These models of hegemonic masculinity also shape ideas of citizenship. Macchiavelli, for example, cast civic virtue, to be embodied by an ideal citizen, as virile political action wedded with armed masculinity. This masculine construction of citizenship was opposed to an effeminacy marked by weakness, impotency, and cowardice (Snyder, 1999, p. 24). Macchiavelli's vision has become a vital part of Anglo-American hegemonic masculinity. In using this model to order my narrative, it will become obvious that when men and women create a discourse centered on hegemonic masculinity, the ideal types discussed above are not completely discrete and do overlap.

Hegemonic masculinity has had a complex relationship with empire and imperialism. Research reveals clearly how the values of hegemonic masculinity colored the imperial lens through which British colonial administrators, military commanders, and historians categorized colonial subjects. Lord Macaulay (1878) claimed that "[t]he mission of England in the east is to elevate the people of India, to emancipate them from the chains of ignorance, error, and superstition, to lead them onward to a higher career of social, intellectual and political life" (p.3). This mission was a masculine affair: "In the 1850s Charles Kingsley helped create a masculinist image of an imperial English nation concerned with formal territorial expansion" (Wee, 1994, p. 66). But the process of masculine categorization guiding imperialism was dynamic. On the one hand, imperialism configured its ideas of hegemonic masculinities by defining itself against a supposedly effeminate colonial "other," and on the other hand, the colonized subject created a masculine cultural space that resisted this effeminization. With colonizer and colonized locked in struggle, the terms of which had been set by Britain's imperial authority, not surprisingly various nationalist responses to incorporating the values of hegemonic masculinity occurred. This incorporation did not merely duplicate British ideas but was itself an imaginative configuration of nationalist myths and icons based on traditional cultural ideas aimed at challenging alien colonial rule. Creation of imaginative constructs of an oppositional masculine identity is not limited to the Indian context; remarkably similar constructions are found in many other cultural settings.

In mid-nineteenth-century Ireland, for example, the nationalist discourse also became marked by values of hegemonic masculinity. McDevitt (1997) notes that "[t]he creations of the Gaelic Athletic Association (GAA) in 1884 and the subsequent standardization of hurling and Gaelic football marked . . . a nation-wide campaign to resurrect the physical stature of the manhood of Ireland, which was deemed debilitated because of the . . . effects of British rule" (p. 262). The Irish forged an ideology of "muscular Catholicism" in opposition to "muscular Christianity"—a concept that will form an integral part of my analysis—to assert their manliness. Masculinity was connected to the Gaelic games in many ways. They were seen to be a civilizing tendency by their imposition on the individual of team ideas (from the bourgeois rational model) of organization, discipline, and control. This configuration was meant to resist British depictions of the Irish as unruly, brutish, and lacking self-control. The GAA promoted "hurling," a dangerous type of sport that functioned as a metaphor for war. This link was further reinforced for the players by the retention of overlapping memberships in both the Association and various sectarian militia. Finally, the games helped define separate spheres for men and women within the nationalist terrain. For example, Ireland was represented as a woman—Eire, Erin, Mother Ireland, Cathleen ni Houlihan, and Shan Van Vocht—whom the manly warriors of Ireland were to protect with their lives if need be. As we shall see, this cultural metaphor—nation as woman (usually mother)—is also visible in Hindu nationalism. Most importantly, this masculinization of Ireland was coupled with a counter effeminization of British men, who were configured as weak, effete fops incapable of martial or athletic prowess (p. 272).

A similar masculinization of nationalism occurred in another colonized cultural space far away from Ireland—Palestine. Despite cultural differences, actors in this arena also resisted the impact of British imperialism rooted in ideas of hegemonic masculinity. The Palestinian national elite view liberation "as a transaction between men over the honor of a woman-mother whose ownership passes through paternity" (Massad, 1995, p. 473). The actors within Palestinian nationalism are masculine, "bourgeois-in-the-making, . . . young and able-bodied—free from the physical vulnerabilities of old age" (p. 479). According to Massad, the Zionist enemy is masculinized, and Palestinian nationalists are urged to equal the enemy in martial prowess and muscular strength as they defend Palestine, embodied as a nation as woman. Although he does not discuss in detail the cultural metaphors defining this masculine Palestinian identity, Massad is very clear that the forging of this vision was shaped by "European colonial culture as a paradigm through which tradition is (re)interpreted" (p. 468).

Finally, in an attempt to reinforce the reach of hegemonic masculinity, two other gendered nationalisms are presented: Australian and Serbian. In Serbian nationalism, again, the nationalist actors—defined by the values of hegemonic masculinity—fight to protect Mother Serbia. The feminine "has been employed to include virtually everyone—men and women alike—not conforming to the accepted 'nationalized' versions of masculinity" (Sofos, 1996, p. 76). Rape is seen as a tool of war. According to this masculinized Serbian nationalist narrative, Serbian women remained in danger of being raped by Kosovar Albanians and it was up to the Serbian manly warriors to protect them.

Australian nationalism also unfolded using the values of hegemonic masculinity. According to Australian national mythology, in the 1915 Battle of Gallipoli, male citizen soldiers—through their martial prowess, bravery, and physical strength—gave birth to the Australian nation. In other words, nation and manliness originate in war; indeed, war becomes the test of manliness and national independence. So, mothers and citizen-soldiers were connected by the act of "giving birth." According to Lake (1992) mothers gave birth to the soldiers who in turn gave birth to the Australian nation. But mothers were not equal in power or value to these male citizen-soldiers. The major actors within the nationalist terrain are masculinized; women's bodies associated with the feminine either become a threat to these masculine citizens because of their unpredictable sexuality or can only enter the fray in roles validated by hegemonic masculinity, for example, as mothers. In Lake's story of Australia, male martial heroism was the basis of nation-making.

The above examples emphasize clearly that masculinity, war, and nation create and inform each other. As George Mosse (1996) argues, "Nationalism, a movement which began and evolved parallel to modern masculinity, . . . adopted the masculine stereotype as one means of self-representation. . . . Modern masculinity from the very first was co-opted by the new nationalist movements of the nineteenth century" (p.7). Most importantly, masculinity needs an image against which it can define itself. Outsiders formed such an image and, more often than not, were constructed with effeminized qualities opposite to those of hegemonic masculinity; that is, outsiders were not strong, not martial, and so on. Further, even within the parameters of hegemonic masculinity, masculinity was multifaceted, never just the sole exercise of raw power. The next chapter's discussion of Christian manliness will illuminate this multiplicity.

The cases described above emphasize that hegemonic masculinity's connection with nation was not limited to the Western world but also found in the non-Western world (e.g., Palestine). In many non-Western cases, hegemonic masculinity became an integral defining component of the nation because of the impact of the British Empire's gaze as it categorized and evaluated its colonized subjects. The pivotal influence of British imperialism also can be highlighted by the example of the emergence of "muscular" Catholicism in Ireland. Although, Ireland is perceived as part of the Western world, it was (and parts of it remain) a British colony. Thus, although Palestine, Ireland, and India were and are located in different social, political, cultural, and economic spaces, certain similarities in the delineation of masculinity underlying their forms of nationalist resistance can be explained to a certain extent by the construct of empire.

My analysis of a case study of India adds depth to the evidence for the existence of a link between nation and hegemonic masculinity in various cultural milieus. This linkage needs to be analyzed for two reasons. One, it contains important implications for female participation in the nation and women's access to national resources. Two, given that the figure of a martial hero is central to this construct, militarism and violence are likely outcomes of assertive nationalism defined by hegemonic masculinity. The war raging between the antiterrorist coalition led by the United States against Osama bin Laden and Al-Qaeda is the most contemporary example of such an outcome. It can easily be seen that hegemonic masculinity comprises part of the nationalism defining the antiterrorist coalition (the United States, Germany, Canada, and the United Kingdom). Al-Qaeda has obviously eagerly incorporated this vision of assertive nationalism as it projects values of hegemonic masculinity (martial prowess, strength, muscularity) on its own actions. The issue is not so much whether the values of hegemonic masculinity are alien to or part of an Islamic politics but that in a world dominated by Western ideas of nationalism, hegemonic masculinity is the language that has to be spoken so that nations can be heard. Al-Qaeda and bin Laden have chosen to speak this language spectacularly.

Additionally, the conflict between Israel and Palestine is also being waged in such terms. I have already alluded to the location of hegemonic masculinity in certain dominant imaginings of the Palestinian nation. Such values also exist in the Israeli nation. Mosse (1996) argues that the most potent "outsider" figure in Western Europe has been the Jew. Jews were defined as dirty, ugly, crooked, diseased, nervous, and sexually promiscuous. "But it was Otto Weiniger's famous and perversely popular book *Geschlecht und Charakter* [*Sex and Character*, 1903] that proved to be the most important source book for the feminization of the Jews. Here Jews and women were equated as creatures of passion and emotions, lacking true creativity; both were without any individuality, devoid of self-worth" (p. 69). A dominant response to this "othering" was the idea of the "New Jew" or the "Muscle Jew" that defined itself both against European feminization as well as in contrast to the diaspora Jew, who was seen as timid and effeminate (Mayer, 2000a). The "muscular Jew" became the martial hero, constructing and defending the Israeli nation at all costs. So once again in the Middle East, we have the clash of hegemonic masculinities: the "Muscle" Jew and the "manly" Palestinian.

A similar clash of masculinities is occurring in Kashmir as India and Pakistan amass their troops along the Line of Control dividing the two states. So as not to appear weak or effeminate the Indian Hindu man and the Pakistani Muslim man are locked in a struggle defined by the valorization of martial prowess, physical strength, and the unwillingess to compromise.

Given the real geopolitical impact of a nationalism constructed with values of hegemonic masculinity, a genealogy and an articulation of this interpretation of nation within various cultural milieus become vital if communities are to resist the dangerous implications of this construct, that is, the exclusion of women, femininity, and womanhood from politics as well as the potential threat of masculine and military violence. This book will provide such an analysis by focusing on Hindu nationalism. In presenting this narrative of gendered nationalism, I would like to draw on the inspiring words of the great philosopher Hannah Arendt, who remarked once that it was far less important (and rather presumptuous) for a scholar to tell others what to do. More fruitful by far would be for scholars to help make society aware of and/or think about what it is doing. In other words, her advice is a variation on the Platonic injunction to lead an examined life. If we do not excavate and trace the values of hegemonic masculinity defining contemporary nationalisms that are eagerly accepted by the elite of both Western and non-Western states because of a legacy of European and British imperialism, then militarism and violence will never cease. We must think about what we are doing.

Having said this, I must again point out that I am not arguing that former colonies were devoid of indigenous martial traditions and heroes and/or values of militarism, nor am I positing that a nationalist elite blindly copied the values of hegemonic masculinity introduced by imperialism. Rather, I have pointed out that nationalist resistance movements creatively incorporated these ideas by drawing on their own cultural memories and vocabularies of militarism.

The point of departure for my analysis is the manner in which women intersect a nationalism defined by hegemonic masculinity. Women as social reproducers of cultural forms teach children rituals and myths aimed at locating them within a specific national context; in other words, by learning about brave warriors or courageous pioneers through song, stories, or pictures, children develop a loyalty to a certain idea of nation (Peterson, 1998). As shown in the brief description of Ireland above, motherland or nation as woman to be protected by brave citizen-warriors is a common metaphor for nationalism. For example, the "Marseilles" implicitly calls upon soldiers to protect the French nation embodied by the beautiful young Marianne. Similarly, many Indian nationalists vow to protect Bharat Mata, "Mother India." Britain is sometimes embodied as "Brittannia," a female figure based on images of Athena, the Greek goddess of war. Nation as woman also intersects the nationalist discourse through socially constructed ideas of honor. In many contexts (e.g., in Serbian nationalism), women symbolize national honor; thus any act (e.g., rape) that defiles and violates their bodies becomes a political weapon aimed at destroying the enemy nation's honor. Consequently, the point of departure of an analysis of the social construction of gender and how it informs nationalism is the relationship between woman as a signifier of the nation and the warriors exhorted to defend the homeland. Further, the gendered manner in which the image of the warrior is constructed within nationalist narratives as well as the notion that women embody national honor influences to a certain extent how women participate in nationalist politics.

Such a process of masculinization does not necessarily eliminate women from active nation-building. Women may simply join the project of nationalism by taking on the masculine traits approved by the hegemonic masculine interpretation of nation. Indeed, it is possible that some women may do so. But we must not forget that when women challenge societal ideas of femininity by taking on masculine traits, they may face censure and sanction from the (usually male) elite leading the project of masculinization. Further, that elite may not welcome such women, seeing their female presence as diluting the resolute masculinity of the nation. Therefore, it can be argued that women as political actors may become invisible when faced with such a process of masculinization. In reality, however, women within the many interpretations of nationalism have created a space within this framework, delicately negotiating their way through culturally dominant ideas of masculinity and femininity by means powerful and visible.

One important way in which this has occurred is by women taking on masculine traits to become citizen-warriors defending the nation. Women may do so in two ways. One is to protect national possessions (goods and land) and the other is by fending off attacks on their bodies. The latter act is crucial because according to the conceit of "nation as woman," women actually embody national honor, which can be sullied if enemy soldiers rape women. Women also intersect the masculinized discourse of nationalism by playing on their roles as wife and mother as well as on culturally endorsed ideas of wifehood and motherhood.

The above ideas shape the gendered lens I employ in analyzing the narrative of Hindu nationalism unfolding in contemporary India. I draw upon the role and construction of masculinity within Hindutva in the Indian context to examine the influence of the masculinization of nationalism on female political participation. I argue that while there are multiple interpretations of Hindu nationalism, an image central to the more militant of these views is that of the male warrior. It is important to acknowledge that the notion of militancy, within the context of Hindu nationalism, is contested. Social organizations such as the VHP and RSS and political parties such as the Shiv Sena and BJP all represent aspects of militant Hindu nationalism. However, ideological differences exist among them. For example, VHP

members define their nationalist mission as conserving tangible representations of Hindu religion (i.e., temples and idols) and participating in religious
rituals. RSS activists visualize themselves as social workers, building a strong
nation with education and discipline. Despite celebrating Hindu spirituality,
however, protecting temples, preserving idols, and observing Hindu rituals
are not the primary features of the RSS's nationalist vision. This difference
is succinctly illustrated by one RSS activist who was interviewed in New
Delhi in February 2002. He stated, "My first allegiance is to Bharat Mata
[Mother India] and not Ram [a Hindu deity revered and used by the VHP to
justify many of its militant activities]."[1] Further difference—for example,
evidence of tensions between BJP Prime Minister Vajpayee and the RSS
leadership, centered on the degree of militancy defining their respective
visions of Hindu nationalism—has been noted by Indian scholars (Kanungo,
2002, pp. 264–71).

However, despite internal dissensions, all these organizations do overlap
somewhat in their ideology because of close interpersonal relations and a
common commitment to establishing a powerful Hindu nation regardless of
certain fine distinctions made in articulating that national vision; for example, Ashok Singhal, VHP leader, was also a member of the RSS. Similarly,
many activists of the Sena, BJP, and the VHP have close ties with the RSS
and at times with each other. The idea of the Hindu warrior referred to above
is an ideological commonality. This image, rooted in a notion of masculinity
defined by attributes of decisiveness, aggression, muscular strength, and a
willingness to engage in battle, is opposed to a notion of femininity that is
defined by traits such as weakness, nonviolence, compassion, and a willingness to compromise. The image of the warrior—reflecting (as I term it) masculine Hinduism—is the culmination of a series of gendered historical and
social processes playing themselves out in the Indian context. In addition to
this model, masculine Hinduism yields another image of manhood, the warrior-monk. This figure although still a valorization of physical strength also
incorporates ideas of spiritual strength and moral fortitude.

Further, militarism has not necessarily been an exclusively masculine
trait in India. Goddesses such as Kali and Durga illustrate that violence and
militarism have also been associated with the divine figure of the feminine.
The cult of the mother goddess as a symbol of martial strength and prowess
even inspired some nineteenth-century nationalist movements. Indeed, the
existence of multiple ways of mapping gender and militarism in India has, to
a certain extent, enabled female visibility in the Hindu nationalist project.
As the discussion below will highlight, women who participate in this project
are aware of and use various strategies to deal with masculinist fears that
female political presence may challenge socially prescribed gender roles and
hence weaken and feminize the image of the powerful, masculine nation.
Three models of female activism that I have chosen to order women's pres-

ence in Hindutva are: heroic mother, chaste wife, and celibate masculinized warrior. Although divergent in their articulation at the grassroots, all three representations of female behavior do draw on a common theme: female virtue and chastity. Whether as mother, wife, or warrior, woman's sexual nature is erased, and the need to be pure, modest, and chaste is emphasized. To sum up, a particular vision of Hindu nation informed by representations of hegemonic masculinity—Hindu soldier and warrior-monk—and associated ideas of femininity—heroic mother, chaste wife, and celibate warrior—has been ascendant in contemporary India over the past decade.

It is important to stress that these cultural processes did not emerge in a material vacuum but unfolded against a context of political and economic anxiety that may have heightened the salience of armed masculinity and models of female behavior rooted in notions of chastity and purity. The story of Mumbai and the Shiv Sena illustrates the background of political and economic frustrations that make this particular incidence of gendered nationalism meaningful. It is important to remember that while the details of the Mumbai case may be unique, the general theme of frustration, given failing industries, political stagnation, and growing inequities, is pervasive at all levels of Indian society (Talbot, 2000, pp. 225–27).

Fifty percent of Mumbai's population lives in horrific urban slums (D'Monte, 1993). The population of these slums keeps growing as migration from surrounding rural areas continues unabated. This demographic change has been occurring in tandem with deindustrialization. As a result the number of jobs in the manufacturing sector is decreasing while the only new jobs being created are service jobs that require sophisticated training and skills not available to the urban poor (D'Monte, 1993).

The failed 1982–1983 strike signalled the almost complete collapse of the textile mill industry in Mumbai. As textile mills were a major employer in the formal sector, this collapse meant the displacement of thousands of securely employed formal sector workers. Jogeshswari, a slum that has seen some of the worst Hindu-Muslim clashes in Mumbai, was home to a large proportion of millworkers. Further, it is significant that Hindu Maharashtrians, who form a majority of the Shiv Sena's followers, are well represented in all levels of the textile industry while they are underrepresented in other industries (Katzenstein, 1979). As the formal sector has shrank, the informal sector—daily wage labor, street vending, and domestic employment—has expanded. But these occupations do not pay well and offer no job security. Rather than dissipating the feeling of economic deprivation, it is possible that jobs in the informal sector may actually increase frustration, as well-paid factory workers who turn to these occupations out of desperation may resent their fall in status.

Additionally, economic hardship creates destructive self/other perceptions. For example, many uneducated Muslim youth in Mumbai feel they are not benefiting from the fruits of modernization because of Hindu biases. In contrast, many poor Hindus in the slums of Mumbai see the presence of televisions and VCRs in some Muslim houses in the slums and immediately assume that these are bought with money sent by a family member working in the Middle East. These remittances, in the Hindu mind, are seen as proof of the fact that other Islamic countries are subsidizing Indian Muslims who are loyal not to the Indian nation but to Islam. Coupled with this belief is the perception that a Congress Party (the Indian National Congress founded in 1885 and until recently the dominant party in India) hungry for votes has been distributing votes to Muslims while ignoring Hindu needs. As a result, there is a view circulating among many Hindus that Muslims are not loyal to India, and in the past the Congress Party, in its greed for electoral power, instead of condemning these alleged traitorous links to other Islamic countries, actually rewarded such behavior. Hindu resentment against Muslims is further exacerbated by Muslim dominance in the powerloom industry in Maharashtra (the state where Mumbai is located). After the 1982 strike destroyed the large textile factories (dominated by Hindu Maharashtrian workers) in Mumbai, textile manufacturing shifted to the powerloom sector. Unlike the factories of Mumbai, the powerloom industry has a low capital outlay, employs very few people, and is housed in a room or a shed on the owner's property. In small towns like Bhiwandi in Maharashtra, the powerloom industry has created a substantial section of middle-class Muslims. Disgruntled and displaced Hindu textile workers and unemployed youth view this affluence as another example of the Muslim community benefiting from Hindu misery (Banerjee, 2000, pp. 61–84).

Coupled with this economic frustration is India's growing crisis of governability. Atul Kohli (1991) points to the following causes for the Indian state's declining capability to govern: the changing role of the elite and the decline of the Congress Party's dominance in Indian politics (until 1996 the Indian state was run by the Congress Party, except for a brief hiatus in 1977), weak and ineffective political organizations, and the mobilization of new groups for electoral participation (pp. 13–21). Many of these new groups have resonated to the ideology of Hindu nationalism disseminated by parties like the BJP and Shiv Sena. Another aspect of the crisis of governability in India is the ever increasing public perception that the Congress Party's allegiance to a politics that is tolerant of diversity and protective of minority rights is faltering. This perception is shored up by the Congress Party's implication in Hindu violence against Sikhs after the assassination of Indira Gandhi, this administration's inability (some would say lack of willingness) to decisively halt both the destruction of the Babri Mosque, and the all-India Hindu-Muslim riots that followed in 1992–1993 as well as its willingness to ally with parties like the Shiv Sena for local political advantage (e.g. during the seventies in Mumbai, the Congress forged electoral alliances with the Sena to defeat the Communist opposition). To sum up, although the exact details of decay and crisis may vary according to region, there is no doubt that economic and political frustration have created a context in India generally wherein Hindu nationalism resonates among a certain section of Hindus.

Against this context, armed masculinity denoting action, resolution, and most importantly the willingness to strike back and seize one's rightful share of the benefits is an extremely powerful cultural construct. While male Hindu warriors are resisting political and economic decay, their women, pure and chaste, are with them in the fray. An emphasis on the chastity of women and control of female sexuality during times of social uncertainty can be interpreted as a form of resistance to uncontrollable external changes. Certainly scholars (e.g., Asfar, 1987; Chhacchi, 1994; Derne, 2000; Mayer, 2000; Nagel, 1998) have argued that regulation of female sexuality occurs in a context where patriarchal authority structures are being challenged as economic changes enable the entry of women into the labor force and the rise of female-headed households. So it is not unreasonable to surmise that this form of control becomes a resistance to political decay situated in a national discourse wherein women's bodies and womanhood actually represent the nation. Consequently, controlling women and womanhood may be read as a metaphorical control of the nation. The theme of chastity and purity running through the multiple expressions of female activism within Hindu nationalism seems to illustrate this form of control. Having made the above argument, I must caution that I am not drawing a direct causal link, but delineating the material context within which the gendered discourse of Hindutva is expressing itself.

But even if women enter the nationalist project as citizen-warriors or mothers, it does not necessarily follow that they become involved in constructing a feminist nationalism. While the concrete political goals of feminist nationalisms will vary according to context, some common goals may include a restructuring of power relations within patriarchal families, fighting violence against women, and insisting on an equality of rights under the law. As will be discussed in this book, women's participation in Hindu nationalism reveals an interesting tension between feminine nationalist activism and feminist nationalism. This tension derives from the ideals of female virtue and chastity defining all three models of female activism and the discourse of the harmonious Hindu family within which they are embedded. As will be discussed more fully in chapter six, ideas of female virtue and the ideal of the Hindu family shunt aside a comprehensive critique of the multiplicity of women's lives, power relations and sexual aggression within families, and ideas of shame and sexual respectability that inhibit many Indian women's freedom. From the point of view of the Indian women's movement, the considerable empowerment Hindutva women derive from activism must be seen in conjunction with the above implications as well as the fact that female political participation is perpetuating a vision of nation built on a monolithic masculinized self/other model closed to negotiation and compromise and implicated in intolerance as well as episodes of violence.

There is a body of work analyzing female participation in militant Hindu nationalism (e.g., Sarkar and Butalia, 1995) as well as gender and nation in India (e.g., Chowdhury, 2001; Gupta, 2001; Mankekar, 2000, 1998; Roy, 1998; Sinha, 1995). The Sarkar and Butalia book offers a collection of studies on women's activism in the Hindutva movement. However, most of these authors neither draw on current feminist theorizing on gender and nation for their analysis nor explicitly discuss the construction and implications of a nation built by hegemonic masculinity for women. Further, most authors who have discussed gendered nationalism in India predominantly focus on colonial India and do not explore various vital aspects of the historical evolution of masculinity in colonial times and its continuity within modern India, and/or do not explicitly link feminist theorizing on gender and nation to the modern Indian context. My work adds to these studies in three ways. One, while the works above do allude to ideas of masculinity, I find that many of them do not provide a detailed examination of an important cultural construct: Christian manliness and its dynamic reciprocal relationship with masculine Hinduism. This concept forms a vital component of my study, as it plays an integral role in illuminating the masculinization of the Hindu nation. Two, although I do discuss colonial India, my discourse primarily highlights the historical evolution of masculine Hinduism. Specifically, then, the main focus of my study is on gender and nation in modern Hindutva. Three, by explicitly locating the gendered Hindu nation within contemporary feminist theorizing on nationalism, I link the Indian case to a global system wherein a certain interpretation of masculinity becomes an important part of the vocabulary and behavior of states and provides cultural depth to current work on gender and nation. In sum, my study weaves together various isolated strands of theorizing on masculinity and nation in an attempt to offer a holistic analysis of gender and nation in an Indian context, currently not found in the literature.

The following chapter traces the gendered impact of British colonialism on Indian society by focusing on the construction, internal evolution, and use of Christian manliness by the imperial gaze. Chapter three highlights elite Indian response to this construct and the early nationalist delineation of masculine Hinduism. Chapter four explores the continuities and discontinuities between colonial visions of masculine Hinduism and modern ideas of Hindu nationalism. Chapter five analyzes the relationship between the masculinization of Hindu nationalism and female participation. Chapter six explores the implications of such participation with particular attention given to the tension attendant between women's activism in nationalism and feminist nationalism.

Finally, I would like to mention a few words on multiplicity before pro-ceeding further with my analysis. Indian, indeed Hindu, nationalism has unfolded in multiple ways as various elite and common folk imaginatively responded to colonial and postcolonial conditions, essentially turning to their own cultural traditions to make sense of their realities. In this work, I shall focus on a single dominant strand—masculine Hinduism—that exists within the whole of the intricately woven cultural cloth that is India, for the reasons delineated above. My emphasis by no means denies the importance or existence of multiple other strands.

TWO

Empire

Christian Manliness and the British Gaze

I hate bookworms. . . . Give me a lad with pluck and spirit. . . . What we want for India are men who can ride and shoot, who are ready at any moment to start on a hundred-mile journey horseback, who will scale hill forts with a handful of men.

> —G. A. Henty, *Through the Sikh War:*
> *A Tale of the Conquest of the Punjaub*

The native strength and soundness of the English race, and of manly English training and discipline, were never more powerfully exhibited, and it was there emphatically proved that the Men of England are, after all, its greatest products.

> —Samuel Smiles, *Self-Help*

SAMUEL SMILES'S BOOK *Self-Help* (1879) promised to "explain the secret of the superior energy and success of the Anglo-Saxons" (p. 230); within a few years he had sold 250,000 copies (Green, 1980, p. 204). While it may indeed be gratifying to be introduced to the roots of one's racial superiority, it must have struck the young men (although not explicitly stated, his book assumed a male audience) who read Smiles that Britain's empire in India was inextricably linked to Anglo-Saxon glory. Smiles (1879) frequently used examples from the Raj to illustrate his moral lessons:

> India has, during the last century, been a great field for the display of British energy. From Clive to Havelock and Clyde there is a long and honourable roll of distinguished names in Indian legislation and warfare—such as Wellesley, Metcalfe, Outram, Edwardes, and the Lawrences. (p. 231)

There can be no doubt that India occupied a dominant place in the British Empire not only economically but also in terms of animating a heroic self in the imperial imagination. British imaginings of India spanned images ranging from experiments in utilitarianism and feats of engineering to, in the slightly paraphrased words of Edward Said (1978), the Englishman's "day dream," conjured with adventure and exoticism. This latter notion is nicely illustrated by Sir Walter Scott's prefatory to *The Surgeon's Daughter*: "India, where gold is won by steel; where a brave man cannot pitch his desire of fame and wealth so high but that he may realize it, if he have fortune to friend" (quoted in Green, 1980, p. 113). However, whatever the construction of India, the actions of an Englishman within this space was shaped by ideas of hegemonic masculinity.

Green (1980) identifies four archetypes of English manliness implied in the idea of empire: the engineer, explorer, missionary, and soldier (pp. 204–14). The engineer tamed unruly nature—rivers, jungles—by using science to build bridges, railroads, and highways; the explorer trekked throughout the mysterious subcontinent mapping terrain; the missionary heralded the civilizing force of Christianity; and the soldier conquered and maintained control over the "effeminate" Hindu. Although each version of manhood perhaps performed a different function within the imperial project, each figure embodied traits of hegemonic masculinity, strength, self-reliance, independence, and confidence as India was controlled, categorized, and conquered.

The linkage between British notions of hegemonic masculinity and institutions as well as imaginings of empire has been a topic of contemporary research (e.g., Alderson, 1998; Chowdhury, 2001; Gilmore, 1996; Gupta, 2001; Hall, 1994; Inden, 1993; Roper and Tosh, 1991; Sinha, 1995; Vance, 1985). Inherent in this relationship is the pejorative judgment of the conquered. In the words of Said (1978) such criticism can be related to a process of feminization wherein the Orient (non-Western colonies in South Asia and the Middle East) was constructed as the weak, irrational, nonmartial "other" in contrast to a rational strong, martial European "self" (p. 207). Ronald Inden (1990) alludes to the European masculine hero who would conquer and create order out of the feminized chaos that was India (p. 17). Said and Inden both imply that the feminization of the Orient encompassed a disparagement of Arab and Indian men who were conquered because they were effeminate and seen as effeminate because they were conquered. Their conquered status constructed them as not muscular, not aggressive, and not skilled in militarism, all values associated with femininity. Thus, gender was a politically salient aspect of colonialism. Gender—a contested term—has little analytical value unless it is socially and culturally situated. In the nineteenth and early twentieth centuries, at the height of imperial expansion, values of hegemonic masculinity within Britain stimulated the construction of a gendered norm commonly known in that era as Christian manliness.

Christian manliness formed the bridge connecting empire and gender both in terms of emphasizing the British need to guide Indians (who were not aware of these values) as well as presenting India as the ideal venue for practicing Christian manhood. Christian manliness was a Protestant construct. It emerged in the mid-nineteenth century when British imperial power was at its zenith and drew upon various traits—self-control, discipline, confidence, martial prowess, military heroism, and rationality—expressed in the typology of hegemonic masculinity.

It is important to remember that British images of empire were not monolithic either in one period or over time. For example, Greenberger (1969) divides British literary attitude toward imperial India into three periods: the era of confidence (1880–1910), the era of doubt (1910–1935), and the era of melancholy (1935–1960). In the first period, many authors voiced confidence in the righteousness of the British presence in India, projecting that "the ideal British hero of this 'era of confidence' is brave forceful, daring, honest, active, and masculine" (p. 11). During the era of doubt, confidence began to recede. Some British supporters of the Raj reacted aggressively to signs that the Empire was crumbling; others attacked the Raj, Western civilization, and mocked the "manly" English in India; still others tried to adopt a balanced approach to argue that though imperialism was problematic, it had wrought some positive change in India. Finally, in the last era, the era of melancholy, most authors accepted that the Empire had collapsed and their focus was on the fate of the English in India. Although Greenberger's emphasis is on the production of literature, it is not inaccurate to posit shifts in literary emphasis as representing general societal attitudes. Further, these are, of course, ideal categories that surely ironed out nuances and multiplicity of opinions within each era. However, these emphases do provide a convenient heuristic device to temporally locate the discussion. My analysis will draw not only on official memos, published histories, and religious pamphlets but also autobiographical and biographical accounts of colonial India and boys' adventure stories. I have used multiple accounts to underscore the reach of these ideas. Finally, most of the narratives are located in the era of confidence, with a few written in the decades before this era.

CHRISTIAN MANLINESS AND EMPIRE

In 1866, the Religious Tract Society of London published a monograph titled "Christian Manliness: A Book of Examples and Principles for Young Men." Its contents outlined several characteristics necessary for constructing an ideal Christian man: faith, personal will to decide, resolve, fidelity, courage, energy, perseverance, strength, gentleness, self-mastery, and prudence. The title as well as the language of the tract very clearly assumed a male audience (p. 95). Reverend John Caird in *Christian Manliness: A Sermon* (1871) similarly observed, "Let inward principle take the place of instinct and outward restraint,—let the thoughtfulness, the intelligence, the earnest devotion, high and noble objects which are the characteristics of Christian manhood, raise you above the temptations of indolence and self-indulgence or the baser lives of appetites and sense" (p. 28). These values constructed the figure of the manly English actor in opposition to an effeminate, native "other" marked by weakness, fickleness, cowardice, laziness, and a lack of self-control.

Other tracts revealed the links between Christianity, militarism, masculinity, and nationalism more clearly. For example, *Christian Manliness: A Sermon Preached to the Third Lancashire Artillery Volunteers in the Bolton Parish Church 1888* stated,

> Samuel, X:12: "Play the *men* for our people, and for the cities of our God, and the Lord do that which seemeth Him good." These are the words of a Commander-in-Chief. They were addressed by Joab to the chosen *men* of Israel, whom he was about to lead out to fight against the Syrians. . . . The subject suggested by the exhortation, "Play the *men*," is *Christian manliness*, and Christian manliness should be the characteristic of the Christian man at arms. (n.p.; italics added)

In this text, the need to defend one's nation is embedded within the idea of Christian manliness. Further, the image of the "Christian man at arms" highlights the notion of armed masculinity wherein war and conquest legitimately measure manliness. Within the discourse of imperialism, the Christian man at arms represented empire and national glory. For example, Sir Henry Lawrence, a much revered colonial administrator and military commander, linked his imperial presence in India with his Christian duty. In his contributions to the *Calcutta Review* (1859) he described the ideology shaping his location as a commander in India: "On the other hand, what may not a Christian soldier do? The man who, a Christian at heart, . . . believes his duty . . . evincing his love to God by performing his duty to man . . . such a man will not be the one to quail in the hour of danger" (p. 43).

John Brookes's book *Manliness: Hints to Young Men* (ca. 1860s) drew a link between national progress and manliness, wherein *manly* nations are sure to progress whereas *unmanly* nations are bound to be conquered: "Nations never remain stationary—they are always either progressing or retrograding. If they are *manly* their march towards perfect civilization is . . . certain . . . but if they become *unmanly* their retrogression is rapid and awful" (p. 150). He argues that the Jewish, Greek, and Roman nations fell because they had lost sight of or were unaware of the proper notions of manliness, best exemplified by ideas of Christian manhood. He then goes on to claim that there is no need to search human history for examples of Christian manliness because the Bible provides us with the most inspiring model, Christ. Drawing on such assumptions, Thomas Hughes penned *The Manliness of Christ* (1879). Hughes draws on Britain's Indian empire to elaborate his story about the manliness of Christ. For example, when describing the social and spatial context of Christ's birth, he writes, "It is not easy to find a parallel case in the modern world, but perhaps the nearest exists in the portion of our own empire. The condition of parts of India in our day resembles in some respects that of Palestine in the year A.D. 30" (p. 17). It seems reasonable to argue that Hughes by drawing parallels between Palestine and India views Britain's role in India as divinely inspired.

Samuel Smiles, author of *Self-Help* (1879) whose words begin this chapter, was one of the more popular voices delineating Christian manliness: "The spirit of self-help, as exhibited in the energetic action of individuals, has in all times been a marked feature in the English character and furnishes the true measure of our power as a nation" (p. 5). In this work, self-help is linked to enterprise, industrialization, and leadership in technology, all traits in turn that are posited as the cause of British imperial glory. The idea of self-help is also embedded within a context of manliness defined by athleticism, hard work, frugality, honesty, and temperance. Further, the virtues of manhood include good manners, courtesy, and chivalry. The overlap among Smiles's ideas of self-help, manhood, and Christian manliness is considerable. For the purposes of this argument, it must again be emphasized that most of his examples embodying the virtues of self-help and manhood were the colonial administrators and soldiers who had served in India.

All the quoted passages above, as well as the one following, clearly distinguish between mere muscular Christianity and Christian manliness, including physical strength/martial prowess but also going beyond mere "muscularity" to emphasize moral dimensions: "We need not fall into the folly of so-called 'muscular Christianity,' but it is a Christian duty to maintain in health and vigour the body to which God has given strength and beauty" (Religious Tract Society, 1866, p. 146). Norman Vance (1985) suggests that " 'manliness' may relate to physical vigour and prowess . . . or to patriotic and military qualities, or to the traditions of chivalry, or to a variety of moral qualities ranging from . . . general benevolence to the most awe inspiring moral rigour" (p. 10). Patriotism was an important trait of Christian manhood as Brookes and Smiles reveal; manliness must serve the nation, and indeed manhood and nation just reinforce one another. Further, despite the allusion to the folly of "muscular Christianity," many proponents of Christian manliness placed a muscular body at the center of their discourse and were avid supporters of athletics as an expression of masculinity. It is also important to note that British interpretations of manliness were not necessarily defined in opposition only to effeminacy but also to childishness and sometimes beastliness. However, the boundaries between effeminacy and childishness become blurred when the qualities of irrationality, emotiveness, weakness, or passivity are seen as traits describing both feminine and childlike behavior.

The difference between them is that male children, with proper training and guidance, will progress beyond this childlike state, whereas adult women remain trapped in it.

The terms of "manliness" and "manhood" shifted in colonial observations. Although some references to Indians commonly conflated effeminacy and a lack of martial prowess, other observations about Indian manhood were based on broader interpretations of Christian manliness. For example, while the martial ability of some groups of Indian men may have been acknowledged, simultaneously these same groups would be condemned for being "unmanly" because of a lack of patriotic fervor and/or honesty.

The discourse on Christian manliness was an important part of late Victorian debates on nation (e.g., Hall, 1994; Vance, 1985). An examination of the factors shaping the English focus on this debate will underscore that Britain's determination to categorize and control Indian men using a gaze defined by the values of Christian manhood emerged from social anxiety about British masculinity. Some British social leaders—such as Charles Kingsley, William Pater, William Blake, and Thomas Hughes—called for a remasculinization of the British nation, which in their eyes had become soft and effeminate. Imperial expansion was very much a part of this project.

Christian manliness and muscular Christianity arose in response to industrialization and the uncertainties created by a changing social order wherein race and gender roles were shifting. In face of these uncertainties, a feeling arose among certain elite that Englishmen had become too effeminate and were losing the manly qualities that had made England great (Hall, 1994). Further, many argued that it was time to recapture this manliness and resist the effeminization and decline of Anglo-Saxon glory (Faulkner, 1994): "His [Charles Dickens] celebration thus reinscribes England's topographical boundaries . . . as natural fortresses against racial infection in the uncertain world of 1870 . . . [the] muscular Christian masquerades as global policeman, guarding Anglo-Saxon virtues and casting out foreign devils" (p. 88). Dilution of Anglo-Saxon racial purity was part and parcel of the anxiety about British masculinity. Another aspect of this national anxiety was the tension between "middle class radicals and the aristocracy. Some elements of the middle class elite believed that one of the reasons for the decline of Anglo-Saxon glory was the presence of an aristocracy that had identified with the effeminate French rather than their own hardy Protestant culture" (Alderson, 1998, p. 26). Finally, while the robust values of Christian manliness were being created as an antidote to the effeminate decline of society, it became clear that an important component of this remasculinization was empire. Conquering and holding British imperial lands were vital aspects of this rejuvenated masculinity. Note that in addition to other factors, this renewed emphasis on imperial masculinity may have been sparked by the Indian War of 1857 wherein the British were amazed at the widespread resistance to their presence and, more importantly, frightened by the fact that they had almost lost India to "native" forces and commanders. This fact, I would argue, strengthened British resolve to prove their masculinity in opposition to, in their view, the effeminate (and sometimes childlike and beastly) native. The War of 1857 occupied considerable space in British memoirs of empire, and it is no accident that Havelock and Lawrence, saviors of imperial India in 1857, are oft-quoted examples embodying the virtues of Christian manliness.

The intersection of Christian manliness and empire was manifested in both fictional and nonfictional narratives. In the fictional realm, adventure books written for British schoolboys incorporated the message of Christian manliness by celebrating its alliance with imperialism; simultaneously, patriotism and military courage were also emphasized as potent traits in this intersection (Green, 1980). The focus on youth and the construction of imperial masculinity formed an integral component of the Christian manliness movement as British society reproduced its values through the socialization of its children.

In 1883 the Boy's Brigade Movement was founded to teach young boys the principles of this vision of manhood. In 1908, Lt. General Robert Baden Powell, believing that the virility and hardiness of British boys were being sapped by domestic urban life, founded the Boy Scouts with the intention of creating a proper breed of "manly" English men to maintain the glory of the Empire (MacDonald, 1993). Another training ground for male empire-builders wherein they were taught the salient aspects of Christian manliness was the public schools, where the harsh treatment meted out was interpreted as a male rite of passage and preparation for "young Oxbridge aristocrats for the self-reliance and fortitude needed to run the British Empire" (Gilmore, 1996, pp. 17–18). The Boy Scouts, the Boy's Brigade, and the English public school all represent modes of hegemonic masculinity wherein women as mothers have disappeared and young boys are actually "reborn" under the tutelage of adult males as true "men." These organizations also emphasize male friendships, camaraderie, and the valorization of military heroism: every English schoolboy's dream was to be a Clive (a founder of the Empire) or Havelock (a savior of the Empire). All three organizations additionally emphasized the muscular body as a symbol of manliness and encouraged athleticism. Participation in team sports such as cricket and rugby was perceived by many as an ideal method of internalizing the values of Christian manliness. One of the famous examples of this belief in the educational role of rugby was portrayed in *Tom Brown's School Days* (1857) written by Thomas Hughes, an enthusiastic proponent of Christian manliness.

Nonfictional accounts also disseminated ideas of Christian manhood. For example, the monograph published by the Religious Tract Society referred to British colonial administrators and military leaders such as Warren Hastings, Henry Lawrence, and General Henry Havelock as living examples of Christian manliness. General Havelock was a favorite icon representing Christian heroism, and books such as *General Havelock and Christian Soldiership* by the Rev. Frederick S. Williams (1858) and *General Havelock or the Christian Soldier* by Lt. Col. B. D. W. Ramsay (1871) celebrated his valor.

In addition, well-known English intellectuals—Gerard Manley Hopkins, Hughes, Dickens, Kingsley, and Pater—debated these ideas in public fora (Alderson, 1998; Hall, 1994; Vance, 1985). Colonial military historians also classified Indian soldiers in terms of both muscular Christianity and the multifaceted notion of Christian manliness. It is important to remember that the views of colonial administrators and commanders formed the basis for many of the adventure stories and tracts on Christian manliness alluded to above. When the colonial observers spoke of the "manly Jat" or the "devious Maratha," these stereotypes then emerged in popular adventure stories and instructional monographs aimed at British boys and young men, many of whom were eager to come to India to seek adventure and fortune.

THE MARTIAL RACES OF INDIA

British gendered lens sorted Indian men in several ways, the categories "martial" and "nonmartial"[1] as depicted in Sir George MacMunn's text *The Martial Races of India* (1933) being the most common:

> We do not speak of the martial races of Britain as distinct from the nonmartial, nor of Germany, nor of France. But in India we speak of the martial races as a thing apart and because the mass of people have neither martial aptitude nor physical courage. (p. 2)

Traits characterizing the martial races were clearly drawn from notions of muscular Christianity—physical hardiness, loyalty, strength—while nonmartial races embodied opposite values. Although some martial races were "discovered" in India, clearly, in British eyes, they were anomalies in a land filled with effeminate beings: "India has a population of 350 millions . . . and perhaps of them thirty-five millions whose young men are *manly* [italics added] young men, there may be three million males between the military ages of 20 and 35! Astounding!" (MacMunn, 1933, p. 3). Further, with the exception of the martial races, the British were quite contemptuous of the effeminate Hindus: "The (Hindoos) are in an awful fright and today most of the shops are shut. It is really a most despicable race, and without any exaggeration . . . [they] have not even the pluck of a mouse."[2] Usually in these British accounts, the effeminacy of Hindus was defined by mention of their feeble bodies, perceived to be the result of little vigorous exercise, an excessive bookishness, a propensity for mercantile occupations—which in turn supposedly supported practices (deceit and dishonesty) violating the morality of Christian manliness—and behavior marked by a cowardly lack of patriotism.

The latter was supposedly demonstrated by the fact that "[a] region of Asia, *equal in extent to the whole of Europe* (exclusive of Russia), with a population of *more than one hundred and thirty millions* [was subjugated by only] *forty thousand* British" (Duff, ca. 1850s, p. 22).

The most potent symbol of general Hindu effeminacy was the Bengali. Much has been written (e.g., Alter, 1994; Chowdhury, 2001; Sinha 1995) about the Bengali babu (government clerk) as the archetypical effeminate figure constructed in opposition to the hardy, masculine, imperial British ruler; the stereotype needs little further elucidation. But it is worth presenting, yet again, Macaulay's famous words (Lord, 1931) describing the Bengali, because this most powerful image of an effeminate India formed the basis of British confidence in their own masculinity, which in turn buttressed their belief that the martial races of India were merely exceptions to the rule in a general body of effeminate Hindus:

> The race by whom this rich tract was peopled, enervated by a soft climate and accustomed to peaceful avocations, bore the same relation to other Asiatics which the Asiatics generally bear to the bold and energetic children of Europe. . . . Whatever the Bengalee does he does languidly. . . . He shrinks from bodily exertion; . . . and scarcely ever enlists as a soldier. We doubt whether there be a hundred genuine Bengalese in the whole army of the East India Company. (p. 31)

> The physical organization of the Bengalee is feeble even to Effeminacy. . . . During many ages he has been trampled upon by men of bolder and more hardy breeds. (pp. 109–10)

In British eyes, these feeble effeminate beings required "the straightforwardness of Christian honesty and the manliness of British energy" (Duff, 1858, p. 286) to enjoy order and stability.

In addition, it is important to remember that when the British first came, in their opinion, none of the races of India were capable of acting as an organized army: "'They are for the most part,' as Sir Lepel Griffin says, 'an undrilled, wretchedly armed rabble, and two or three of our regiments, with a battery of horse artillery, would disperse 50,000 of them.' With the exceptions that I haved named [armies of Gwalior (Maratha), the Nizam of Hyderabad, and the Sikhs], they cannot cause us anxiety. They are not armies in the ordinary sense of the term" (Strachey, 1888, p. 327). As discussed above in the Introduction, hegemonic masculinity not only emphasizes martial prowess but also discipline, rationality, and control. Consequently, "scientific war" and an organized army were important reflections of these traits. In an 1873 memo to the India Office Major Owen T. Burne despaired of the native armies:

> But however large the armies of Native states may sound numerically, they are in reality a mere rabble. Undrilled and unorganized, the men are kept up

for the purposes of rivalry and show, and considering the large area for
whose peace and well-being they are supposed to be answerable, their number is not much large[r] than might be expected.[3]

In British eyes, this population had "no real discipline or organization, no
knowledge of modern warfare, and their arms were antiquated." They simply
existed to "pander to the love of display of an *effete* [italics added]."[4]

Floating in the general pool of native rabble were the martial races who
had the potential to be trained as good soldiers: "Although these troops [the
reference here is to Sikhs, one of the martial races] are good, they are not
quite good enough. The material is excellent but has not been worked in the
right shape."[5] In *The Annual Report on Indian State Forces 1922–1923*, an
anonymous military commander writes, "In the mean time all states concerned are busy reorganizing their troops of Indian Army Establishments, and
in the place of the old undisciplined rag tag and bobtail, small, efficient, well
disciplined forces are being raised, which will be of considerable value to the
Empire."[6] Lt. Col. Aga Durand (quoted in Beastson, 1903) praised the efforts
of his officers in training the martial races in a memorandum to the India
Office in 1892:

> I have had these regiments under my orders for two years and have seen
> them grow in efficiency under the careful instruction of Captain Twigg and
> Lt. Townsend, and the steady efforts of some of their own officers. The result
> has been most satisfactory and they have proved themselves fit to take place
> in line with our own regiments. (p. 140)

This memo alludes to the issue of "native" officers. Whether the martial races
of India were fit to command troops or not was a topic constantly debated in
the British army guarding India. Some natives (Caplan, 1991) were allowed
low-level leadership roles within the ranks, but "native" officers would never
command British troops and were not allowed to rise to high levels. This
debate over leadership reveals the explicit racism embedded in the British
gendered vision of India. Even martial races were endowed with only some
aspects of Christian manliness—loyalty, virility, hardiness—but other facets—
control, discipline, courtesy, chivalry, independence, self-reliance—were miss-
ing. Indeed, the lack of such traits meant Indians would never be leaders like
the British and certainly were not capable of leading or governing themselves.
Even a very young British officer who had the benefit of training in Christian
manliness could lead mature Indian troops: "Ensign Allan, a youth of seven-
teen, left to the unaided resources of his own mind, reclaimed this disorderly
and unpaid rabble to obedience and energy; . . . [exhibiting] all the vigor and
enterprise of manly youth" (Wilks, 1932, p. 5). Because of the lack of certain
key traits of hegemonic masculinity, Indian men, regardless of martial ability,
were childlike and effeminate, unable to govern themselves.

This gendered categorization of the Indian populace facilitated the rise of several popular stereotypes that still resonate in certain contemporary milieus in both India and the United Kingdom: the manly Sikh, the devious Maratha, and the loyal Gurkha. It is worthwhile to mine the values of manhood implicit in these images.

THE MANLY SIKH

In the post-1857 recruitment for the Indian army, the British became attracted to the sturdy peasant inhabitant of Punjab (Wuhrgaft, 1983). Colonial administrators found the Sikh and Hindu Punjabi peasants more amenable to civil improvements, such as road, sanitation, and irrigation projects. Agriculture flourished in the area. Its physically hardy inhabitants were compared favorably against the urbanized Hindus, who were symbolized by the effeminate Bengali who (in British opinion) constantly carped about minutiae and made life difficult for colonial authorities. Indeed, the most famous colonial administrators of this area, John and Henry Lawrence (the latter it should be remembered was an admired icon embodying Christian manliness), invented the term "Punjab style of rule," seen as active, independent, self-reliant, strong, and militaristic (Wuhrgaft, 1983)—in other words, manly.

Ranjeet Singh, the famous Sikh leader, had particularly impressed the British army commanders with his military acumen: "Runjeet Singh's military achievement, in short, was to seize upon the masses of brave but militarily ignorant horsemen of the Punjab and with foreign help transform them into a disciplined regular army" (Bruce, 1969, p. 58). The foreign help Singh drew on was the services of an ex-officer of Napoleon's army and an American soldier of fortune, Col. Alexander Gardner. But, perhaps even more importantly, Ranjeet Singh had been impressed by British martial prowess: "The Rajah said, . . . [h]is French officers and others had told him that English discipline was nothing. . . . 'But now,' he said, 'I see what liars they are; you have shewn me not only how troops can be moved but also how those movements can be brought to bear upon a hostile force.' He added that it was now no matter of wonder to him why the English had always been victorious in the East" (Fane, 1862, p. 161). Thus, Sikhs and some Punjabis embodied some of the raw material—strength, bravery, loyalty—and after proper training could be forged into disciplined soldiers. Consequently, during the era of confidence, a Punjabization of the Indian army took place wherein seventy-five percent of its troops were recruited from this area (Talbot, 2001, p. 123). While deemed capable soldiers, they were still seen to be lacking other traits critical to the English masculinization project—self-control, rationality, prudence—and in British eyes, they remained childlike, that is, volatile and emotive. Put another way, like all other Indian men, they were incapable of expressing a fully developed sense of masculinity and hence were not capable of governing themselves.

DEVIOUS MARATHA

Even within the ranks of martial races, a hierarchy existed in terms of British approval. The Sikhs and the Gurkhas were most favored by the British military authorities and historians, while the Marathas were not so favored. Indeed, at times, even though their martial prowess was praised, they were deemed inferior in terms of all other masculine traits. Shivaji and the Marathas, able warriors who harassed colonial troops, occupied much of the British imagination: "I place the Mahrattas first, both because they possess the greatest military power and also on account of their having been our most formidable opponents in the past."[7] But even as historians spoke of their prowess in battle, these achievements were denigrated by references to the moral laxity of Maratha troops: "Maharattas are total strangers to charity, and possess an insensibility of heart with which other nations are unacquainted" (Tone, 1818, p. 31). Even their martial ability was not "manly" because it did not fit the features of the Christian man at arms, that is, it did not adhere to the "proper" rules of war: "Fighting is neither their object nor inclination; nor indeed are they properly qualified for it. Their single aim is plunder; and their glory consists in effecting an inroad by surprise and making a secure retreat" (Thorn, 1818, p. 519). As a result of their guerrilla-like tactics, that is, a so-called dishonorable conduct in war, they were deemed unworthwhile opponents (even though their troops needed to be defeated for the security of the Empire): "[T]here is something noble in the carriage of an ordinary Rajput; and something vulgar in that of the most distinguished Mahratta. The Rajput is the most worthy antagonist, the Mahratta the most formidable enemy" (Lawrence, 1859, p. 144).

But most of British anger seemed aimed at the famed Maratha warrior Shivaji: "Sevjaee's system of cold-blooded plunder was regulated with a degree of skill and vigilance which suffered not the most minute article of theft or robbery to escape his observations and control" (Wilks, 1930, p. 100). Another passage states, "[W]ith many of the great qualities of a hero as they are falsely called, he possessed the vices of a robber and an assassin" (Waring, 1810, p. 88). Such comments are relevant to this narrative because contemporary Hindu nationalist groups forming the basis of this analysis do focus on Shivaji fundamentally as an icon of Hindu martial power and celebrate the military history of the Marathas. In other words, an aspect of the masculinizing project of Hindu nationalism includes reclaiming and celebrating warriors who were dismissed as "unmanly" by the colonial rulers. The effeminization of the Bengali along with the denigration of Maratha martiality within the British discourse present important implications for the construction of Hindu nationalism. The popularly recognized figures implicated in both the colonial and postcolonial imaginings of masculine Hinduism examined in this study came from within these two regions—Sister Nivedita, Sarala Ghosal, Swami Vivekananda, and Bankimchandra Chatterjee from Bengal; Savarkar, Hedgewar, Golwalkar, and Madam Cama from Maharashtra.

THE LOYAL GURKHA

In contrast to the Marathas, the Gurkhas occupied a favored position in the British classification of martial races. Again, they were praised for their bravery in battle but failed to demonstrate other "manly" traits. The original story of the British army's "discovery" of the Gurkhas as a martial race during the Anglo-Nepal War of 1814–1816 illustrates this inequity. During the war campaign, a Lt. Young was sent in with a force of two thousand sepoys (indigenous Indian soldiers) to intercept two hundred Nepali soldiers who were on their way to protect a besieged fort. The Nepalis easily defeated the sepoys, who ran away, but the lieutenant and his colleagues stayed to face the Nepali soldiers. Impressed by their bravery, the latter exclaimed, "Ah, you are brave men. We could serve *under* men like you" (Caplan, 1991, p. 580). In other words, the Nepalis may reflect some traits of masculinity (bravery, martial prowess) but in terms of other ones—discipline, self-control, rationality—they did not measure up and hence were only capable of serving *under* Englishmen. Although in this particular scenario, it is the Nepalis themselves who acknowledge the superiority of British leadership, the account was disseminated throughout British sources and hence was seen to reflect popular colonial biases. The Gurkhas, like the Sikhs, gained a prominent position within the British Indian army because of their martial prowess. Again, in British eyes, the Gurkhas excelled in some qualities of hegemonic masculinity—bravery, martiality, loyalty—but could not be counted as fully formed men in the tradition of English manhood. This limitation of Nepali men is most emphatically illustrated by the words used by British authors to describe the Gurkha men: "They are tykes, little highlanders, little Gurkhs, little blighters, doughty little Mongolian hillmen." Animal metaphors also abound: they are "tigers, ferrets, mountain goats, and gambolling bull pups" (p. 587).

BOYS' ADVENTURE STORIES

It is important to emphasize that the beliefs outlined above were not limited to an elite circle of Englishmen serving in India. Such beliefs achieved common currency among a large proportion of the British population. Their popularity can be illustrated literally by the circulation of such cultural constructs as adventure stories written for boys during the era of confidence. It is worthwhile to look closeup at some of these stories to grasp the wide reach of ideas of Christian manliness and empire in Britian.

G. A. Henty (1832–1902), one of the more popular adventure writers, had, by the 1890s, sold more than 150,000 books a year (Rutherford, 1997). The heroes of Henty's books were muscular, fearless, athletic boys who were natural leaders and served Britain's Empire in India well. One of them, *At the Point of the Bayonet: A Tale of the Mahratta War* (1902), tells the story of Harry Lindsay who had been saved by his Maratha nurse (named Soyera) after his parents had been killed by her own people. The boy was brought to live with her relatives; soon it becomes apparent that Harry is superior to other little boys in the village. Soyera has no choice but to inform Harry of his true heritage. The conversation between them after the revelation is made is rooted in the ideas I have discussed above:

> *Harry:* But the Mahrattas are strong, mother.
>
> *Soyera:* Yes, they can stand great fatigues, living as they do, so constantly on horseback but like all people of India, they are not fond of exercise save when at war; that is the difference between us and the English. . . . Exercise to them is a pleasure. . . . I came to understand that it was to this love of theirs for outdoor exercises that they owed their strength and firmness of their courage. None can say that the Mahrattas are not brave, but although they will charge gallantly, they soon disperse if the day goes against them. (p. 33)

This dialogue illustrates several of the themes I have already discussed. The Marathas are praised for their martial prowess, but a Maratha woman herself recognizes that they lack discipline and perseverance as well as a commitment to vigorous physical exercise. In an effective literary tactic, the voice of an Indian woman celebrates English manliness. This simultaneously justifies the Empire and shames Indian men in the eyes of their women, who notice and disapprove of the lack of appropriate manly traits.

Soyera then goes on to praise the just and fair government of the British while condemning the rule of local Maratha lords. She urges Harry Lindsay to take up his rightful role as a leader in imperial India. He does so, and the rest of the book describes his exploits as he fights natives, saves Britons, and retires in England after a long and distinguished military career in India. Many of the Indian men he meets along the way (women, both Indian and British, are peripheral to these stories) are brave and skilled warriors but generally volatile, emotional, and almost childlike in their erratic behavior, in contrast to the "manly" Harry Lindsay.

Henty's *Through the Sikh War: A Tale of the Conquest of the Punjaub* (1894) tells a similar tale but with a different protagonist (Percy Groves) and draws on a different war of conquest in India. Percy embarks for India to join his uncle, Col. Roland Groves, who was "Europeanizing" Ranjeet Singh's army. Percy gets involved in various adventures and is rewarded for his courage and heroism during the 1857 "mutiny." The book ends with Percy and his wife retiring in England after a successful time in India. Again, masculinity is an important theme in the story. For example, when Percy first shares his interest in going to India with a retired colonial administrator, the older man encourages the young one, affirming that he has the right physical hardiness for India. On arrival in India, Percy's Uncle Roland teaches him to deal with natives: "it is a standard rule with us out here, Percy . . . never count upon the natives unless you are with them yourself. The Sikhs are brave, but they want good leaders, and are not to be relied upon unless under the eye of an officer they respect. . . . They will fight, and fight pluckily, but without Europeans to lead them they will fall into disorder. . . . Given English officers, the natives of India fight as well as our own men" (p. 113). According to Percy's uncle and (as argued in this chapter) most of the colonial military commanders and administrators deemed that even the "martial" Sikh needed the strong leadership of an Englishman.

Frederick Gibbon's *The Disputed V. C.: A Tale of the Indian Mutiny* (1909) presented a similar story. The hero Ted Russell, athletic, honest, and muscular, traveled to India as a young officer, inspired by the tales of an old "India hand": "Ted listened attentively but said nothing. He too was already filled with admiration for those Christian soldiers and statesmen who were soon to save India" (p. 38). When Ted arrives in India, he notices "with amazement the difference between the strong fighting men of the north west—the sturdy Jat and stalwart Pathan—and the fat, mild, shrinking Babu from Bengal or the slender and weaker Hindu from the South" (p. 41) and remarks that most natives are childlike, " a bundle of tenderness, love, crankiness and cruelty" (p. 63). Like Percy and Harry, Ted is involved in various hair-raising adventures in which English manliness triumphs over native treachery. The novel ends with Ted married and settled in England.

Henty and Gibbon were not the only authors who wrote adventure stories that used ideas of masculinity to create energizing myths for empire-building. H. Rider Haggard, Arthur Ransome, and R. M. Ballantyne also added to this discourse (Gittings, 1996; Phillips, 1997). The Religious Tract Society in 1879 launched the *Boy's Own Paper (BOP)*, which in short order reached a circulation of one million (Phillips, 1997). Christian manliness comprised an important component of this publication, as authors such as Ballantyne—praised by the *BOP* for being "at once amongst the manliest of men and the sincerest of Christians" (quoted in Phillips, 1997, p. 54)— wrote action-packed, Christian adventure stories for boys. The magazine published adventure stories set in the United Kingdom as well as various other parts of the Empire: India, Africa, and the American frontier. Another staple of this publication was "the public school story." These events set in English public schools taught boys the values of Christian manliness by characters who were rewarded for proper "manly" behavior (honesty, courage, strength, and courtesy) and punished for "effeminacy" (excessive emotionality, manipulation, lying, deceit, and weakness). Additionally, the *BOP* underscored the need to be athletic by running articles on how to excel in rugby, cricket, swimming, and rowing.

These themes continued in another BOP publication aptly titled *The Empire Annual for Boys*, which began publication in 1909. The four models of English manhood—explorer, missionary, engineer, and soldier—form the basis of these stories as English men and boys roam the far reaches of the Empire. In Volume 25, for example, there are stories set in Australia, Thailand, India, Burma, and South Africa. As a general rule the protagonists are English boys who overcome obstacles created by the treachery of natives. In the white settler colonies (i.e., Canada, the United States, and Australia), the white settlers retreat to the background and the English boy heroes face the "fierce Red Indian" or "savage Blacks." An adventure story set in Africa, titled "White Magic," describes African spiritual beliefs as follows: "To anyone not acquainted with the mentality of the African savage, the plan might have seemed an impossible one. But Bill knew how prone the native was to anything that smacked of magic" (p. 87). In the same story the traditional healer's suspicion of the vaccinations brought by an English doctor is interpreted thus: "I fancy he feels a kind of professional jealousy of me, . . . And that's why he told these woolly headed savages that I was casting evil spells every time I took their temperature" (p. 86). In every tale the traits of Christian manliness inherent in each of the boy heroes (it should be emphasized that many of these heroes were members of the Boy Scouts) enables them to conquer the multifarious dangers within each colonial realm. As in other *BOP* publications, short articles describing specific athletic and survival skills (presumably needed for the jungles in England's empire) were interspersed among the stories.

Thus, we can see that boys' adventure stories brought the ideas of Christian manliness and empire into the popular realm. The heroes of these stories, embodying all the qualities of Christian manliness, were ideal empire-builders.

SCIENCE AND MANLINESS

The gendered classification so far described in this chapter intersected with and was supported by the production of scientific knowledge developed in the late eighteenth and nineteenth centuries. "Scientific racism" justified itself by two major arguments: monogenism and polygenism. Monogenism argued that human beings descended from a single source but became degraded at differential rates because of environmental factors, climate being the most popular explanation. White Europeans were the least degraded, blacks the most (Gould, 1981, p. 39). Presumably, racial groups in India occupied intermediate positions on a gradated hierarchy between the two extremes. Polygenism argued that human beings comprised separate biological species and that "inferior" races were completely different biological entities from the "superior" races.

Monogenism and degradation as the more popular explanations for racial inferiority were further linked to traits of passivity, uncontrolled sexuality, emotionality, and physical weakness of the "lesser" races, all deriving from a tropical climate. Note that the indicators of racial inferiority delineated above are traits associated with effeminacy. One famous French proponent of this view argued, "The most temperate climate lies between the 40th and 50th degree of latitude, and it produces the most handsome and beautiful *men* [italics added]" (quoted in Gould, 1981, p. 40). Polygeny also had its implications for the Empire. David Hume, the famous philosopher, held the stewardship of the English Colonial Office in the late eighteenth century and was a passionate proponent of this view, claiming that "negroes and in general all other species of men . . . [are] naturally inferior to the whites. There never was a civilized nation of any other complexion than white" (quoted in Gould, 1981, p. 41). The century wore on and the Darwinian revolution introduced evolutionary theory into the monogeny and polygeny debate. Both sides enthusiastically embraced it and reconstituted their versions of scientific racism. As Gould points out, "The monogenists continued to construct linear hierarchies of races according to mental and moral worth; the polygenists now admitted a common ancestry in the prehistoric mists, but affirmed that races had been separate long enough to evolve major inherited differences in talent and intelligence" (p. 73).

Among the many scientific discoveries in late nineteenth-century Britain, two had immediate effect on the gendered discourse under discussion here. One was the emergence of evolutionary anthropology as a scientific field, and two, a fetishization of numbers, that is, an overemphasis on the belief that rigorous numerical measurements guaranteed irrefutable scientific truth. These two trends were reflected in the work of Francis Galton, a leading intellect of the Victorian era. He pioneered the field of modern statistics and coined the word *eugenics*. But Galton's leading work was on the inheritance of intelligence—*Hereditary Genius* (1869)—that sought to prove the genetic nature of intelligence by mapping and measuring skulls and bodies. Not surprisingly, Galton's scientific work found that whites were more intelligent than any other race (p. 76). Both monogenism and Galton's celebration of measurement served to buttress the gendered discourse of colonial administrators and observers in Britain. Another scientific theory that implicitly or explicitly shaped the gendered colonial gaze was recapitulation, which argued that "[t]he *adults of inferior* groups must be like *children of superior* groups" (p. 115; italics added). When the British soldiers affectionately referred to Gurkhas as little tykes or little highlanders or when Sir Henry Lawrence, Christian soldier-hero of 1857 and revered colonial administrator, observed, "Most native chiefs are mere children in mind, and in the ways of the world; and as children they should be treated not with affectionate sympathy, but with systematic firmness" (Lawrence, 1859, p. 191), contemporary scientific knowledge provided justification for this cultural perspective.

Monogenism and the theory of racial degeneration also constructed the lens of masculinized colonial observation. Ethnographic studies such as those of Sir Herbert Risley's *The People of India* (1915) and John Anderson's *The Peoples of India* (1913) presented scientific measurements of the skulls and bodies of the people of India, who then became categorized and classified according to various traits, one of which was martiality. Some groups like the Jats and Sikhs were warlike, while others, such as the Bengalis, were not. Risley did not hesitate to make sociological comments when presenting his classification based on scientific measurements: "The Arya Samaj . . . [may] almost be described as a nationalist development of Hinduism . . . their teaching is of a bold and *masculine* type and is free from the *limp* eclectism which has proved to be fatal to the Brahmo Samaj" (Risley, 1969, p. 21; italics added). The inference of male potency and impotency as a measure of masculinity in the words of Risley cannot be ignored. Such gendered comments found their way into other objective scientific reports, for example, the 1911 *Census Report for Uttar Pradesh:* "The Arya Samaj alone has provided a *manly* and straightforward creed which is in all essentials thoroughly Hindu" (quoted in Rai, 1967, p. 69; italics added).

An interesting fusion of "science" and the gendered imperial gaze is also reflected in observations about Swami Vivekananda during his tours of England and America. One famous Western doctor viewed Vivekananda's physical stature, as reported in the *Indian Mirror* of October 5, 1895, in the following terms: "Narrow-headed people are indifferent or averse to war and commerce. This is particularly true of the believers in the Vedas. . . . One of the most striking peculiarities of the man is the femininity indicated in nearly every contour of the figure, face, head and hands. He has probably as perfect a conic hand as could be imagined. . . . The oriental nations generally have been noted for the conic hand" (quoted in Basu and Ghosh, 1969, p. 77). This observation about Vivekananda forms a relevant footnote to our narrative on masculinity and nation because the Swami, one of the most passionate advocates of masculine Hinduism in nineteenth-century India, is among the select array of historical figures revered by contemporary Hindu nationalists groups for his embodiment of masculine traits.

In addition to physical measurements, the British provided various other "scientific" explanations for the inferiority of Indian manhood, for example, climate (heat saps masculinity), disease (malaria and hookworm make men weak), and Hindu rituals (child marriage and consequent juvenile sexual activity erode manhood) (MacMunn, 1933, p. 2; see also Sinha, 2000). The argument for degradation based on early marriage and premature

sexual intercourse entered the gendered discourse by drawing on British fas-
cination with India as a land of unbridled sexuality. Both Indian men and
women became incorporated into this discourse. Indian women, viewed as
seductive sirens, threatened the righteousness of the manly Christian and
Indian men, who as weak beings lacking the discipline and strength to control their sexual urges, needed the guidance of the masculine, imperial English. The premises of scientific knowledge of that era simply became embedded in a racist discourse wherein the more manly races of Risley's
classification were seen by some commentators to be racially determined:
"[T]the point here is that some four thousand years ago a white race akin to
our British selves, which became the mother of the Hindu race of today, . . .
swirled up and round the mountains we now call Afghanistan" (MacMunn,
1933, p. 7). The martial races of India retained some of the original racial
features of this great white migration, while the rest became degraded
through climate, disease, and bad cultural habits.

The gendered gaze of the British intersected with two other common
European imperial views that were dominant in India—the construction of a
mythic, golden, Hindu Vedic past and ambiguity about Islam and its practi-
tioners (Talbot, 2001, pp. 22–34). Some like Max Mueller regarded Muslims
as vicious destroyers of this golden age and the source of the present degradation of Hindu culture (Chowdhury, 2001, p. 54). As we will see in the next
chapter, both interpretations—the golden Vedic past and demonic Muslim
invader—were used by Hindu nationalists to construct their own cultural
vocabulary of resistance to British rule. However, some observers were not so
positive about Hinduism, past or present, declaring: "I hear the clarion-blast
of triumph for civilization, and progress, and Christianity, over the caste-
bound systems of Asia, over its petty and sanguinary tyrannies and over its
hoary and blood-stained idolatries" (Ryder, 1853, p. viii) and "not less than a
HUNDRED AND THIRTY MILLION SUBJECTS, sunk beneath a load of
most debasing superstitions, and the cruelest idolatries that ever polluted the
surface of the earth, or brutalized the nature of man" (Duff, ca. 1850s, p. 2;
emphasis in the original).

But as the era of confidence receded and the era of doubt emerged in
response to growing nationalist resistance, a slightly different view of Hindus
and Muslims began to circulate within the colonial milieu. Valentine Chirol
in his influential *Indian Unrest* (1910) wrote, "It is important to note . . . that
the more dangerous forms of unrest are practically confined to the Hindus. . . . Not a single Mahomedan has been implicated in . . . the criminal
conspiracies . . . the Mahomedans of India as a whole identified their interests . . . with the consolidation and permanence of British rule. It is almost a
misnomer to speak of Indian unrest. Hindu unrest would be a far more accurate term" (p. 6).[8] The effeminate Bengali bore the brunt of British wrath for
being the prime instigator of this "Hindu" unrest. As Greenberger (1969)

noted in this context, the Bengali cannot win his right to manhood even when he is involved in resistance because, in British eyes, the effete babus were not stirred by a noble desire to create a manly independent nation but only motivated by narrowly self-interested monetary interests (pp. 129–30).

In contrast, Chirol (1910), although disapproving of the militant tactics of young Bengali revolutionaries, acknowledges that perhaps some Bengalis can reach for masculinity: "In its moral aspects the revolt of young Bengal represents very frequently a healthy reaction against sloth and self-indulgence and the premature exhaustion of manhood which is such a common feature in a society that has for centuries been taught to disregard physiological laws in the enforcement of child marriage" (p. 102). It must also be remembered that most Hindus, with the exception of the martial races were constructed with the same effeminate traits as the Bengalis. The observations made about Bengali involvement—depending on one's perspective—in the "unrest" or "resistance to alien rule" held true for most Hindus (pp. 43–46). However, whether the British viewed Hindu involvement in anti-British movements as a self-interested elite movement striving to gain power at the expense of the masses of people who benefited from British rule or as a Hindu bid to gain lost manhood, the resistance itself was viewed as illegitimate because

> India is neither a nation like France nor a collection of nations like Europe. . . . If the strong hand of England were withdrawn, the different races and creeds would never agree to a common line of action . . . they would not consent for long to subordinate their racial and religious jealousies to the common good. (Morison, 1899, p. 3)

While patriotism was a trait to be found in Christian manliness, obviously, the martial races of India did not embody it, as the following passage reveals:

> the martial races of India are brave and make excellent soldiers, . . . the native civilians are possessed of great intelligence. . . . But India is wanting in the one qualification essential to independence, inasmuch as she possesses no sentiment of nationality. (p. 2)

Ultimately, since an India under Indians was not a "manly" nation in all senses of that word, it could not exist.

CONCLUSION

Christian manliness formed a central component in the lens that the British used to focus their gaze on India. Its multifaceted and shifting interpretation of manhood shaped the classification and categorization of the populace, which colonial administrators found so alien, exotic, and, to a certain extent, baffling. India became the realm where British masculinity was tested as Britain reached for supremacy in the world. Imperial masculinity was inextricably linked with British and Anglo-Saxon glory. Imperialism, nationalism, manliness, and conquest all reinforced one another. In hierarchies constructed by Christian manliness, the Englishman was always deemed superior even to Indian "martial races," who might be brave soldiers but lacked all other "manly" traits. The multiple values shaping Christian manliness and its relevance for the Empire were socially and generationally reproduced as young boys received exposure to these values through fiction, instructional monographs, and education in public schools.

This masculinized gaze shaped the creation of a vast interconnected network of knowledge about India circulating through and disseminated by colonial accounts, biographies, autobiographies, and light fiction. As a result, stereotypes such as the effeminate Hindu, the manly Sikh, the devious Maratha, and the loyal Gurkha became embedded in Britain's cultural vocabulary. Further, these culturally and socially produced narratives were endowed—by a new scientific discourse—with the status of universal and objective truth. One vital impact of this complex gendered hierarchy was the innovative manner in which various Indian elite constructed an oppositional masculine identity, one built with Hindu symbols and icons to resist the effeminization of Hindus, the denigration of Maratha martial honor, and the British rejection of Indian demands for self-rule.

THREE

Nationalism

Masculine Hinduism and Resisting the British Gaze

"Away! Away to the battlefield!
Sing your loudest songs of triumph:
Guard your faith imperiled!" Mother India cries. . . .
Rush to war! Rush to war!
We shall disperse the troops of the enemy. There will be left no
Traces of the foe in old and sacred Aryavarta.
We shall make our ablutions in the blood of the enemy
And, with it, we shall tint Hindustan red!
—*Bande Mataram*, Front Page, December 1911

THE TENOR OF THE sentiments expressed in the martial invocation above, penned in growing reaction to British colonialism, clearly reflected the tide of resistance forming in India as well as the motifs underlying the greater battle of cultures, East and West.[1] Its discourse, constructed with ideas of manhood circulating through the Indian cultural terrain, became mediated through indigenous categories as well as British ideas of manliness.[2]

In this chapter, I will examine more closely how notions of masculinity and male bodies shaped the Indian nationalist discourse in the nineteenth century and interplayed with a specific British interpretation of hegemonic masculinity: Christian manliness. Again, the argument is not that such nationalist responses mechanistically incorporated British categories but that a dynamic dialogue occurred instead, with a responsiveness and resistance to those colonial observations embedded in both Christian manliness and muscular Christianity. Ideas of hegemonic masculinity ordering intersections of

gender and nation are evident within the writings of three prominent nine-
teenth- and twentieth-century nationalist ideologues that I have chosen as
representative of a certain masculinist nationalist discourse: Swami
Vivekananda (1863–1902); V. D. Savarkar (1883–1966); and Madam Cama
(1861–1936). Also influential in promulgating certain interpretations of
nationalist masculinity were Bankimchandra Chatterjee (1838–1894), as
reflected in his novel *Anandamath* (1882); Sarala Debi Ghosal (later Choud-
hury, 1872–1946); and Margaret Noble (1867–1911), also known as Sister
Nivedita, an Anglo-Irish follower of Vivekananda. The works of these individuals will be presented singly here; in their own lives, however, most of
them had either close personal contact with or had read the works of the others. Collectively, their ties and efforts joined to give voice to a larger interre-
lated web of nationalist discourse.

The intellectual legacy of these leaders clearly lives on in present-day
debates defining Hindu nationalism. For example, in conducting field
research during one visit to a Shiv Sena *shakha* (branch office), I was taken
back by a young *shakha pramukh*'s (local leader) assumption that I would be
sympathetic to his party's aggressive Hindu stance. In his mind, my Bengali
ethnicity automatically conferred a receptivity to Swami Vivekananda and
by association a presumed support for the Sena's cause. Indeed most Sena,
BJP, RSS, and VHP activists spoke approvingly of the Swami's attempts to
revive Hindu pride and his courage to celebrate the idea of a Hindu nation.
Frequently, in the offices of these organizations hangs a widely known and
well-loved portrait of Vivekananda, one that captures the revolutionary masculinist zeitgeist of the Indian nationalist movement: Vivekananda's saffron-
clad shoulders are thrown back, his crossed arms project strength, his eyes
gaze fearlessly ahead. My extensive interviews with the editors of the RSS
affiliated newspapers *Organiser* (English) and *Panchyajanya* (Hindi) as well as
numerous VHP, BJP, and RSS activists confirmed the foundational location
of Vivekananda, Savarkar, and Chatterjee within the ongoing Hindu nationalist project in India.[3]

Interestingly, Madam Cama, Sister Nivedita, and Sarala Ghosal, who
were also significant figures of that same era, were not mentioned by these
men. Perhaps the omission was rooted simply in patriarchal blindness to the
contribution of many women to nationalism. Or perhaps it represented a
more selective omission by intention in that none of the three women listed
above adhered to traditional roles of womanhood in advancing the nationalist cause of their era, neither as mothers nurturing potential nationalist
heroes nor as wives providing support to the same male figures. Thus, in effect
the three women were unmentionables, unworthy of recognition. Regardless
of the reasons, the contribution of Indian women to the construction of
nationalism (and indeed other facets of political activity) is no longer being
ignored. Recently, the publications of *Kali for Women*, a feminist press estab-

lished in 1984, coupled with the work of feminists including Grewal (1996), Kumar (1993), Ray (1995), and Vaid and Sangari (1989) have begun the process of moving the achievements of many colonial women to the foreground. My focus on Madam Cama, Sister Nivedita, and Sarala Ghosal attempts to add to such an excavation of women's lives and works. These three individuals defied traditional roles to become active proponents of masculine Hinduism in their own pursuit, even aggressive quests, to build a strong Indian nation.

Masculine Hinduism anchored the image of strength within the Hindu nationalist discourse. While the discourse that centered on masculine Hinduism constituted a form of resistance to colonial British hierarchy, which itself was founded upon ideas of hegemonic masculinity, Indian masculine Hinduism was *not* a mechanical incorporation of British ideas dressed in Hindu cultural garb, nor was it monolithic. Rather, the Indian construct essentially was a creative response to British disparagement of Indian men. Savarkar clearly perceived masculine Hinduism in terms of virile Aryan warriors riding onward from a legacy of Indian (i.e., Hindu) imperialism; Vivekananda's image of masculine Hinduism—reflecting the purity and stance of a warrior-monk and derived from notions of a mythic ascetic warriorhood—was delineated most eloquently in Chatterjee's *Anandamath*. In Vivekananda's vision of masculine Hinduism, spiritual strength sat in the foreground; Savarkar's vision emphasized martial prowess. Both viewed physical strength as an important condition for expressing images of masculinity. Madam Cama, Sister Nivedita, and Sarala Debi drew on a figure of manhood that was closer to Savarkar's Aryan soldier than Vivekananda's fighting monk. These masculine images, created in opposition to an effeminate "other," did not display physical weakness, cowardice, passivity, or a nonmartial spirit, qualities that could threaten the construction of a strong and independent Indian nation. Thus, as will be seen, only extraordinary women were able to enter this masculine landscape by becoming warriors themselves and by shedding outer markers of their femininity. These particular nationalist imaginings played out within a Hindu context. Put another way, an integral aspect of this particular interpretation of nation is the Hindu perspective, one that needs to be located within the contemporary debate surrounding nationalism in India.

SECULARISM AND COMMUNALISM IN INDIA

The tension between secularism (civic nationalism) and communalism (cultural nationalism) defines the nationalist debate in India, as we saw above in the Introduction. T. N. Madan (1993) underscores the idea that secularism is the state ideology of India (p. 674). However, a secular state is not a homogenous entity. Multiple interpretations of secularism and its relationship to the state are anchored in unique and specific conceptions of politics as well as political and cultural milieus. For example, the secular state in the United States may differ from the one in the United Kingdom, Germany, or India.

Madan argues for two major schools of secularism in India: Gandhian and Nehruvian. Nehru considered religion as bigoted and dogmatic. In his eyes, science, reason, and a socialist ideology provide the true basis for a modern nation (p. 683). In contrast, Gandhi did not reject religion so categorically. He was secular in that he placed religion in the private realm and believed that the state should respect all religions equally (*sarvadharma sambhava*). He also felt that the state should be responsible for the welfare of its citizens. But, concurrently, Gandhi also asserted notions of civic virtue and spirituality as necessary for living a moral life. In his eyes, a state that only emphasized material well-being and promoted consumerism would not be moral, as it would be rooted in individual selfishness from which a good society cannot be elaborated. To the extent that virtue defined by religion signified living a good life, Gandhi was not secular; further, he had begun to blur the lines between civic and cultural nationalism. What kind of morality should define society? Most ordinary folk shape morality particularly, within the outline of their own religious beliefs. Under the principle of *sarvadharma sambhava*, was Gandhi suggesting that Islamic, Christian, and Hindu religious moralities were equally valid? Has Indian secularism supported this equality? Given that almost eighty-five percent of the Indian population practice Hinduism in one form or another, how would religious minorities figure within this majority?

Cultural nationalists defining nation within Hindu markers would presumably celebrate the dominance of Hinduism and categorically claim that India is a Hindu country. In that context, religious minorities would have to respectfully acknowledge this dominance. But this interpretation of Hindu nationalism, according to Pandey (1993), did not come to the foreground of Indian society until after the 1920s. Before that, even prominent leaders like Madan Mohan Malaviya, who celebrated Hinduism and Hindu culture, claimed, "Hindustan is not just the land of the Hindus. . . . Hindustan is the much beloved homeland of both Hindus and Muslims. These two communities live together harmoniously and will continue to do so in the future" (quoted in Hindi in Pandey, 1993, p. 260; my translation). However, after the 1920s, argues Pandey, both civic and cultural nationalists—rather than emphasizing the heterogeneous nature of Indian society by acknowledging the multiple ties shaping an individual's identity—began to think of a homogenous, unified India. Both groups focused on "the Spirit of India, the Essence, an already existing Oneness, seeking to realize its eternal mission" (p. 252). Some claimed that the "Spirit of India" was Hindu, others (like Nehru), that it was secular and rational, while still others such as Gandhi dealt with the notion of Oneness and diversity by removing religion to the private sphere, where all paths to God were equally valid.

However, some scholars argue that whether it is discussed as civic or cultural nationalism, as Gandhian or Nehruvian or Hindu nationalism, the historical legacy of Indian nationalism has always recognized "a single source of Indian tradition, viz. ancient Hindu civilization. Islam here is either the history of foreign conquest or a domesticated element of everyday popular life. The classical heritage of Islam remains external to Indian history" (Chatterjee, 1992, p. 149). Other scholars agree by arguing that Indian secularism is embedded within a Hindu context (Srivastava, 1998). By describing implicit Hindu cultural echoes even within a self-conscious secular institution—the Doon School—responsible for educating the secular (Nehruvian) elite of India, Srivastava persuasively argues that both in the past and present, Hindu contexualism is part of the Indian secular landscape. For example, the Doon school symbol, the lamp as an image resonates and is reminiscent of the *diyas* (earthen lamps) that are lit as an integral part of Hindu worship. Further, on occasions when dignitaries visit the school, Indian culture is celebrated through songs, chants, and mythic icons, all embedded in the mystique of Hindu context (pp. 90–130). As a result, Srivastava also voices suspicion of any clear-cut demarcation of secularism/communalism or civic/cultural nationalism in the Indian context.

Clearly, Hinduism becomes the specter that haunted and continues to haunt Indian nationalism. The principle difference between self-styled Hindu nationalists and Indian civic nationalists or secularists seemingly is the degree of emphasis that each places on Hindu superiority and dominance. The first group unabashedly claims Hindu cultural superiority both within India and on the international scene, cautioning non-Hindus to accept and be tolerant of this dominant culture. The second group circumvents the implicit (and, to be fair, unconscious) Hindu contextualization by focusing on minority rights and equality and rejecting claims of national exclusion based on Hindu supremacy. However, at times, this distinction becomes problematic. For example, Swami Vivekananda spoke enthusiastically of *Hindu* spiritual superiority and condemned the West for its spiritually bankrupt and overly consumerist culture. By utilizing such a focus on Hindu superiority, was the Swami preaching an exclusionary (read anti-Islamic) view of nation? In modern India, Vivekananda is revered not only by members of the RSS, VHP, and BJP but by many others who would encamp themselves as "secular."

Finally, as we will discover, Hindu superiority itself occurs as a recurrent theme in Hindu nationalist discourse. Indeed, it is possible to argue that the tensions between "us" and "them" in the context of cultural nationalism stem from a hierarchy of cultures, where either one, buttressed by political and military might, has subjugated the other or competes culturally to determine that question of superiority. In order to resist cultural imperialism or emerge as the cultural victor, the first imperative for self-professed nationalists is to assert the preeminence of the nation they are defining and protecting. Its articulation may occur in religious, economic, or political terms or in a vocabulary combining all three. As British cultural imperialism, shored up by a discourse centered on Christian manliness, became an integral part of the Empire's march forward, some Indian nationalists within this colonial milieu fought back by holding aloft images of masculine Hinduism—whether configured as Aryan soldier or warrior-monk—to declare the cultural supremacy of India.

THE COLONIAL MILIEU

British engagement in India, beginning in the seventeenth century, gradually evolved into a combined direct and indirect control over the entire subcontinent by mid-nineteenth century. By the late nineteenth century, the British colonial presence had begun to penetrate indigenous society significantly. As the degree of British control increased, so too did the measure to which Indian culture was transformed. Indeed, increasing pressure was brought to bear upon every facet of India's national life. Interaction between the two cultures stimulated a wide spectrum of responses as Indians sought to reorder their traditional relationships of secular and religious authority, both irreparably altered by British imperialism. These diverse responses coalesced into the socioreligious movements that collectively came to be known as the Hindu renaissance.

Its roots took sustenance adroitly within the colonial milieu, that is, within the physical space and time when British colonialism met with indigenous Indian culture. The defining agents of the milieu, British colonial administrators and missionaries, introduced Western political and socioreligious ideologies to Indian society. The new perspectives and ideas posed challenges not only to India's existing political framework but also to traditional Indian thought, religion, and concepts of social duty. The disturbance compelled the development of a new dialectic between indigenous traditions and the colonial world. The movements that arose in response to the colonial milieu, however, did not simply fuse Indian tradition and a British paradigm or insert a mechanistic incorporation of British categories within Indian society. Rather, they innovatively (re)configured a legacy of cultural patterns and symbols to a rapidly changing social context.

Of the wide-ranging movements that sprang up within the Hindu renaissance, encompassing many ideologies from conservative revivalism to radical reform, almost all reflected the desire to define, assert, and defend a Hindu identity at both individual and societal levels. In this sense, the term "renaissance" may mislead: the movement was less a spontaneous reawakening of interest in historical cultural roots and more of a self-conscious desire to resist or adjust to radical changes forced upon Indian culture by external forces. Hindu revivalism comprised part of this cultural movement. Both the renaissance and the revivalism followed multiple and complex trajectories, and it may not be fruitful to place these in hierarchal orders of importance. Recon-

figurations of the idea of Hindu manhood became one of these cultural trajectories. As I have argued above, this particular trajectory had vital consequences for the manner in which certain Indians imagined and related with
their constructed Hindu nation. It is also important at this juncture to highlight the flexibility of the heuristic terms "Hindu renaissance" or "Hindu
revivalism." While V. D. Savarkar and Swami Vivekananda may be placed
squarely in the midst of such a movement, it is possible that Madam Cama
(as a Zoarastrian) may not be recognized or accepted as members of those
ranks. However, an examination of her words and actions illustrates that
whether or not she identified herself as part of a Hindu movement, what Srivastava refers to as "Hindu contextualism" was very much a part of her
nationalist vision.

The impact of this late nineteenth-century (and early twentieth-century) movement on modern Indian society was profound. However, it is
important to remember that an argument for an unbroken continuity
between these thinkers and their late twentieth- and early twenty-first-century followers is not being articulated here. When British and Indian thought
intersected in the colonial milieu, certain images about manhood and nation
became released into the cultural context and available for use by later generations, regardless of whether BJP or Shiv Sena or RSS activists have been
cognizant of these origins. Further, it is also possible that as modern-day
activists draw on these same images, they may again become reconfigured and
used in contemporary India, and in ways contrary to earlier intent and use.

The poem cited at the beginning of this chapter reflects various general
themes concerning the vision of manhood emerging to the foreground of the
Indian nation in the late nineteenth and early twentieth centuries. Its martial tone depicts armed masculinity in dominant metaphors of brave warriorhood. Further, its patriotism, couched as the desire to protect the motherland,
is denoted by lines and phrasing such as "Will the shiny sword rest in its
sheath / When the Indian is offended?" and "the trampling of the British."
The vocabulary is quite significant: the intersection of gender and nation is
explicit. The nation is created as a mother figure ("Guard your faith imperiled!" Mother India cries) and the warriors protecting it are men ("Will you
consider but your lives / When peril threatens mothers, wives?"). At least in
this vision, women have no place as warriors of the nation but are visualized
as symbols of national honor in need of protection. Finally, in the poem India
is constructed as an old and united land, its origins obscured in the mists of
time ("There will be left no / Traces of the foe in old and sacred Aryavarta").
Aryavarta refers to the land of the Aryans and draws on the belief in an
ancient Vedic golden age and nation, existing before the various Mongol,
Persian, and Afghan conquests. The image of Aryavarta, together with pleas
to Mother Kali (Hindu goddess), and reference to Hindustan infer a strong
Hindu contexualization of this particular vision of the Indian nation.

Indeed, the poem creatively resists two themes of the British colonial critique of India constructed with ideas of Christian manliness—the lack of a proper martial spirit and the absence of patriotism—by using Indian interpretations of gender. For example, Mother Kali personifies both a martial spirit and the Indian nation. Such a divine female embodiment of martial spirit is not prevalent in ideas of Christian manliness. Kali, usually imagined as a ferocious female deity, blood dripping from her lips, a garland of human skulls encircling her neck, and weapons held aloft in her four arms, provides an effective icon for the male Indian warrior's martial determination to overthrow British subjugation. Thus, the beginnings of a Hindu cultural appropriation of the ideas of hegemonic masculinity—masculine Hinduism—can be seen here in opposition to the British articulation of Christian manliness. The Hindu contexualization also anticipates the creation of Islam as the "other" of the Hindu nation. As we examine additional texts below, it will be clear that although there is reference (as in the poem) to the humiliating presence of the British, Islam and the Muslim conquests are, at times, seen as the greater enemy of the nationalism expressed by masculine Hinduism.

V. D. SAVARKAR

Savarkar, neither the first nor perhaps the most articulate voice delineating ideas of Hindu nationalism, was certainly one of the most political and hence played an influential role in the expression of Hindu nationalism, as visualized by the BJP, RSS, VHP, and Shiv Sena. Vinayak Damodar Savarkar was born on May 28, 1883, in the western Indian state of Maharashtra. In 1899, he formed, along with his brother, a secret revolutionary society—the Abhinava Bharat Society (Young India Society)—dedicated to reviving Hindu pride and overthrowing British rule. The society developed ties with a similar organization in Bengal known as the Anushilan Samiti. Most of Savarkar's early schooling occurred in his home state until he left for London in June 1906. There, he came into contact with Madam Cama and other Indian expatriates. In 1910, Savarkar was arrested because of an alleged involvement in a conspiracy against the British government and deported to India. There he was tried and sentenced to a term of fifty years in the Andaman Islands, home to a maximum-security British penitentiary. Savarkar was released in 1924, subject to the condition that he not leave the district of Ratnagiri in Maharashtra (Grover, 1990, p. xi). This ban was lifted in 1937, when he then became president of the Hindu Maha Sabha, an organization bent on the political mobilization of Hindus and Hinduism (Anderson and Damle, 1987, p. 36).

Savarkar wrote profusely, both in and out of jail, but among his works *The Indian War of Independence* (1909), *Hindutva* (1923), *Hindu Pad-Padashahi or a Review of the Hindu Empire of Maharashtra* (1925), and *Six Glo-*

rious Epochs of Indian History (1963) were the most influential in developing and framing ideas of masculine Hinduism in modern Hindu nationalism. His annual addresses to the Hindu Mahasabha during his term as president also facilitated the politicization of the Hindu nation. Masculine Hinduism very much comprised part of his nationalist vision.

An exploration of India's weak martial spirit—demonstrated, in Savarkar's mind, by the subjugation of millions of Indians by about one hundred and fifty thousand Englishmen—formed the thematic framework of almost all of his work. Savarkar rejected the British solution—that is, the effeminate nature of Indian men—to this conundrum. He posited instead that the British victory could be explained by the degeneration of a once powerful and mature masculine Hinduism, one that had reached its zenith during the rule of the Marathas under Shivaji and sparked briefly during the War of 1857. The latter was identified by him as the first war of Indian independence. As Savarkar outlined his configuration of masculine Hinduism, it becomes clear that "Hindu Swaraj" (Hindu nation) animated the warrior's patriotic fervor.

In most of Savarkar's work, the "other" of the Hindu nation is not the British but the Muslims. Indeed, at points Savarkar accepts the superiority of British martial tactics. In *Hindu-Pad-Padashahi* (1942), while explaining the defeat of the Marathas in the Anglo-Maratha wars, he commented:

> For, England was then relatively far better equipped in all these essentials that contributed to great conquests. Their nation had long since passed the period of incubation, civil feuds and Wars of the Roses and religious persecutions. . . . Unlike the Marathas, they had long been trained into all those public virtues of how to obey and order . . . of patriotic loyalty to their country . . . above all, racial cohesion and solidarity of aim . . . which a strongly consolidated nation-state engenders in a people. Even the Marathas—who of all Indian people were the best fitted in all these qualities—were woefully lacking in them relatively to the English. . . . But we grudge not England her victory. Like a good sportsman we admire her skill and might that . . . *snatched an Indian Empire from our struggling hand* and on that foundation has raised a magnificent World-Empire, the like of which history has scarcely recorded. (p. 288; italics added)

And in *Six Glorious Epochs of Indian History* (1985) he voiced a similar sentiment:

> [British traits] shine all the more gloriously when contrasted with the confused way of doing things prevalent in *our country at that time* . . . our lack of order, political instability, and our complete disregard for well-organized work . . . it was on the whole natural that the British who were *at that time* superior to us in the art of war and strength should succeed us. (p. 460; italics added)

Although Savarkar seemingly accepts the vision of Indian effeminacy located at the center of the discourse surrounding Christian manliness, a more nuanced reading might perceive that he is, actually, resisting such a view. The portions of the quotations I have emphasized above reveal Savarkar's belief that events had conspired to temporarily weaken Hindu manhood, and they underscore his confidence that the Indian nation would soon awaken to realize its martial spirit. Further with the phrase "snatched an Indian Empire from our struggling hand," he constructs an India equal in martial power to the British Empire. In his narrative, India's imperial stature is eroding because of a temporary decline in Hindu militarism; hence India, as a "good sport," ruefully acknowledges the martial skill of an equal as it surrenders to British might.

But what was this spirit of masculine Hinduism that had been vanquished by adverse circumstances? Even though Savarkar never explicitly described his ideal, it can be detected within most of his observations. For example, the following passage reveals the rationale guiding his choice of the glorious epochs of Hindu history: "But by the Glorious Epoch I mean the one from the history of that warlike generation and the brave leaders and successful warriors who inspire and lead it to a war of liberation" (p. 3). Savarkar's view of masculinity includes martial prowess, courage, muscular strength, as well as the ability to be organized and efficient. Although, his image of masculinity centered on male bodies, it is clear that extraordinary women could also embody these traits of masculine Hinduism. One example is Lakshmibai, the Rani (Queen) of Jhansi who defiantly declared, "Give up my Jhansi? I will not. Let him try who dares!" (Savarkar, 1960, p. 147). But the Rani could claim this warrior status only by erasing all visible markers of herself as a woman: "Her hair was tied up into a bun on the nape of her neck. She wore a white saree and a plain white choli [blouse]. Thus, sometimes in male attire and sometimes in female, the Bai Sahib [madam queen] used to honour the Durbar [the public court where people met the monarch] with her presence. Those assembled never used to see her person" (p. 148). Savarkar called her the Goddess Kali and extolled her courage: "A mere woman, hardly twenty-three yet, beautiful of conduct, she wielded a power over her subjects, exhibited by very few, even among men" (p. 160).

The Rani could emulate the model of masculine Hinduism not because of, but despite, her femininity. She ruled her subjects behind a screen, thus adhering to the rules of modesty guiding female presence in the public. When she did appear outside the inner realm of the palace, her figure was devoid of color, jewelry, and other adornments. Indeed, because she was a widow and regent for her son, her sexual nature had receded to the background: her maternal nature moved to the fore. The figure of the Rani embodies two models of "woman in the nation" that recur in other texts examined here as

NATIONALISM 53

well as in modern Hindutva: the heroic mother and masculinized, celibate woman warrior. The Rani fought in the guise of a masculine warrior (literally donning male clothing) to defend her son's birthright. Savarkar's texts also draw on another heroic mother—Jijabai—who according to myth taught her son, the powerful Maratha warrior Shivaji, the value of martial valor and encouraged him to resist Mughal imperialism. The Rani and Jijabai are still celebrated in the narrative of Hindu nationalism.

The brave warriors of Savarkar's story strove to protect a powerful nation, worthy of their loyalty. In his influential *Indian War of Independence* (1960) Savarkar described his ideal nation, the primary trait of which was martial strength deriving from unity: "And, hence Nana's programme was first to fight a united fight to make India free and by removing internecine warfare to establish the rule of the United States of India which would, thus, take its rightful place in the council of the free nations of the world" (p. 30). Further, in this text—unlike his later work—Hindus and Muslims united to defeat British imperialism:

> Men and women, rich and poor, young and old, sepoys and citizens, moulvies and Pandits, Hindus and Mahomedans—all attacked the foreign enslaver with their swords drawn under the banner of their country. (p. 54)

But, this attempt to establish *swaraj* (an independent nation) failed. Although courageous leaders—Nana Sahib, Rani of Jhansi, Tatia Tope— bravely embodied the virtues of Hindu soldiers, the treachery of their own compatriots sabotaged their valorous bid for freedom:

> The Revolution of 1857 was a test to see how far India had come towards unity, independence, and popular power. The fault of failure lies with the idle, *effeminate*, selfish, and treacherous men who ruined it. (p. 179; italics added)

It becomes clear that Hindu effeminacy (weakness, treachery, lack of martial ability, cowardice) constructed in opposition to masculine Hinduism (strength, patriotism, martial prowess, valor) is an internal threat to the proper establishment of an independent, united, martial nation. The authors represented in this study imagine a nation wherein this fatal flaw in national character has been overcome. However, Savarkar ended his treatise on 1857 hopefully by quoting a poem written by the heir to the Mogul throne, Bahadur Shah:

> As long as there remains the least trace
> Of loyalty in the hearts of our heroes,
> So long, the sword of Hindustan shall be
> Sharp, and one day shall flash even at the
> Gates of London. (p. 180)

In Savarkar's interpretation of the lament of a Moghul emperor—the nominal head of a failed war aimed at restoring his throne—India is read as "Hindustan" (land of the Hindus). In this vision, Bahadur Shah, though a descendant of India's Moghul conquerors (who were Muslim and originally from Kabul in Afghanistan), accepts the cultural dominance of the Hindus in the geographical space known as India. Further, his image of the flashing sword conflates nation and martial prowess to underscore Savarkar's dream that once Hindu manhood awakened, the sword of Hindustan would be capable of conquering even mighty Britain. Finally, despite some perfunctory acceptance of Hindu-Muslim unity, Savarkar's ideal failed to mute its Hindu colors. Hindu heroes (i.e., Nanasaheb, Tatia Tope, and the Rani of Jhansi) stand guard, while in the case of an Indian victory Bahadur Shah was to be returned not to the throne of the Moghuls, an alien people, but to a free and united (Hindu) India.

In later works, Savarkar moved away from even this cursory idea of Hindustan, symbolizing a homeland for both Hindus and Muslim, and used masculine Hinduism to narrate a martial Hindu nation with a long imperial history. For example, in *Hindutva* (1949) he writes,

> The day when the Horse of Victory returned to Ayodhya unchallenged and unchallengeable, the great white umbrella of sovereignty was unfurled over the Imperial throne of Ramchandra, the brave, Ramchandra the good, and a loving allegiance was sworn, not only by Princes of Aryan blood, but Hanuman—Sugriva—Bibhishana from the south—that day was the real birthday of our *Hindu people*. (p. 10; italics added)

This passage was integral to Savarkar's national vision as well as to the ideal of nationhood underlying modern Hindutva politics. The events and actors used to explain the origin of the Hindu nation imply, unequivocally, that Hindustan was born out of war and conquest. "Horse of Victory" signifies the Ashwamedhya Yagna, wherein, according to myth, an ancient Hindu king released a white horse, which was then followed by his army as it wandered to various other kingdoms of the land. If the horse returned unchallenged by the armies of the monarchies it passed through, this was an acknowledgement by all other rulers that the horse's owner was the supreme emperor. In Savarkar's text, the return of the "Horse of Victory" consolidated a Hindu India under Ramchandra's martial strength. It is interesting to note that Ram, unlike Shivaji or Rana Pratap and other favored Hindu icons, is not a historical figure but actually the protagonist of a long and sacred Hindu epic, *Ramayana*. A debate exists as to whether or not Ram is a historical figure. In Savarkar's story of the origin of the Hindu nation, myth and history are bridged by valorizing Ram as the founder. Further, by alluding to "Princes of Aryan blood," Savarkar alluded to a warrior culture created by Aryans, marked by "political virility" and "manly nobility" (p. 17).

Hindutva elaborated on this warrior culture and the environmental factors that led to its demise. It also advocated the construction of an exclusionary, strong, warlike, and unified nation clearly separated from the "other":

> When the nation grew intensely self-conscious as an organism . . . it instinctively turned to draw the line of division and mark well the position it occupied so as to make it clear to themselves where they exactly stood and to the world how they were unmistakably a people by themselves. (p. 23)

In *Hindutva*, Savarkar sketched the national boundaries he envisioned by distinguishing between Sindhustan—the land between the River Indus and the Indian Ocean—and Mlechhastan, representing the domicile land of foreigners outside these geographical boundaries. The Aryans, noble Hindu warriors, inhabited Sindhustan, which later became distorted (by the tongues of foreign conquerors) to Hindustan. Invaders from Mlechhastan—Huns, *Shakhas*, Afghans, Persians—conquered Hindustan repeatedly. However, although brave, warriors born of this land, could not resist the onslaughts. Why not? Savarkar faults Buddhism as a cause. The fanatic embrace of nonviolence by Buddhism "had no argument that could efficiently meet this strange bible of Fire and Steel" (p. 18) and "nations and civilizations fell in heaps before the sword of Islam of Peace" (p. 35). Mlechhastan, configured as Islamic, conquered the Hindu homeland.

Although Marathas and Rajputs all fought valiantly to reestablish the martial empire of the Aryans, in Savarkar's eyes, when Ashoka converted to Buddhism, the "martial prowess [that] mainly guided the administration of the magnificent empire of Chandragupta" (Savarkar, 1985, p. 51) lost its vitality and Hindu India did not recover its manhood for centuries. By his continual emphasis on the nonviolent, nonmartial spirit of Buddhism and its role in the destruction of Hindu India's manly, martial energy, Savarkar revealed his almost obsessive valorization of masculine Hinduism as the basis for a strong nation. The focus on Buddhism also enabled a narrative wherein the masculine Hindu spirit has only temporarily retreated to the background, waiting to be resurrected, rather than being absolutely and inevitably absent, as the colonial authorities contended.

In his construction of Mlechhastan as the "other" of Hindustan, Savarkar soon focused solely on Islam as the enemy:

> That is why . . . some of our Mohamedan or Christian countrymen who had originally been forcibly converted to Non-Hindu religion . . . are not and cannot be recognized as Hindus. . . . Their holy land is far off in Arabia or Palestine. . . . Their mythology and Godmen . . . are not the children of this soil. . . . Their love is divided. . . . Nay if some of them be really believing what they profess to do, there can be no choice, they must . . . set their Holy-land above their Father-land in their love and allegiance. (1960, p. 94)

The Islamic "other," represented by millions residing within India, derives its
malevolent energy from divided loyalty. The Christian and Muslim reverence
for prophets and sacred spaces outside the ancient geographical territory
known as Hindustan makes followers of these faiths suspect and potential
traitors in Savarkar's eyes. He contended that Muslims and Christians (originally Hindus) can redeem themselves by freely choosing to reject their conversion and returning to Hinduism (p. 94).

In his narrative of the Hindu nation and Islam, Savarkar evoked a culture based on masculine Hinduism that despite the valiant attempts of the
Rajputs and Marathas failed to resist Islamic conquest and the forcible conversion of its people. In explaining this weakness, Savarkar returned to his
former arguments against *ahimsa* (nonviolence). Whether because of its close
contact with Buddhism or other forces, Hinduism during the various Afghan,
Mongol, and Persian invasions could not resist because its martial valor had
been weakened by ideas of tolerance, kindness, chivalry, and forgiveness.
Savarkar does not demean these values absolutely but argues that if one is to
resist the "sword of Islam," a celebration of such ideas weakens (effeminizes)
masculine Hinduism and makes a nation vulnerable. He illustrates this weakness with very explicit gendered imagery.

In his view, Muslim conquerors raped Hindu women both to sully the
honor of Hindu national manhood and to spread Islam "and these [Hindu]
women . . . were distributed by fives or tens amongst the most faithful followers of Islam. The future progeny of these conquered women were born Muslim" (p. 176). Even Muslim women "did everything in their power to harass
such captured and kidnapped Hindu women" (p. 178). However, Hindus
could not resist such threats "because [of] the then prevalent perverted religious ideas about chivalry to women, which ultimately proved highly detri-
mental to the Hindu community" (p. 179). Adopting the voice of the plaintive, raped Hindu women, Savarkar chided the great Hindu warrior Shivaji:
"Did not the plaintive screams and pitiful lamentations of the millions of
molested Hindu women . . . reach the ears of Shivaji Maharaj?" (p. 179).

In the above material, women signify national honor; the capture and
rape of Hindu women highlights an effeminization of Hinduism as Hindu
warriors, weakened by "perverted religious ideas," fail to resist this attack on
their honor. Savarkar's denigration of Hindu notions of chivalry seems to
indicate his belief that the only response to the sullying of national honor by
Muslim men was retaliatory rape of Muslim women by Hindu men. Such a
chilling expectation resides in Savarkar's delineation of masculine Hinduism;
echoes of his stance resonate in modern Hindu nationalist actions, especially,
as will be illustrated in chapter five, in the recent (2002) violence in Gujarat.

In Savarkar's mind, Muslim machinations coupled with the Gandhian
doctrine of nonviolence (presumably a legacy of Buddhist influence) conspired to make Hindus vulnerable. His advocacy of this belief became most

passionate during his term as president of the Hindu Mahasabha. In his 1937 presidential address, he claimed, "To the Hindus independence of Hindustan can only be worth having if that ensures their Hindutva—their religious, racial, and cultural identity" (Savarkar, 1949, p. 17). He publicly denounced Muslims: "Let us not be blind to the fact that they as a community will continue to cherish fanatical designs to establish a Moslem rule in India" (p. 26). He posed a hierarchy of the minorities of India in terms of their good will to Hindus, with Parsees being the most benevolent and Muslims the most malevolent, with Christians and Jews falling in between in that order. While the existence of non-Hindu minorities in India challenged the idea of a homogenous nation, his hierarchy indicated that Savarkar was quite aware of possible challenges to his dream of a monolithic India, devoid of diversity.

In 1938 at the twenty-first session of the Mahasabha in Calcutta, Savarkar constructed a formal stance toward a policy on minorities in India by declaring, "The Hindu Sanghatanist Party [a reference to the Mahasabha, loosely translated, the party for the unified organization of Hindus] aims to base the future constitution of Hindustan on the broad principle that all citizens should have equal rights and obligations irrespective of caste or creed, race or religion, provided they avow and owe an exclusive and devoted allegiance to the Hindustani state" (p. 120). Of course, the statement "devoted allegiance to the Hindustani state" is deliberately vague and remains open to interpretation such that the "other" of the Hindu nation may be suitably denounced when necessary if proper "allegiance" fails to be shown to the "Hindustani state."

In Savarkar's eyes, Congress's pandering to Muslims and Gandhi's disastrous policy of nonviolence had yet again destroyed the opportunity for building an Indian nation with the values of masculine Hinduism: "[W]henever the Hindus are oppressed as Hindus and especially at the hands of the Moslems, the Congress simply will not raise a finger in their defence" (p. 93). At the twenty-second session in Madras, he declared,

> We denounce your doctrine of absolute non-violence not because we are less saintly but because we are more sensible than you are. Relative non-violence is our creed and therefore, we worship the arms as the symbols of the Shakti, the Kali, and Guru Govindsingh sang his hymn to the sword and we also join with the great Guru in the refrain and sing with him, "Hail to Thee Sword." . . . I want all Hindus to get themselves reanimated and re-born into a *martial race*. Manu and Shri Krishna are our lawgivers and Shri Rama the commander of our forces. Let us re-learn the *manly* lessons they taught us and our Hindu nation shall prove again as unconquerable and conquering a race as we proved once when they led us. (p. 201; italics added)

> . . . the teachings of the so-called satyagraha creed sought to kill the very *martial* instinct of the Hindu race and had succeeded to an alarming extent

in doing so. . . . I made it my duty . . . to give a fillip to military awakening
amongst the Hindus by addressing thousands and thousands of Hindu
youths. (p. 204; italics added)

This speech together with the historical narratives presented in previous sections above unequivocally illustrate that Savarkar dreamed of an
India energized by masculine Hinduism read as martial prowess and valor
in battle. In resisting British gendered critiques, he skillfully constructed a
Vedic golden age embodied by a Hindu warrior culture and narrated the
degradation of this spirit. Further, by acknowledging British superiority in
war tactics, he implicitly placed India on equal footing with Britain.
Embedded in the language used to concede British martial prowess was the
assumption that the British Empire now and the Indian Empire in the past
were equally great. He recognized British military might not as a member
of a weak and subjugated race but as a representative of an equal and worthy national adversary. At that moment when Britain has most weakened
the Indian spirit, he believed that spirit would reassert itself within a
strong, unified, militarized, Hindu nation. Indeed, as president of the
Mahasabha, Savarkar stressed that it was the duty of young Hindu men to
join the Indian army to fight for their country and to resist Islamic conta-
mination of the Hindu army. He ended his address to the twenty-fourth
session of the Mahasabha by exclaiming: "Hinduise all politics and Militarise Hinduism!" (p. 302). In his nation, extraordinary women like the
Rani of Jhansi could take on the traits of masculine Hinduism but only if
they shed explicit markers of their femininity. Women would otherwise
remain the repository of national honor and enter the national landscape
only as wives supporting warriors and heroic mothers nurturing future
(male) warriors.

SWAMI VIVEKANANDA

In contrast to Savarkar's vision of masculine Hinduism, constructed predominantly with ideas of martial prowess, military strength, and unquestioning
patriotism to the motherland, Swami Vivekananda, another proponent of
masculinist nationalism, moved beyond ideas of physical strength and martial
prowess to include notions of "muscular" spirituality. His vision of manhood
embodied the figure of a warrior-monk. Just as notions of Christian manliness
moved beyond ideas of muscular Christianity to incorporate spirituality and
moral rigor, so too did Vivekananda's image of warrior spirituality transcend
Savarkar's muscular Hindu or Aryan warrior to include a focus on morality
and social justice.

Swami Vivekananda, born as Narendranath Datta, the son of a fairly
prosperous lawyer in 1863, matured in a society in flux; the lives of the colo-

nial elite were rapidly transforming as the conflict between the old Hindu orthodoxy and the liberal ideals championed by many members of this community reached a peak. For various reasons (Kakar, 1978, pp. 167–79), Vivekananda was attracted to the ascetic life. When he came in contact with the remarkable spiritual being Sri Ramakrishna, he experienced a religious epiphany. For him India's redemption from foreign rule was both a political goal and a variety of religious salvation. In his mind, no religion could be vital unless it was strong and independent. Vivekananda not only aroused Indian awareness and appreciation of Hindu philosophy but also exhorted his countrymen (and sometimes women) to unite religious introspection with worldly and moral battles against both alien British rule as well as social injustices. In his opinion, the method that best expressed his beliefs was a "man-making" education.

Vivekananda's vision became institutionalized in the Ramakrishna Mission and several affiliated schools and organizations (for example, the Vedanta Society) both in India and abroad. These organizations combine his religious theories, represented by Advaita Vedanta, with practice through action in education, self-sufficiency, and social work. Vivekananda died in 1902 after a brief but incredibly dynamic life that provided inspiration for diverse forms of Indian nationalism, including the present Hindutva movement.

As argued above, the model of the warrior-monk formed an integral part of Vivekananda's vision. His eloquent speeches (Jyotirmayananda, 1992) reverberated with masculinist Hindu language. In his younger days, he excelled in wrestling and fencing and stressed that all young men should be physically active and strong. He repeatedly emphasized the need for masculine action in his country's struggle with the British as well as against indigenous forms of injustice and exploitation:

> Make your nerves strong. What we want [are] muscles of iron and nerves of steel, inside which dwells a mind of the same material as that of which the thunderbolt is made. Strength, manhood, Kshatra-Virya [warrior strength]. . . . We have wept long enough. No more weeping, but stand on your feet and be men. It is man-making religion that we want. It is man-making theories we want. It is man-making education that we want. And here is the test of truth—anything that makes you weak, physically, intellectually, and spiritually reject as poison. (p. 29)

> First of all our young men must be strong. Religion will come afterwards. Be strong my young friends; that is my advice to you. You will be nearer to Heaven through football than through the study of the Gita. These are bold words; but I have to say them, for I love you. . . . You will understand the Gita better with your biceps, your muscles, a little stronger. (Majumdar, 1963, p. 491)

The passages in these speeches clearly delineate notions of physical strength and, to an extent, martial power embedded in hegemonic masculinity. Implicitly, he positioned the values of hegemonic masculinity articulated through masculine Hinduism against a femininity defined by weakness, indecisiveness, and a lack of virility. Those men who embodied these feminine attributes were Hinduism's greatest enemies.

> There is another defect in us . . . but through centuries of slavery, we have become like a nation of women. You can scarcely get three women together for five minutes in this country or any other country but they quarrel. . . . Women we are. If a woman comes to lead women they all begin immediately to criticize her, tear her to pieces, . . . If a man comes and gives them a little harsh treatment, scolds them now and then, . . . it is all right. . . . In the same way, if one of our countrymen stands up and tries to become great, we all try to hold him down, but if a foreigner comes and tries to kick us it is all right. We have been used to it, have we not? . . . So give up being a slave. For the next fifty years this alone shall be our keynote—this our great mother India. (p. 129)

Further, he condemned the Vaishnavas (followers of the sixteenth-century Saint Sri Chaitanaya of Bengal, who preached nonviolence and love for all beings) of Orissa and Bengal for becoming "effeminate": "Through the preaching of that love broadcast, the nation has become effeminate—a race of women! The whole of Orissa has been turned into a land of cowards, and Bengal . . . has almost lost all sense of manliness" (quoted in Sil, 1997, p. 117). These effeminate beings were seen to pose a danger to a masculine Hinduism combining invincible muscular strength and awe-inspiring spiritual power.

In his mind (Kakar, 1978) India had been conquered first by the Muslims and then the British because Hindu culture had become weak and effeminate.

> This obsession with manliness carried over into an admiration for India's conquerors, the Muslims and the British. Vivekananda often proclaimed that he wanted to build an India with a Muslim body and a Vedantist brain, and maintained that no race understood as the British did "what should be the glory of a man." For the young men of India who were Vivekananda's primary constituency, this was (and still is) a powerful call for freedom from the conflicting embrace of the Great Mother; the appeal of this kind of masculinist campaign touching a deep current of potential militance and aggressive activity in Indian society. (p. 175)

The works of Savarkar, clearly attempted, through his model of masculine Hinduism, to harness this "potential militance" and "aggressive activity" for nationalism by delineating a golden age of Aryan warrior culture, equal in its masculine strength to the British Empire; Aryan warrior culture was only temporarily declined and awaiting resurrection. In contrast, Vivekananda, with his model of the warrior-monk, actually envisioned dominance, not equality. His vision of dominance, although acknowledging the importance of muscular politics, predominantly focused on the spiritual superiority of Hinduism (Jyotirmayananda, 1992):

> Not politics nor military power, not commercial supremacy nor mechanical genius furnishes India with that backbone, but religion; and religion alone is all that we have and mean to have. Spirituality has been always in India. (p. 52)

> I am an imaginative man, and my idea, is the conquest of the whole world by the Hindu race. . . . The story of our conquest . . . [is] . . . the conquest of religion. . . . We have to conquer the world. That we have to! India must conquer the world, and nothing less than [that] is my ideal. . . . We must conquer the world or die. There is no other alternative. (p. 53)

The above speeches emphasize two themes shaping the role of masculine Hinduism performed by the warrior-monk in Vivekananda's view of nation. One, the monk protects a Hindu nation; and, two, the warrior-monk, though physically strong, conquers (indeed must conquer if India's greatness is to be expressed) through moral and spiritual fortitude. In other words, the warrior-monk cleverly changes the rules of conquest and redefines manliness within the gendered discourse of imperialism created by the British. Warrior-monks test their manhood through spiritual rather than martial prowess. Perhaps, the British may be more manly in terms of coarse muscularity, implies Vivekananda, but in terms of spiritual strength Hindu men will conquer the world to reflect India's cultural superiority. In the notions of Christian manliness heretofore brought to the reader's attention, it may be useful to move beyond what has been previously emphasized in its definition. That is, our look at mere muscular Christianity can be extended to encompass consideration of the construct of morality as well. While Christian missionaries perhaps hoped to overawe the pagan Hindu with a spiritually superior Christian manliness, for the most part British discourse about the effeminate Hindu did not enlist morality within its repertoire. Rather, to an overwhelming extent, British discourse about the effeminate Hindu constrained itself to emphasize particularly a lack of martial ability and military power. Vivekananda did actually embark on a journey of spiritual conquest of sorts when he toured Britain and the United States in the 1890s. His speech about the spiritual strength of Hinduism delivered to the 1893 Parliament of Religions in Chicago has become legendary in the annals of Hindu nationalism.

Although Vivekananda's model of the warrior-monk emphasized the notion of spiritual conquest, that emphasis coexisted with his focus on the importance of martial prowess and physical strength. Indeed, it is possible that Vivekananda's vision of the warrior-monk and Bankimchandra Chatterjee's delineation of freedom fighters in *Anandamath* (first published 1882; this edition reprinted 2002) mutually reinforced one another. The ascetic warriors of this novel, donning the saffron robe of Hindu holy men, remained pure, removing themselves from the temptation provided by female sexuality by not touching women or being alone with them. These warriors saw their quest to free Mother India as spiritual and informed by the religious tenets of Hinduism. Chatterjee's novel very clearly demonstrated an awareness of the colonial gendered critique and the need to reformulate a muscular Hindu warrior culture to resist:

> *Mahendra:* Then what makes this difference between the British and the Indian soldier?
>
> *Bhavan:* Because the British soldier would never run away even to save his life. The Indian soldier runs away when he begins to perspire; he seeks cold drinks. The Englishman surpasses the Indian in tenacity. He never abandons his duty before he finishes it. Then consider the question of courage: A cannon ball falls only on one spot. But a whole company of Indian soldiers would run away if one single cannon ball fell among them. On the other hand, British soldiers would not run away even if dozens of cannon balls should fall in their midst.
>
> *Mahendra:* Do you think you Children [a reference to the ascetic warriors] have acquired these virtues?
>
> *Bhavan:* We have to acquire them by patient practice. (p. 43)

This "patient practice" involved a reconfiguration of Hindu masculinity, and this quest for manly virtue, according to Chatterjee's novel, required asceticism and celibacy, untainted by female sexuality. However, women were not completely removed from this Hindu masculine practice. Shanti, the wife of one of the warriors, dons male armor, takes up weapons, and vows to lead a celibate life to join the struggle for freedom. It is also made clear in the novel that Shanti will return to her role as wife and mother once Mother India is freed. Thus, in this narrative of ascetic, masculine Hinduism within the nation, women can negotiate a space if they are willing to *temporarily* take on masculine attributes, that is, to erase outer markers of their femininity and return willingly to their roles as wife and mother once danger to the motherland is over. To a certain extent, Vivekananda's warrior-monk draws on the legacy of such a vision of masculinity. In his image of manhood, then, asceticism, physical strength, and to a certain extent martial prowess combine to construct a virile figure ready to fight for India's rightful position as a moral and spiritual leader in the world.

Both Chatterjee and Vivekananda seem to inject this notion of spirituality into manhood to emphasize Hindu men's refusal to give into, in their perception, the crass physicality of the British version of armed masculinity. The thematic dichotomy of "India (Hindu) equals spirituality" versus "the West equals crass materialism"—wherein spirituality is deemed more valuable and hence provides a measure of India's superiority—still resonates in constructions of Hindu nationalism and informs a vital part of its modern ideology. However, it should be noted that in Vivekananda's work, and even more so in modern versions, this binary opposition erases out nuances and uncertainties both in India (as a monolithic Hindu, Vedic culture) and "the West" (that ambiguous term referring to multiple diverse cultures in western Europe, Britain, Canada, the United States, Australia, and New Zealand). But as a form of resistance to British views disparaging Hindu manhood, his position took an innovative and creative stance. Although Vivekananda may not have, like Chatterjee, explicitly demonstrated his cognizance of British disparagement of Hindu masculinity, one would have to be culturally isolated in the colonial milieu to be unaware of its discourse.

Further, the nation that the warrior-monk was building and protecting was Hindu. Although Vivekananda (1963) did not paint Islam absolutely as the enemy of the Hindu nation with the fiery eloquence of Savarkar, a focus on Hindu contextualization and fear of foreigners are implicit in his views:

> [T]he name of religion and Hindu have become one. This is the national characteristic, and this cannot be touched. Barbarians with sword and fire, barbarians bringing barbarous religions, not one of them could touch the core [of Hinduism]. . . . If the Hindu is not spiritual I do not call him a Hindu. (p. 139)

Although he did not clearly state that the barbarians are Muslim, given the history of Afghan and Persian conquests of "Hindu" India, it seems reasonable to interpret the passage above as a suspicion of Islamic conquerors.

If warrior-monks were to construct and protect the nation, then how were these men to be created? While Savarkar did not explicitly delineate a method that would facilitate the creation of men who could emulate Aryan soldiers, Vivekananda was very clear that education was the means of socializing warrior-monks. According to him, the education of his time made "parrots of boys" and "slowly reduced them into machines" (Mukherji, 1971, p. 186). He advocated a return to the ancient Vedic system of schooling wherein a boy lived with a teacher for several years to learn philosophy, recommending that such a system would create the self-reliance and strength required of the new warrior-monks of India. It would be infinitely better than the British system wherein "the teacher has become a mere lecturer, the teacher expecting his five dollars and the person taught expecting his brain to be filled with the teacher's words and each going his way after this much is done" (quoted in Mukherji, 1971, p. 188). Again, the Swami resisted Western claims of superiority by rejecting its model of a "man-making" education, even though the English public school might be a training ground for future empire-builders, inculcated in the arts of Christian manliness.

In terms of female activism and its relation to masculinity, it behooves us to query whether in Vivekananda's view women could take on the traits of masculine Hinduism to serve the nation as warrior-monks. The answer is a qualified no. Vivekananda held a rather ambiguous position toward women. On the one hand, he extolled the virtues of historical figures such as the Rani of Jhansi and even celebrated various women of his time—Sister Nivedita and Sarala Debi—who had transcended traditional gender roles to enter the public sphere as nationalists. Yet, on the other hand "wife" and "mother" (2000) were held up as potent images in his interpretation of women's role in the nation: "The height of a woman's ambition is to be like Sita . . . the patient, the all-suffering, the ever-faithful, the ever-pure wife" (pp. 11–12), and "Now the ideal woman, in India, is the mother, the mother first, and the mother last. The word woman calls up to the mind of Hindu motherhood" (pp. 26–27).

The valorization of such images led him to ignore actual women when he was organizing the Ramakrishna Mission as a training ground for warrior-monks. Women, because of their potential for seducing a warrior-monk away from a path of spiritual righteousness, were to be kept under strict surveillance in the religious organization (Chowdhury, 2001, p. 134). Celibacy, as in Chatterjee's delineation of the ascetic warriors, was a vital part of Vivekananda's vision of the warrior-monk. All dedicated followers of the Ramakrishna Order were to be monks who had embraced celibacy and accepted the wearing of the saffron robe (as did Vivekananda) of Hindu holy men. In this narrative of male celibacy, the sexuality of women becomes a perceived threat. Thus, it became necessary for women not to enter the Ramakrishna monasteries. Further, because of their primary roles as mothers and wives, "woman-making" education was to be kept separate from "man-making" education and to include only a rudimentary introduction to religion, arts, and science, with an emphasis on "housekeeping, cooking, sewing, hygiene. . . . It is not good to let them touch novels and fictions" (Vivekananada, 2000, p. 37). Likewise, women ascetics, skilled in such arts, could be trained as educators of women in separate institutions. Wife (pure and chaste), heroic mother, and celibate female ascetic represented the entirety of women's role in the nation. We may note that female sexuality has been erased, and it can be inferred that women who do embody markers of femininity—jewelry, makeup, colorful clothing—thus enhancing their sexual nature, are not deemed as appropriate participants in the nationalist struggle.

Further, another inconsistency in Vivekananda's view of women in the nation also can be seen in his attempts to eliminate the actual realities of their lives in India. He made such generalizations that declared "[t]he Indian woman is generally very happy; there are not many cases of quarrelling between husband and wife" (p. 33). He would even sometimes deny that women, for example, child widows, were in any way ill treated in India (Chowdhury, 2001, p. 133). Some scholars (Sil, 1997, pp. 117–26) argue that such utopian (and simplistic) statements reflected Vivekananda's misogyny. Others (Chowdhury, 2001, p. 133), in offering a motive for his words, focus on his deliberate *public* creation, at times, of a national utopia formed as a resistance to British critiques of Hindu manliness that were based on, in Vivekananda's opinion, greatly exaggerated and generalizing comments on the country's brutal and exploitative treatment of women. This latter explanation can be buttressed by the existence of internal speeches he made to his disciples that were exceedingly critical of Hindu society's treatment of women (Vivekananda, 2000).

Another strategy deployed to resist gendered colonial critique centering on Indian womanhood was to, again, draw on the argument of Hindu India's spiritual superiority over the West. By idealizing Hindu women as wife and mother, he attacked Western women as impure and improper: "No sooner are a young man and young woman left alone than he pays compliments to her. . . . I was told it is mere pleasantry, and I believed it. But . . . I know it is not right.'. . . It is wrong, only you of the West shut your eyes and call it good" (p. 26). Obviously, the Swami held women responsible for their chastity; it is they who must be modest to prevent such improper interaction. At other times, he referred to Western women (that is, American and British women) as fickle, "masculine," and even vulgar and loose (Sil, 1997, pp. 116–17). Yet at other times Vivekananda extolled their virtues: "there are no women in the world comparable to the American. . . . How pure, free, self-reliant, and kind they are . . . pure as the icicle on Diana's temple and withal with much culture, education, and spirituality in the highest sense" (quoted in Sil, p. 115).

The inconsistency in his views of women, both Indian and Western, could derive from an embedded misogyny. Or it could merely express a nationalist resistance to colonial critique. His idealization of women as pure wife, selfless mother, and chaste warrior-monk must have conflicted with the reality of complex flesh-and-blood women he met in India as well as in the United States and United Kingdom, women who defied neat categorization. On the other hand, his act of holding women or femininity within parameters of a monolithic binary opposition—that is, of erasing nuances in the lives of all women, Indian and Western, for the sake of the ideal—allowed Vivekananda to glorify the Indian woman's perceived purity over the Western woman's perceived impurity. Put another way, his dichotomy of pure versus impure, although not accurately representing a complex reality, still effectively challenged British manhood by defiling the honor of their women. Such a tactic, of course, fits in nicely within a masculine narrative defining nation as woman and woman as a symbol of national honor, wherein any defilement of a woman's body uncovers a weakness in the nation's manhood.

Finally, the Hindu context of Vivekananda's view of Indian womanhood is clear. His models—Sita (consort of Ram, hero of the epic *Ramayana*), Rani of Jhansi, Savitri (lauded in Hindu mythology as the model of a devoted wife), Mirabai (a princess who left her family to search for divine enlightenment), Ahalyabai (the powerful queen of Indore)—all derived from Hindu folklore. At times he did make comments that could be construed as critical of Islam: "To the Arab, marriage is a contract or a forceful possession, to be dissolved at will, and we do not find there the development of the idea of the virgin or Brahmacharin" (Vivekananda, 2000, p. 22). Rather than "Muslim," he used the term "Arab"; however, it would be difficult to argue that Vivekananda was referring to non-Muslim Arabs. Through his construction of warrior-monk, pure wife, heroic mother within a Hindu context, the Swami both creatively resisted British gendered observations about India and simultaneously released into the nationalist discourse models that could be used and incorporated by future cultural nationalist movements.

MADAM CAMA

A concern with the location of Hindu manhood within the nation was not limited to the thoughts and ideas of men. Women of the nineteenth century also contributed to this discourse within the colonial milieu. Madam Bhikaji Rustomji Cama, popularly known as Madam Cama, born in 1861 to a wealthy Parsee family, was also an ardent advocate of militant nationalism constructed with the ideas of masculine Hinduism. Exiled by the British, Madam Cama articulated most of her nationalist thought while residing with other Indian expatriates in London, Paris, and Geneva. In 1907 at the Internationalist Socialist Congress in Stuttgart, she unfurled her own version of the Indian national flag, decorated with the phrase Bande (Hail) Mataram (Mother, i.e., India) written in Devnagari script (used in writing Sanskrit) (Kumar, 1993, 46). As one of the founders and editors, most of her nationalist ideologies became explicated in the pages of the *Bande Mataram* (*BM*), defined on its masthead as the "monthly organ of Indian independence." This paper had been founded in 1909 in response to the British ban on Chatterjee's poem "Bande Mataram." Although she did not sign all the articles she wrote, Madam Cama played an enormous role in publishing and editing the publication.

    She believed that the Indian nation's hope for independence lay in the articulation of masculine Hinduism. Military violence was clearly stipulated as necessary to save India:

> I also appeal to your patriotism to make the best of your stay in the West by taking all kinds of physical training (which is not allowed in our country). Above all learn how to shoot straight, because the day is not far when to

attain *swaraj* and *swadeshi* you will be called upon to shoot the English out
of the land which we love so passionately. (quoted in Yadav and Bakshi,
1991, p. 160)

The BM repeatedly mentioned Savarkar's work, both announcing his book
in March 1910 (1:7, p. 4), and reviewing it favorably a month later (April,
1:8, p. 1). However, the paper disagreed with him about the causes behind
the failure of the 1857 war. Rather than focusing on the treachery of Indians as Savarkar did, the BM argued that the English army, numbering five
thousand, defeated Tatia Tope's twenty-two thousand soldiers because
"[t]hey were more determined men" (April 1910, p. 4). Consequently, the
paper urged that the time to "set to work in earnest spirit to renovate the
lost *manhood* [italics added] of the nation so that in the coming revolution
the tables may be turned on our enemies and a charge of a few of our soldiers should scatter before it the serried ranks of Highlanders like chaff
before the wind" (p. 4). This loss of manhood purportedly occurred
because "India became conquered and remains so because Indians are
indolent and love the pleasures of life. They have no conscience and/or
commitment to duty" (October 10, 1909, p. 2). The pages of the paper eloquently urged Indians to recapture their lost manhood and regenerate the
martial spirit of India. This notion is dramatically illustrated in one passage, the Sikh Invocation to the Sword: "I bow with love and devotion to
the Holy Sword. . . . I bow to the Arrow and the Cannon which destroy
the enemy. I bow to the Sword and the Rapier which destroy the evil"
(BM, July 1911, p. 1). These lines encircle India depicted as a woman
holding a sword with a lion by her side.
    Elsewhere, the BM (August 1910) ridiculed men for not defending their
honor: "[W]e do not sympathise with our afflicted Hindu brethren who have
been plundered and insulted. Now, how can we accord generous recognition
to cowardice and social atrophy? How can we esteem a population devoid of
manliness. It is inconceivable that a self-respecting *manly* community should
be so helpless. . . . Is the Hindu community of Peshawar composed of old
women and children? Are there no young *men* among them?" (p. 2; italics
added). This passage explicitly equates martial prowess with manliness and
weakness with effeminacy; its angry tone targets *Hindu* men who did not
stand up to *Muslim* rowdies, harassing the women of the village. Women, as
signifiers of honor, shaped conflict between men as a test of manhood. Put
another way, Hindu men failed as men because they could not protect their
women's honor. Thus, Madam Cama configured Islam as the enemy and celebrated the Hindu context of nation by drawing on familiar Hindu icons—
Rama, Krishna, Shivaji, Rana Pratap, Lakshmibai—to call for the reawakening of a manly Hindu nation. The figure of the Hindu soldier rather than the
warrior-monk animated Madam Cama's nationalist writings. Similarly, Sister

Nivedita and Sarala Ghosal, also ardent female proponents of masculine Hinduism, emphasized the figure of the virile Hindu soldier rather than the celibate warrior-monk implicit in Vivekananda's texts.

SISTER NIVEDITA

Sister Nivedita, an Anglo-Irish follower of Vivekananda, in an essay titled "Aggressive Hinduism," urged Indians to precipitate a war, if necessary, to win independence from the British.

Margaret Noble, a schoolteacher, met Vivekananda in 1895 during his tour of the West, a covert mission of conquest of sorts, driven by his belief in the superiority of Hindu spirituality. Noble traveled to India in 1898 after receiving an invitation from the Swami; he wanted her to take on the role of an ascetic monk and contribute to the education of Indian women. Margaret became his closest female disciple and was renamed Nivedita. Not discerning female education as separate from the debate over Indian nationalism unfolding in the colonial milieu, she plunged enthusiastically into the argument over the construction of the Indian nation. Delegates attending the 1906 Congress session in Calcutta witnessed the unfurling of one of the first Indian national flags, designed by Nivedita and sewn by the pupils of her school. Colored red and yellow and featuring a thunderbolt in its center, the flag was flanked by "Vande" (Hail) on the left and "Mataram" (the Mother, in this instance referring to India as mother) on the right, written in Bengali. In 1909, under a pen name Nivedita later wrote an essay titled "Vajra as Design for the National Flag" (Evolution of Indian Flag). The thunderbolt, in Hindu mythology, symbolizes many aspects but one predominant interpretation is martial strength. In certain myths, the thunderbolt is affiliated with Lord Indra, god of war. The thunderbolt symbolized both the Hindu context of Nivedita's vision of the Indian nation and her support for a strong, aggressive, martial nationalism:

> Above all, we find out how to distinguish effectively between the social idea and religion. It is thus that it becomes possible to talk of "an aggressive Hinduism. . . . Aggression is to be the dominant characteristic of the India that is to-day in school and classroom,—aggression, and the thought and ideals of aggression. Instead of passivity, activity; for the standard of weakness, the standard of strength; in place of a steadily-yielding defence, the ringing cheer of the invading host. (1960, p. 5)

In the above passage, Nivedita, clearly sees Hinduism as being able to facilitate a social movement based on strength and offensive action. The phrase "the ringing cheer of the invading host" clearly imagines martial prowess as an important component of aggressive Hinduism. Further, male bodies embody this prowess:

The Indian mind has not reached out to conquer and possess its own land as its own inalienable share and trust, in the world as a whole. It has been content, even in things modern, to take obediently whatever was given to it. And the newness and strangeness of the thing given, has dazed it. The Indian people as a whole, for the last two generations have been *as men walking in a dream, without manhood* without power to react freely against conditions, without even common-sense. (p. 26)

. . . Herewith then let us sound the charge. *Sons* of the Indian past do ye fear to sleep at nightfall on your shields? On, on, in the name of a new spirituality, to command the treasures of the modern world sack! On, on, *soldiers of the Indian motherland* seize ye the battlements and penetrate to the citadel! Place garrison and watch within the hard-won towers, or fall, that others may climb on your dead bodies, to the height ye strove to win. (p. 33; italics added)

In the above selections, Nivedita's construction of a masculinity based on martial prowess, offensive action, and physical strength become explicit. Like Vivekananda, she believed that Indian men suffered from a malaise of effeminate passivity and weakness in a rapidly changing world, which required "muscles of iron" and "nerves of steel" for success. In the latter passage above, she called on Indian men to reformulate their masculinity in a martial form and seize their nation back from the British. Although in these particular selections she does not explicitly allude to Hinduism, the title of her essay in which the exhortations appear does; the "Aggressive Hinduism" piece, along with the Hindu context of her vision of a national flag, underscore that her imagined nation is rooted in masculine *Hinduism*. In her mind, the *warrior* seems to be given priority over the *monk*. In other parts of the essay, however, allusion is made to the necessity of a spiritual quest for nation.

Nivedita's gendered imagery constructed the figure of a male warrior and seemingly women cannot perform this role. In referring to the "Sons" of India and the "Indian Motherland," at least in this particular articulation of nationalism, Nivedita presented the nation as woman protected by brave male warriors. Although Nivedita was a proponent of female education, her representation of Indian women did not underline traits—independence and equity—that such an advocacy would imply. In her configuration of Indian gender roles, the conjugal relationship was signified by a wife's unequivocal surrender to her husband's wishes: "as a child might do, she cooks for him, and serves him, sitting before him as he eats to fan away the flies. As a disciple might, she prostrates herself before him. . . . It is not equality. . . . But who talks of a vulgar equality, asks the Hindu wife, when she may have instead the unspeakable blessedness of offering worship" (quoted in Neogi, 2000, p. 137).[4] Given her rather conventional stance on feminine identity, it would be reasonable to argue that Nivedita did not envision women as warriors but rather as wives and mothers who could support and cheer the nationalists, give birth to heroic sons, but not transcend their roles to actually enter the battle as soldiers. Nevertheless, Sister Nivedita remains one of the few non-Indian people who have been incorporated into the Indian pantheon of spiritual freedom fighters. The image of masculinity underlying her vision of the Hindu nation emulates Savarkar's strong, Aryan soldier rather than Vivekananda's figure of the warrior-monk

SARALA DEBI GHOSAL

Sarala Debi Ghosal, niece of the famous Bengali novelist and poet Rabindranath Tagore, admired Vivekananda and in turn was admired for her outspoken nature. As a member of the Bengali colonial milieu, Ghosal was well acquainted with Chatterjee's ascetic warriors in *Anandamath*, a model of masculinity she admired. Sarala Debi, born in 1872, grew up to be a rebellious and independent woman. She completed her B.A. at Calcutta University and challenged the social conventions of her time by, at the age of twenty three, taking a job in a school in Mysore. For an unmarried young woman to leave home and reside in a distant city was unheard of in 1895 Calcutta. Returning after a year's time, Sarala Debi came into contact with the militant nationalism in Bengal advocated by leaders such as Aurobindo Ghosh (Kumar, 1993, p. 40).

Immersing herself in militant ideology, her own practice became shaped by the intersection of ideas of masculinity and nation. Like Savarkar, Vivekananda, Chatterjee, and Nivedita, Sarala Debi believed that Indian men (specifically Bengali men) had lost their manhood and become cowardly (p. 39). In articles written for the journal *Bharati*, she urged them to regain their masculinity, that is, martial courage and prowess.[5] In 1902 Sarala Debi organized the first Pratapaditya Brata (loosely translated, the rites of Pratapaditya, a Hindu landlord, whom Sarala Debi characterized as a brave warrior resisting imperial Moghul power). Under the mantle of Pratapaditya, young men would learn and practice wrestling, boxing, and swordplay. In the following year, she organized a Birashtami Festival (to celebrate martial valor) on the second day of Durga Puja (Durga being a female divinity embodying cosmic power that includes but is not limited to martial courage and prowess). To this goddess, young men were to vow in the name of bygone *Hindu* martial heroes—Krishna, Rama, Bhishma, Drona, Arjuna, Bhima, Meghnad, Rana Pratap, Shivaji, Ranjeet Singh, and Pratapaditya—to fight for independence and dedicate their lives to building a strong and manly nation (p. 40). All these heroes, both historic and mythic, were (and are) celebrated as warriors in India. Rana Pratap, Shivaji, and Pratapaditya's martial valor is commemorated in the context of honoring their defensive stance against Islamic conquest of India; Ranjeet Singh is known for his valor against the British. As discussed previously, Ranjeet Singh was recognized by the British as a member of the martial race who understood, because of his European advisors, the intricacies of organized warfare. Finally, Sarala Debi encouraged the celebration of another Hindu festival, Rakhi. By binding dec-orative threads on the wrists of young men, women pledged their chaste sis-terly love; men used the same ritual to establish fraternal ties with other men. Under Sarala Debi's tutelage (she was an enthusiastic participant in the Rakhi ritual), women urged their "brothers" to join the battle for indepen-dence, while men as members of a national fraternity vowed to join the fight for freedom (p. 45).

Her use of Pratapaditya Brata, Birashtami, and Rakhi, all traditional and accepted Hindu rituals, as well as the presence of a divine feminine figure (Durga) representing militant anger, enabled her effort as a woman—one who was articulating a message of aggression and martial power—to go forth without the appearance of being a radical challenge to the norms of her con-temporary patriarchy. The Hindu tone of Sarala Debi's national narrative cannot be ignored. Indeed, rituals and icons disseminating this vision at times moved beyond a muted Hindu context into the chant of a more strident interpretation, projecting Islam as the enemy of the nation articulated by the valorization of masculine Hinduism. Although the nation was embodied as a woman, it was to the young men that Sarala Debi called out to enter the fray and rejuvenate masculine Hinduism. Women supported the men, nurtured them, and instilled the values of patriotism and nationalism but in invoking the martial men of India's past did not themselves vow to fight as warriors for the motherland (Ray, 1995).

The writings of Sister Nivedita, Sarala Ghosal, and Madam Cama cele-brated the masculinized nation, tracing the ambiguity of its relationship to female activism within the confines of this nation, and in the process high-lighted their own precarious location as feminine nationalists within mascu-line Hinduism. Sister Nivedita, as a Western disciple of Vivekananda who traveled freely and spoke in public, legitimized her position by expressing an unreflective admiration for ideal Hindu models of femininity: chaste wife and heroic mother.[6] Further, her advocacy of conventional models of Hindu womanhood could also be interpreted as a personal desire to perform the "proper" role of female disciple and please her master, that is, Swami Vivekananda (Roy, 1998, p. 123). Such propriety may have been expected of one who, as a Western woman, was suspect in the eyes of Hindu society. Sarala Debi, too, negotiated a delicate balance between her fervent advo-cacy of political aggression and contemporary mores dictating female mod-esty (Ray, 1995).

Madam Cama also was aware that her passionate calls for bloodletting might not be seen by some as a womanly attribute. She once commented, "Some of you say that as a woman I should object to violence. . . . Three years

ago it was repugnant to me even to talk of violence as a subject of discussion . . . but owing to the heartlessness, the hypocrisy . . . of the Liberals . . .
that feeling is gone. . . . Why should we deplore the use of violence when our
enemies drive us to it?" (quoted in Yadav and Bakshi, 1991, p. 231). At the
same time, her belief that women had to enter the struggle for freedom as
independent actors was unassailable. Attending the meeting of the 1910
Egyptian National Congress in Brussels, she exclaimed, "I see here the repre-
sentatives of only half the population of Egypt. May I ask, where is the other
half? Sons of Egypt, where are the mothers of Egypt? Where are your mothers and sister? Your wives and daughters?" (Cama, n.d.).

The lives and words of Sister Nivedita, Sarala Debi, and Madam Cama
eloquently highlight the dilemma of strong, independent women living in
nineteenth-century India, women who felt an affinity for the figures of Hindu
soldier and warrior-monk but could not aspire, because of gendered social
restrictions, to live life as such. Thus, they advanced the project of masculine
Hinduism through their speeches and written texts in supporting roles of
chaste wife and heroic mother. While it was possible for a few to temporarily
enter the political landscape as ascetic, masculinized warrior (in fact, a few
female revolutionaries did follow Madam Cama's command to learn how to
shoot straight, using British officers as their targets), embracing such a role
risked a high social cost.

In contrast, Sister Nivedita, Madam Cama, and Sarala Debi steered cau-
tiously on their course through this masculinist terrain. Sister Nivedita traveled and spoke widely, but as a celibate disciple of the Swami—wearing the
holy saffron robes of a feminized warrior-monk and advocating traditional
roles of devoted wife and heroic mother for women—her stance prevented
her from being a threat to patriarchal norms of contemporary society. Madam
Cama, although not celibate, lived most of her life outside India; she down-
played her femininity to demonstrate devotion to the motherland. Indeed,
most of the fiery and aggressive articles she wrote in the *Bande Mataram* were,
perhaps modestly, not signed. Sarala Debi, also a vocal and confident woman,
confined her fervor to words and contained her celebration of martial heroism within the limits of Hindu ritualistic practice. She justified her devotion
to masculine Hinduism by constructing herself as a chaste sister who encouraged her brothers to join the nationalist struggle.

CONCLUSION

Masculine Hinduism grew out of a nationalist effort to resist a gendered colonial justification for the British presence in India. This cultural construct
intersected the masculinist narrative shaping the colonial gaze by asserting
Indian martial prowess and physical strength with icons and historical-
mythic figures drawn from indigenous tradition. Masculine Hinduism did not

merely parrot British categories but rather developed an innovative and dynamic model of resistance, a discourse based on hegemonic masculinity framing colonial rule.

The Hindu soldier and the warrior-monk were two dominant representations of this interpretation of masculinity. The former configured manhood by emphasizing martial prowess, physical strength, and patriotic fervor in battle; the latter model moved beyond these traits to emphasize spiritual strength and moral fortitude, traits essential for Hindu masculinity. While these images offer a convenient heuristic device for ordering this gendered nationalist challenge to colonial domination, reality often eluded such neat categorization. Frequently, both constructs of manhood overlapped or were configured with minor modifications in the texts and speeches of nationalists. Further, the language and context of this particular nationalist narrative was Hindu. Women's voices and models of femininity were not completely absent from its interpretation of nationalism, as masculine Hinduism attracted female advocates while simultaneously stimulating the creation of corresponding female images within the nation: nation as woman (Mother India), heroic mother, pure wife, and masculinized, celibate woman-warrior. Female advocates had to negotiate a delicate social compromise in taking up the standard of nationalism within this masculinized terrain to avoid transgressing society's gendered norms. These gendered models coupled with women's attempt to maintain a vocal presence within a masculinist narrative, with some modification, still resonate in modern Hindutva politics.

FOUR

Cultural Nationalism, Masculine Hinduism, and Contemporary Hindutva

The foremost task before us, therefore, is the moulding of . . . a . . . disciplined and virile national manhood. And verily, this is the one mission to which the RSS is wholly and solely dedicated.

—M. S. Golwalkar, *Bunch of Thoughts*

Yet, six months ago, during the battle of Kargil, Indian army proved that when it is given a free hand . . . its soldiers and officers are among the best in the world. . . . And for the first time in five hundred years, . . . the Kshatriya spirit [warrior spirit] was revived in India. Once again, what the Bhagavad Gita had preached became alive: that violence is sometimes necessary to protect one's children, women and borders . . .

—Excerpt from the VHP website

How does our Shiv Sainik appear as he is marching towards Ayodhya? Like the roaring lion spreading terror, with the gait of an intoxicated elephant, like the assault of a rhino which reduces to powder a rocky mountain, like the manoeuvres of a leopard: Our infinite blessings to these Hindu warriors who are marching towards Ayodhya.

—Bal Thackeray, Shiv Sena leader

HINDUTVA IS NOT A monolithic cultural construct. It has varied over time as well as according to the context within which it has been articulated. Although the RSS, VHP, BJP, and Shiv Sena are frequently described as Hindu nationalist organizations, it is possible to tease out ideological and tactical differences among them. However, a comprehensive discussion of such differences is not the goal of this chapter.[1] Rather, drawing on the ideals of masculine Hinduism and the models of masculinity outlined in the previous chapters, it analyzes the intersection of gender and nationalism within Hindutva. Put another way, this chapter argues that ideals of masculinity, central to various interpretations of Hindutva, is anchored within this discourse through the figures of the Hindu soldier and the warrior-monk. These archetypes are not rigid totalizing categories but rather gender constructs in flux, which are modified to reflect the ideological biases of each organization. However, they remain an efficient heuristic device with which to analyze the articulation of masculinity and nation in Hindutva. Further, given that militarism is a central conceit of these representations of nationalism, violence is always one of the practices available to Hindutva and whether or not it chooses to use it depends on the strategic stance of each organization. Competing nationalisms—Hindutva and secularism—form the background against which this chapter's analysis of the space occupied by and tensions between social constructions of masculinity and femininity unfolds.

Advocates of both types of nationalism state that they have the interests of the country at heart and that under the sway of the other group the Indian state will descend into political chaos. The forces of secularism argue that Hindutva is a dangerous ideology that will lead to more and more sectarian violence in India, and there is no dearth of examples that they can point to: the involvement of the VHP in the Gujarat riots of 2002, the BJP/Sena's implication in the destruction of the Babri masjid, and the Sena's role in the 1992–1993 riots in Mumbai as well as earlier riots in Bhiwandi. Further, secularists also fear that minorities will lose their constitutional protection under a Hindu nationalist government. But Hindutva can also hold secularists responsible for many episodes of violence: the Congress Party's implication in the violence against Sikhs after the assassination of Mrs. Gandhi and caste violence under Laloo Yadav's Janata Dal. Indeed, let us not forget that India's most flagrant violation of civil liberties (the Emergency) happened under a party, the Congress, that considers itself a vocal advocate of secular nationalism.

The question is, of course, whether any or all interpretations of Hindutva contain unique features (not found in secular nationalism) open to manipulation by leaders for the purpose of facilitating violence or expressing aggressive action against minorities. Put bluntly, are the various forms of Hindu nationalism circulating in the modern Indian context inherently more violent than the nationalism shaping Congress's ideology and various forms of Indian communism and socialism? Indeed given that almost any ideology can be used to foment violence against the enemy of the nation, this is a fruitless path of inquiry. Rather, an analysis of the manner in which Hindutva incorporates a cultural vocabulary to construct a particular vision of the nation might illuminate the implications of the rise of cultural nationalism within the Indian polity.

In recent years an uneasy tension has emerged between cultural nationalism and the Nehruvian vision of secular nationalism as interpreted by the Congress Party. At the all-India level, the tacit Congress support for the Hindu violence against Sikhs after the death of Indira Gandhi is the most extreme example of its betrayal of the Nehruvian ideal. At a more local level, for example in Mumbai, an erstwhile center of Congress power, the willingness of the Congress to ally with the Shiv Sena in the seventies, its use of this party to break up communist unions, its failure to quell the spread of violence during the 1992–1993 Mumbai riots, and local Congress politicians' active participation in attacks against Muslim slum dwellers indicate that the division between civic nationalism (Nehruvian secularism) and cultural nationalism (communalism) has become blurred at least at the lower levels of the Congress's organization. Given the previous discussion of the slippage between civic and cultural nationalism in the Indian context as well as the allusions to the above incidents of violence, its seems that civic and cultural nationalisms are so entangled that it is impossible to neatly distinguish one from the other.

Hindu nationalists accuse their opponents of being "pseudo-secularists" and "traitors to the nation" while these opponents in turn accuse Hindu nationalists of being "Fascists."[2] This give and take of insults further illustrates the confusion of civic and cultural nationalism in India. Anti-Hindutva forces are making the equation that civic nationalism=secularism=good=nonviolent tolerance of democracy, while in contrast Hindutva forces are altering this equation to read cultural nationalism=Hindu nationalism=good=nonviolent tolerance of democracy. The point is, of course, that anti-Hindutva forces do not accept the equation of nonviolence and democracy with cultural nationalism, and given the destruction of the recent Gujarat riots, Ayodhya, and the riots that it followed it, this skepticism may be justified. Yet let us not forget that in many instances civic nationalism—Emergency in India, McCarthyism in the United States, as well as the internment of citizens of Japanese descent in both the United States and Canada—has also suppressed civil liberties and temporarily facilitated violence. So the debate continues. This debate, although not an integral part of this chapter, frames its interrogation of nation and manhood in the RSS, VHP, BJP, and Shiv Sena.

RASHTRIYA SWAYAMSEVAK SANGH (RSS)

The RSS has been the most consistent and articulate institutional voice of Hindutva in India. Founded in 1925 by Dr. Hedgewar, it remains a dominant advocate of this perspective, efficiently disseminating its ideology through local centers of activity known as *shakhas*. Although Hedgewar remains

revered as the founding father, it was actually the second *sarsanghchalak* or
supreme head of the RSS, M. S. Golwalkar, who synthesized and consolidated
its ideology in various texts, the most famous being *Bunch of Thoughts*, first
published in 1966. This section draws on this publication, pamphlets available at the RSS book store in New Delhi, and interviews conducted with various activists to unpack the ideology of this organization in an attempt to
reveal the location of manhood as a dominant metaphor ordering its vision
of nation.

SHAKHA AND MASCULINITY

Every morning, night, or evening young men and boys gather in open spaces
in rural and urban India to participate in the daily activities of the RSS
shakha. There are about forty thousand *shakhas*, with about ten to eighty volunteers scattered throughout the country (MacDonald, 2000, p. 351). Golwalkar's description of *shakha* routine reveals an almost elegaic celebration of
an unified, disciplined brotherhood:

> There is an open playground. Under a saffron flag groups of youths and boys
> are absorbed in a variety of Bharatiya games. Resounding shouts of joyous
> enthusiasm fill the air. The sight of the daring young men pressing forward
> with the cry 'Kabbadi, Kabbadi' on their lips thrills the heart. The leader's
> whistle or order has a magical effect on them; there is instant perfect order
> and silence. Then exercises follow—wielding the lathi [literally stout bam-
> boo stick, but also a weapon used in Indian martial arts], Suryanamaskar
> [salutation to the sun], marching, etc. The spirit of collective effort and
> spontaneous discipline pervades every programme. Then they sit down and
> sing in chorus songs charged with patriotism.
>
> Discussions follows. They delve deep into the problems affecting the
> national life. And finally, they stand in rows before the flag and recite the
> prayer: *Many salutations to Thee, O loving Motherland* whose echoes fill the
> air and stir the soul. 'Bharat Mata ki jai' [victory to Mother India] uttered
> in utmost earnest furnishes the finishing and inspiring touch to the entire
> programme. (2000, p. 393)

The *shakhas* provide the public fora wherein boys and men are taught the
proper ideals of manliness necessary for creation of the true patriot: discipline, martial prowess, and loyalty to the collective, in this case, the nation
imagined as Mother India. In other words, "being a man" is integral for
national glory,

> Today, more than anything else, Mother needs such men—young, intelligent,
> dedicated and more than all virile and masculine. When Narayana—eternal
> knowledge and Nara—eternal manliness—combine, victory is ensured. And
> such are the men who make history—men with capital 'M.' (p. 448)

Manliness indicates the nation's resolve to overcome the internal effeminacy that remains the greatest threat to its strength and never allow an external aggressor to subjugate its people:

> After all, nations can stand only upon the solid foundation of their organized strength. . . . Then, what are the qualities required of individuals who will form the living limbs of such an organized strength? . . . The first thing is invincible physical strength. We have to be so strong that none in the whole world will be able to overawe and subdue us. For that, we require strong and healthy bodies. . . . Swami Vivekananda used to say, "I want men with muscles of iron and nerves of steel." He himself was like that. Finding that some co-disciples were always sitting down and shedding tears, he would thunder, "That is not *bhakti* [faith]. That is nervous weakness. Don't sit down and weep like little girls." What do we see today when we look at ourselves in a mirror? Do we find any sign of manliness and strength? . . . Without an able body, we cannot achieve anything. Even to see God, a healthy and strong body is required. God is not for the weak. . . . The present-day fashion of our young men of decorating the skin and discarding the sinews must be given up and they should, with proper exercises and healthy habits, develop strong bodies capable of . . . undergoing all the hardships of life with good cheer. (Golwalkar, 1981, p. 66)

Golwalkar's reference to the Swami underlines his attempts to locate the RSS in a nationalist lineage deriving from the nineteenth century. He also acknowledges Sister Nivedita as a source of inspiration for RSS ideology:

> Once Sister Nivedita, the chosen disciple of Swami Vivekananda, said, "If only Hindus collectively pray daily for ten minutes in the morning and in the evening, they will become an invincible society." The daily *Shakha* of the Rashtriya Swayamsevak Sangh augurs the realisation of the passionate dream of that dedicated soul. (p. 421)

By drawing on the ideas of Vivekananda and Nivedita (and Savarkar in other texts), he may be combating accusations of "Fascism" by removing the RSS from the right-wing margins of Indian political thought to the center of mainstream nationalism. In addition, by acknowledging his debt to these nationalists, ardent advocates of manliness, he reinvigorates ideas of masculine Hinduism within the RSS brand of Hindutva. Further reading of Golwalkar's ideas indicate his rather uneasy negotiation between the Swami's model of the warrior-monk and Savarkar's aggressive Hindu soldier. On one hand, he admits that Hindu manhood should move beyond physical prowess and martial ability (Golwalkar, 2000, pp. 43–53) to incorporate self-sacrifice, service, restraint, and displine, but on the other hand, for example, writing during India's confrontations with China and Pakistan, he conflates masculinity and military might.

The Hindu Soldier in RSS Thought

In face of the "yellow peril" (his term for Chinese aggression), Golwalkar urges, "Let all persons physically fit be ready for military service. And let their mothers bless and send forth their sons at this hour of trial. When the five Pandavas [exiled warriors of the epic *Mahabharata*] went to seek the blessings of their mother Kunti before the commencement of the *Mahabharata* war, she blessed them saying, 'Go ye all to the battle. This is the occasion for which Kshatriya [warrior caste] women give birth to sons. . . .' Let every mother speak in the same heroic strain to her sons even now" (Golwalkar, 2000, p. 291). In the above selections he not only equates manhood and militarism but by using the phrase "all persons," he seems to indicate that women can also enter the fray as soldiers, but in the lines following this assertion, such an assumption becomes moot as he valorizes women as heroic mothers who bear and nurture male warriors to fight for their country. He uses a similar vocabulary to describe Indian actions during the 1965 Indo-Pakistan war:

> Our Jawans have in these few days smashed the myth assiduously built up by the British, and believed by the world and many of our own country men, that we are a meek and weak lot who have always been at the mercy of any and every freebooter who chose to trample upon us. . . . In fact, no society which could give birth to a Rama, a Krishna, Pratap, a Shivaji, and a Ranjit Singh could be considered anything but virile and valiant. A distorted presentation of our national history depicting all such great national heroes as either mythological . . . and naming only some sections of our people as martial races had so far misrepresented the true heroic ring of our national character. Our valiant Jawans have given lie direct to that mischievous propaganda and proved that very son of soil inherits the blood of those peerless ancestors. They have projected before the world the real mighty image of Bharatmata [Mother India] with Her millions of arms raised to strike down evil forces on the face of the earth. (2000, p. 317)

The above selection, rich in imagery and icons, weaves together various strands of cultural imagination to create the tapestry reflecting Golwalkar's and, as a consequence, the RSS's image of Hindu manhood. The valiant "Jawans" or the foot soldiers of the Indian army are glorified. Jawan also means young and muscular, and although not necessarily gender specific, it usually connotes a male body. In this vision, the valor of the Jawans in battle erases any remaining internalized legacy of the British contempt for Indian manhood; further, this defiant stance is buttressed by the construction of a now familiar Hindu martial tradition built around historical-mythic warrior figures. Note that in an act of cultural resistance he constructs Ram and Krishna (usually thought to be mythic figures) as flesh and blood heroes, and dismisses their mythic status as disinformation disseminated by foreigners in an attempt to denigrate Indian martial history.

The phrase "yellow peril" and the celebration of brave Jawans in the 1965 Indo-Pakistan war clearly indicate the "enemies" of the Indian nation: China and Pakistan representing Islamic aggression. Europe and Britain also are viewed with suspicion, but again, like Savarkar, there is some ambivalence towards the British, and a reluctant admiration of their disciplined approach to war emerges. India's loss of manhood, seen as the result of a long history of aggression is lamented. Indeed, Golwalkar contends that Indian humiliation on the battlefield flowed from the effeminate nature bred in them because of centuries of aggressive attacks: "In our own history we have seen that the British armies could put rout to our armies several times their number. The obvious reason was their superior discipline" (Golwalkar, 2000, p. 410). In this narative, Indian manhood disintegrated in face of vicious attacks by Islamic invaders, "But what does history say? After the death of Mohammed Pygamber, his followers poured out from Arabstan in waves after waves with their sword dripping with blood and overran vast portions of the globe . . ." (Golwalkar, 2000, p. 109). This quotation, clearly equates Islam and violence. Further, it exonerates India or at least downplays its weakness by claiming that India was not unqiue since many parts of the world capitulated to the sword of Islam. Never again, urges Golwalkar, should India become so weak and effeminate: "To remain weak is the most heinous sin in this world" (Golwalkar, 2000, p. 271).

Islam (represented by Pakistan), China, Christianity, and the West (Britain in the past and America in the future) remain modern India's greatest threat. When urging India to resist Chinese and Pakistani aggression, the anger explicit in Golwalkar's tone dehumanizes and demonizes the citizens of these states (Golwalkar, 2000, pp. 177–87 and pp. 290–98). Although he is suspicious of Christian missionaries who are in his view converting people with false promises of riches and as a result threatening national cohesion represented by an united Hindu community, his words do not reflect the violent rage used to describe Pakistan and China. Finally, the United States as a superpower is also located in relation to India's global position; in an imagined battle of masculinities, Golwalkar feminizes the U.S. polity. He elaborates this theme by recounting his words to an American journalist,

> America is moving fast on the road to self-destruction. Just see your own clothes. The loose fashionable garments that you wear and the comb in your pocket betray the effeminate nature of the average American today. . . . I sincerely hope that America will wake up in time and stop this internal corrosion of its manhood. (2000, p. 241)

Golwalkar's choice to use clothing and vanity to demonstrate and condemn American effeminacy, rather than failing military might or defeat in

war, is surprising and to an extent not very effective, given his reasons for
such condemnation. For what he does not explicitly mention, but implies
later on, is the need for India to take advantage of this supposed American
effeminization and reclaim its masculinity by reaching for global power to
replace the United States as a hegemon. Consequently, if the only mark of
American effeminization is excessive attention to fashion and not weak
armies, India's bid for hegemonic status may not be so easily attained. However, it is possible that he leaves much unspoken. That is, this male focus on
fashion is equated with effeminization that in turn will corrode American
martial prowess and hence its military supremacy.

In this elaboration of masculine power, Golwalkar does not reject Gandhian nonviolence but rather reinterprets it to dovetail with his image of
Hindu manhood. He states that Gandhiji would never advocate running
away in face of danger or remaining passive when threatened by physical
force. He buttresses his point by recounting an incident during Hindu-Muslim riots in Ahmedabad when supposedly Gandhi rebuked Hindu men for
deserting their families and not resisting Muslim aggression (Golwalkar,
2000, p. 276). Again, Golwalkar attempts to strengthen the RSS position
within mainstream Indian nationalism by invoking its philosopical proximity
to a revered national leader.

The cultural festivals of the RSS further highlight its valorization of the
link between manliness and martial prowess. For example, according to Golwalkar some important celebrations include Varsha Partipada or Hindu New
Year commemorating Hindu heroes; Hindu Samrajya Dinostav (loosely
translated, "celebration of the Hindu Empire") marking the victory of resurgent Hindu power under Shivaji who ascended his throne in 1674 on this
day; and Vijaya Dashami (loosely translated, "the tenth day celebrating victory") glorifying the divine Ram's conquest of the demon Ravana (Golwalkar,
2000, p. 397). Even the title of the RSS Hindi weekly—*Panchajanya*—
reflects this martial tone. It refers to the conch shell blown by Lord Krishna
in his guise of charioteer, announcing the arrival of the warrior Arjuna on the
mythic battle field described in the popular Hindu epic *Mahabharata*.

To sum up, masculine Hinduism interpreted in terms of physical strength
and martial ability is central to the image of nation underlying RSS ideology.

THE WARRIOR-MONK IN THE RSS

The image of Hindu soldier, although vital to RSS ideology, captures only a
partial aspect of this organization's vision of manhood. The gates opening
into the RSS compound in the Jhandewala area of New Delhi reveal a space
that is occupied by men and marked by an aura of piety. Many of the men
residing there don the saffron robe of Hindu ascetics. The role of *pracharak*,
an important position in the RSS hierarchy, draws on Vivekananda's vision

of the warrior-monk. *Pracharaks*, men who have dedicated their life to the RSS, are celibate and frugal. Joseph Alter suggests that this asceticism continues to be an important way for some Hindu men to reclaim a masculinity that many feel has been threatened by external domination (Alter, 1994). It is also possible that British condemnation of Indians as sexually deviant because of child marriage and its resultant juvenile sexual activity may have also encouraged some Indian men to resist this discourse by embracing celibacy. However, it should be remembered that holy men or *sadhus* who have rejected materialism as well as sexual activity in their search for enlightenment have been a part of the Indian cultural fabric well before the arrival of the British. Whatever its historical and cultural antecedents, this deliberate rejection of the feminine through abstinence marks masculine fear that somehow female sexuality remains a threat to a male heroic quest whether it be for self-enlightenment or for the manly nation.

Golwalkar anticipates this model of manhood when he extols the spiritual superiority of Hinduism:

> It is clear, therefore, that the mission of reorganising the Hindu people on the lines of their unique national genius which the Sangh has taken up is not only a great process of true national regeneration of Bharat but also the inevitable precondition to realise the dream of world unity and human welfare. For, as we have seen, it is the grand world-unifying thought of Hindus alone that can supply the abiding basis for human brotherhood, that knowledge of the Inner Spirit which charge the human mind with the sublime urge to toil for the happiness of mankind. (2000, p. 6)

This spiritual strength and moral fortitude, ideally, forms the basis of the *pracharak's* role in the RSS.

THE NATION TO BE DEFENDED

The Hindu soldier and the warrior-monk not only protect the Hindu nation but they are the nation. One very important trait embodied by both models is disciplined unity. Put another way, Hindus have to work for national glory as a cohesive collective. Such collective action presupposes a fairly homogenized society, and caste hierarchies have to be explained away as do the existence of various interpretations of Hinduism (for example, Vaishanvism, Shaivism) along with Sikhism, Jainism, Buddhism, Islam, and Christianity.

Golwalkar eloquently decries the curse of untouchability and calls for other Hindus to uplift their "neglected brethren" (Golwalkar, 2000, pp. 358–70). To be sure, this attitude is rife with paternalism and marked by a reluctance to admit that high-caste Hindus exploit Dalits (literally, the downtrodden, a title appropriated by untouchables and lower-caste Hindus in India to emphasize their exploitation in the Hindu caste hierarchy) in cruel

ways. Despite the RSS's self-reporting of the work done among Dalits, there
is no actual evidence whether or not this organization will support a Brahmin
marrying a Dalit or if Dalits will be allowed to occupy powerful positions in
the RSS hierarchy. Further, the diverse body of Hindu thought along with the
message spread by Guru Nanak (founder of Sikhism), Mahavir (founder of
Jainism), and the Buddha are incorporated within one monolithic cultural
construction known as "Hinduism." The presence of Islam and Christianity
is explained by the conversion of native Hindus to these faiths through coercion and bribery. Therefore, in a bid to challenge this action, it becomes the
national duty of the RSS to present the Hindu nation in such a positive light
that these converts will return, of their own volition, to the Hindu fold.

A final group remains as an obstacle to the RSS's dream of an unified,
homogenous, disciplined India: scheduled tribes or Adivasis (indigenous people). Adivasis form an extremely marginalized group in India. They have lost
access to the fruits of the lands that sustained their traditional way of life
because of deforestation and economic development while their religions,
languages, and music are slowly vanishing. There is a common historical perspective held by some ordinary folk (who are not privy to various academic
debates) that Adivasis were the original inhabitants of India when invaders
(sometimes referred to as Aryans) came in from central and west Asia centuries ago. Such a perspective disrupts the RSS's "sons of the soil" narrative
of nationalism and hence is violently rejected by Golwalkar:

> In the natural course of our national life, there are some who live in
> cities, . . . some others . . . live in villages and some have as yet remained in
> the jungle and hills. But those forest-dwellers, the *vanavasis* are now called
> *adivasis*, aboriginals, as if all others are upstarts and settlers coming here
> from somewhere outside! (2000, p. 115)

Adivasis have been renamed "vanavasis" and the myth of a nation,
immutable and permanent, is maintained.

Coupled with the erasure of diversity within the nation is the RSS's
claim that India as it is configured now, stretching from the Himalayas to
Kanykumari, is not a recent construct, but of ancient origin as is Hindu devotion and loyalty to this territory:

> But there are persons who say that Hindus did not know what motherland
> was, that they were all divided into various warring clans, that patriotism,
> i.e. devotion to the one single motherland, was unknown to them and if at
> all they were to a certain extent devoted, it was only to certain fragments of
> the land and not to the country as a whole from the Himalayas to Kanyaku-
> mari. (p. 82)

In conclusion, the master narrative of nationalism underlying RSS ideology projects an ancient, virile, manly, unified Hindu community striving

to eradicate India's past humiliations and enhance its glory both domestically and internationally.

This master narrative as constructed by Golwalkar continues on today in publications available at the RSS bookstore, including *The R.S.S. at a Glance; RSS: A Vision in Action; Hinduttva: a view and a way of life; Global Hindutva in 21st Century and Rashtriya Swayamsevak Sangh;* and *Manu, Sangh, and I.*

MEN OF THE RSS

Obviously, the personal experience and interests of activists shape their location within this narrative. For example, interviews with two workers—quiet, well-spoken men—in the international (or SEWA) division of the RSS highlighted their dedication to social work as a patriotic means of reaching for national glory on the global stage.[3] One with a Ph.D. in Biology was introduced to the RSS by his brother, residing in the United States who turned to the RSS as means of maintaining his ties to his heritage. The other, although not as well educated, radiated a quiet confidence in the national value of his work targeted at reaching out to the Hindu diaspora in Asia, Europe, and North America and disseminating the image of a strong and united India. Both emphasized a focus on discipline as a means of transforming Hindu India into a powerful country (personal interview, New Delhi, February 7, 2002).

The editors of the RSS newspapers (both Hindi and English) revealed a fierce pride in Hindu India and drew on the superiority of Hindu spirituality to construct a robust, unified Hindu nation on the brink of becoming a major player in the international arena despite Western attempts to subjugate it. The editor of the Hindi newspaper was rather more passionate in his expression of national pride and the need for a "new generation of Hindus" who were forward-looking, patriotic, and disciplined. In his opinion, the *shakhas* were vital in creating the "new Hindu": "Through games we learn . . . patriotism" (personal interview, New Delhi, March 10, 2002). He seemed incensed at Western hypocrisy: "The West can pile up weapons but when India does so, it must be stopped" (personal interview, New Delhi, March 10, 2002).

The most ominous interpretation of the master narrative was articulated by a former editor of the *Organiser* who for a time also sat in the Indian Parliament as a member of the BJP (personal interview, New Delhi, March 13, 2002). When describing the RSS's national ideology, he began musing on the state of American morality [a train of thought that may have been provoked by the presence of my (white) American husband]. He described American society as morally unstable, then linked this instability to cowardice and lack of martial prowess concluding with his stated belief that the Indian army could defeat American soldiers in hand-to-hand combat any day. In his view, by focusing on discipline and patriotism, the RSS was enabling the creation of a strong military capable of shifting India from the margins of global power to the center. It is not pertinent whether or not this is an accurate description of Indian and American martial ability, but rather that this speaker's vehemence in configuring Indian nationalism in the model of Hindu soldier and offering, as it were, a martial challenge to the United States in the interests of vindicating Indian manhood indicates a willingness to use violence as a means of expressing aggressive nationalism. Indeed, given the wars in Afghanistan and the Middle East, such a view of violence is neither unique to Hindutva specifically or to cultural nationalism in general. But it does stand as a warning that the masculinization of Hindu nationalism can be used in dangerous ways.

Finally, an RSS activist's delineation of his location within the narrative offered by this organization reveals why the *shakha* remains such an effective method of disseminating this image of robust nationalism. Ramesh Patange, an important activist, describes his life in the slums of Mumbai as a "harrowing experience" (Patange, n.d., p. 5). According to him, his father had retreated from his responsibility as a provider and his mother supported the family by working as a maid in various households. When he was a young child, Patange began to attend the local RSS *shakha*, and "all the drawbacks in my household were more than made up during my one hour in the *shakha*. That one hour gave us a sense of being special" (Patange, n.d., p. 5). He learned that "Hindu aggressiveness and disquiet today are responses to humiliating stimuli of appeasement of Muslims, and the calumny and ridicule heaped on Hinduism" (Patange, n.d., p. 2). A child, regardless of class background, will resonate to any message taught in a hour during which he feels special. However, if the child comes from the chaotic background of an urban Indian slum, then the message learned in the *shakha* will play an even more heightened normative role in the formation of his ideology. A socioeconomic analysis of the location of RSS *shakhas* has not been undertaken, but it is reasonable to assert that many of the forty thousand *shakhas* are located either in slums or lower middle-class areas. For example, I visited an active *shakha* in Andheri (East) in Mumbai run by a young man who lived in a two-room apartment with his mother, father, and sister where the family shared a toilet with two other households. Many of the boys attending the *shakha* either came from similar situations or lived in the nearby slums. Using the *shakha* as the fundamental unit of their organization, the RSS effectively draws young boys into their fold by providing a normative framework through which to order their lives and simultaneously offering them an "imaginative response to the overwhelming burden of human suffering—disease, mutilation, grief, age, and death" (Anderson, 1991, p. 10). The images of manhood embedded in Hindutva enable Indian men to make sense of an inconsistent and frustrating economic and political context by endowing them with pride, strength, and unity.

The men of the RSS do not rigidly adhere to the models of the Hindu soldier and the warrior-monk. As the above examples indicate Golwalkar's message of manliness is interpreted in various ways. The workers of SEWA International and the editors visualize it as a quiet, disciplined dedication to social work as well as the forceful dissemination of thought through texts, while the former editor and member of parliament elaborates manhood as a raw exercise of power. "Discipline" constructed as a collective assertion of strength (interpreted variously as aggression, dedication, and martial power) frames these various images of "manhood." These men have not embraced asceticism and celibacy as an expression of self-control and strength of will (as expressed by the warrior-monk). In contrast, Patange, a *pracharak*, does draw on this legacy of monasticism to order his vision of manhood and nation.

To sum up, through its *shakhas*, publications, and speeches, the RSS circulates a master narrative emphasizing the need for an organized and united India represented by its valorization of the figures of Hindu soldier and warrior monk.

VISHWA HINDU PARISHAD

The Vishwa Hindu Parishad (or VHP) draws on a similar interpretation of nation, with perhaps a more militant readiness to use aggressive, even violent action to express national virility.[4] Founded in 1964, the outcome of a meeting between Golwalkar and Hindu spiritual teachers, this organization aims to bring the image of a united, strong, and nonsectarian Hindu community to ordinary folk (Basu, Datta, Sarkar, Sarkar, and Sen, 1993, p. 64). On its website, the VHP clearly states that it aims "to consolidate, strengthen and make invincible the *global* [italics added] Hindu fraternity by following the eternal and universal life values based on Sanatan Dharma [ancient religion] and work for total welfare of humanity on the basis of the unique cultural ethos of Bharatvarsha " (VHP, Aims and Objects). The organization's focus on the masses as well as its global reach distinguishes it from the RSS. SEWA International does underline the RSS's move towards a more international profile; however, India, still remains its primary arena of mobilization. A further difference as articulated by an official spokesperson of the VHP lies in the objective of each organization, while the VHP declares itself as a mass organization, the RSS through its *shakhas*, training camps, and *pracharak* system envisions the creation of an elite cadre of leaders devoted to patriotic duty (personal interview, New Delhi, Feb. 8, 2002). Through schools in rural areas, medical camps, cultural events, and *satsangs* (devotional meetings), the VHP reaches out to Hindus everywhere, even Christians and Muslims seen as converted Hindus are urged to return to the Hindu fold by rejecting their conversion.

MANHOOD IN THE VHP

Masculinity configured in the image of the warrior-monk and the Hindu soldier frames this organization's activities. For example, the VHP's headquarters in New Delhi—Sankat Mochan Ashram—is constructed as an ashram or a devotional retreat. Saffron flags are evident everywhere while a temple occupies the central courtyard. Our hosts kindly invited us to a vegetarian lunch served on the floor in traditional Indian style. The atmosphere of the building mimicked the quiet, muted tones of a space occupied by Hindu ascetics or *sadhus*. One of the official spokespeople we met further illustrated this theme of asceticism. After retiring from his job as an engineer, he had left his family and come to New Delhi to embrace a monastic life in an all-male institution. In his mind, after fulfilling the duties of a householder, he was now a renunciate, dedicated to an ascetic life style to serve the Hindu nation. Women were not prominently visible in Sankat Mochan Ashram. Dressed in saffron robes, this man drew on the tradition of Hindu asceticism. However, when interviewed, his unconscious (or perhaps conscious) echo of the aggressive militarism advocated by Savarkar was unmistakable. When overcome with passion, he banged on the table in front of him to declare that if nonviolence did not enable national glory, then Hindus had to win back their respect with violence if necessary (personal interview, New Delhi, February 8, 2002). This sentiment also reverberates on the VHP website: "Are Hindus cowards then? Are they forever going to take things lying down? Have centuries of Muslim conquests, rape, looting, forced conversion, razing of thousands of temples, imprinted so much on India's psyche, that we can only endlessly produce Vijay Amritrajes [Indian tennis player]; talented, nice, but unable to fight, to win, to defeat the opponent. . . . COME ON INDIA: Stand up and fight" (Gautier, Import of the Bomb Blasts).

The figure of the warrior-monk, although visible, is perhaps not the most dominant interpretation of masculinity within VHP ideology. Lacking an institutionalized expresssion such as the prachark system, monastic ideology is not incorporated within its organizational framework. It is the other prevalent image of Hindu masculinity—the warrior—that seems to be most prominent in the VHP. The general secretary of the Indraprastha VHP office in New Delhi professed admiration for the nation-state of Israel; in his opinion, the Israelis, by adopting a militaristic view of citizenship, were expressing their dedication to the creation of a strong and muscular nation. This was the model, he declared, that India needs to emulate and to this end the Vishwa Hindu Parishad encourages its young men and women to learn martial arts while pledging their lives in service to the Hindu nation (personal interview, New Delhi, March 10, 2002). Elsewhere, the organization endorses such an approach to patriotism most eloquently: "But look again at the Israelis: like the Indians, they were slaughtered for centuries; and during the Second World War, six million of them went to Hitler's gas chambers without even a whimper. But after the war, when the new State of Israel was founded, its leaders decided that enough was enough: henceforth it will be 'an eye for an eye and a tooth for a tooth'" (Gautier, Where is our Shivaji?).

The members of the Bajrang Dal, a youth group affiliated with the VHP, perhaps embody the fury and aggression represented by this interpretation of citizenship most effectively. The Dal declares it is the "security ring of Hindu Society" and whenever "there is an attack on Hindu Society, Faith, and Religion, the workers of the Bajrang Dal come forward for their rescue." Such defense is necessary because "Hindu Society and its faith are being kicked and insulted by various forces for the last fourteen hundred years" (VHP, Dimensions of VHP).

The youthful members of the Bajrang Dal have taken on the role of soldiers protecting the motherland. Although, officially they reject violence and declare they only resist insults to Hinduism through democratic means (VHP, Dimensions of VHP), this support for democracy seems weakened in face of their avowed intention to not appear submissive to their foes. As Dr. Surendra Jain, a Dal leader claims, "The Bajrang Dal is assertive not militant . . . missionaries consider Hindus a soft target. Even words 'soft target' were used in the missionary literature. However, now the Hindus have woken up. We are no more a soft target for their unholy activities" (Diwanji, Hindus are a Soft Target). Although it is possible to demonstrate invincible strength and resistance through democratic means, reality challenges this professed support for democracy claimed by the Dal. The most recent challenge derives from the Dal's implication in the Ahmedabad riots of 2002. A dramatic portrait of a Dal activist on the cover of the news magazine *Outlook* (March 11, 2002) captures the mode of participation undertaken by this group: a young bearded man whose very being radiates fury with a steel rod upheld in one hand and a saffron bandana tied around his forehead.

On February 27, 2002, coach S-6 of the Sabarmati Express on its way to New Delhi pulled out of Godhra—a small station just outside the city of Baroda in Gujarat—and stopped a little less than a mile outside the station. VHP activists who occupied S-6 were suddenly attacked with acid-filled containers, stones, and burning rags. The railway carriages caught on fire and fifty-eight people, including twenty-six women and sixteen children burned to death. There was no question that this was a well-orchestrated attack undertaken by Islamic militants. Such aggressive behavior was seen by the Bajrang Dal as a call to battle for the protection of the Hindu homeland. Cities in Gujarat erupted into violence as Hindu activists targeted Muslim homes and

90   MAKE ME A MAN!

businesses to exact retribution for the horrific attack on the Sabarmati
Express (Aiyar, 2002; Kaifee, 2002; Mahurkar, 2002). When asked about his
views on the atrocities committed in the riots against Muslims, Haraeshbhai
Bhatt, the central vice-president of the Bajrang Dal and a key founding member of the Dal in Gujarat, replied, "There was no rioting. This was just an
expression of the way the majority community [Hindus] has felt. For years,
Hindus have been pushed around. There is no outcry when Amarnath pil-
grims are murdered or Hindus are massacred in Kashmir, . . . How is it that
when innocent men, women and children are burnt alive in a train in
Godhra there is no outrage but when Muslims die in riots there is such a hue
and cry? . . . The Hindu 'samaj' [society] is reacting here. . . . We have our
ways. But it all revolves around Hindu anger" (Bhusan, 2002, p. 28). Bhatt's
language can be read as advocacy for the values of armed masculinity nested
within the ideology of Hindutva.

THE NATION TO BE DEFENDED

Aggression and violence of this sort is one possible outcome of a cultural
nationalism articulated with images of warriors and the vocabulary of martial prowess. Indeed the VHP incorporates the name of a revered book of
Hinduism—the Gita—to vindicate its masculinized image of nation: "Yet,
the Gita says that while protecting one's borders, wives, children and culture, and when all other means have failed, war can become dharma [some-
times dharma is translated as "religion," yet this word denotes a broader concept: duty or even a way of life]" (Gautier, When War Becomes Dharma).
Further, such language within the VHP narrates a monolithic nation devoid
of diversity and nuance: "In place of 'India that is Bharat,' we should have
said 'Bharat that is Hindustan.' Official documents refer to the 'composite
culture,' but ours is certainly not a composite culture. . . . In a very fundamental sense, this country has a unique cultural *oneness* [italics added]. No
country if it has to survive can have compartments" (VHP, Unifying Heritage). The VHP rejection of "composite culture" or diversity is tied to its
fear that an acceptance of "compartments" will usher in chaos and seemingly
obstruct the unity required for a disciplined, masculine nation. It follows a
chain of reasoning similar to that of the RSS to configure a homogenous,
monolithic India: caste hierarchies as well as diverse interpretations and
manners of Hindu worship are erased, Sikhs, Jains, and Buddhists are
included into the Hindu fold, while Christians and Muslims are constructed
as "original" Hindus converted to an alien religion. Finally, like the RSS, the
VHP objects to the notion of Adivasis or indigenous peoples of India, pre-
ferring the term "vanavasis."
      An integral component of a Hindu nation defined by a monolithic cul-
ture is a Manichean vision of good and evil. The binary opposition—Babar

or Ram—eloquently illustrates this stance: "Do India [sic] Muslims want to worship Babar, a man who destroyed everything which was good, beautiful and holy and lived by the power of violence, or do they want to imbibe the qualities of Ram, who believed in the equality of all, who gave-up [sic] all riches and honors of the world because he thought his b[r]other deserved the throne more than him?" (Gautier, Indian Muslims: Babar or Ram). The above sentiments illustrate two unique implications of the VHP's worldview. One, in traditional Hindu mythology the opposition between good and evil is presented through the figures of Ram and Ravana, the demon who sullied Ram's honor by abducting his wife Sita. However, this dichotomy has been recast by the VHP as Babar (the founder of the Mughal empire in India) and Ram. It seems Ravana is visualized as a part of an essential Hindu culture and Babar's figure is deemed as a more appropriate metaphor for enemies of the nation lying outside national borders. Two, only Indian Muslims are offered the choice to follow Babar versus Ram, the assumption being that *all* Hindus have already accepted Ram's path. Again, diversity within the Hindu community is erased. The binary opposition above casts Muslim aggression against Hindu nonviolence. The repetition of the myth of Muslim aggression can justify acts taken to protect Hindu property and lives. The Babar/Ram dichotomy also reflects a host of popular stereotypes of Muslims that inform this masculinized vision of nation.

Origins of the stereotypes about the innate aggressiveness and violent tendencies of Muslims are hard to pin down. Historically, long periods of Muslim rule in India generated stories about the brutality of Islamic rulers who had destroyed Hindu temples and raped Hindu women, likely leading to traditional myths about the Muslim man's voracious appetite for blood and sex. One famous story dramatizing Muslim desire for Hindu women features Padmini, a Rajput queen, who ultimately chose death by fire rather than dishonor in a Muslim ruler's harem. The *jowhar* ceremony (ritualistic death by fire) she and her attending ladies committed to escape the clutches of the Muslim ruler culminated a long siege against the Rajput king. The attack had been initiated by the Muslim ruler who purportedly was smitten by Padmini's beauty and wanted to take her as his wife. Such stories still circulate among the Hindus in India.

Another contemporary myth is the stereotype that all butchers in India are Muslim. Some Hindus like to claim that the Muslim proclivity for killing animals derives from their inherent bloodthirsty nature. Even if the overwhelming majority of butchers in India are Muslim, the prevalence may reflect the fact that Hindus rejected this occupation as polluted, which allowed Muslims to dominate the profession. Some Hindus also believe that most criminals in India are Muslim; Daoud Ibrahim has received almost legendary status as the famous crook of Mumbai. Such prejudices taken against Muslims are akin to Western maligning of Jewish moneylenders and

African American criminals. In India, these types of unfounded sentiments became reactivated when political mobilization efforts roused and exploited Hindu-Muslim differences during times of contemporary social crises. The stereotypes have been hammered again and again in many of the speeches of VHP activists.

To sum up, the VHP, through devotional meetings, texts, electronic media, and schools, disseminates the notion of a united, homogenous Hindu nation embodying martial prowess and invincible strength. Put another way, masculine Hinduism—interpreted as Hindu soldier—represents the ideal citizen of a strong Indian nation. In the VHP's vision manhood becomes quite unidimensional as ideas of spiritual vigor, moral fortitude, and asceticism popularized by Vivekananda retreat to the background and Savarkar's view of Hindu manhood as an expression of raw military power moves to the fore.

The VHP as well as the RSS are not political parties; rather, they define themselves as social organizations aiming to build a strong and proud Hindu India. In contrast, the Bharatiya Janata Party is political, it contests elections, and until recently (2004) Atul Behari Vajpayee of the BJP was the Prime Minister of India. However, for many Indian social observers the BJP's status as a participant in electoral democracy does not mute this party's affiliation with strident cultural nationalism, and they argue that the BJP as a member of the "Sangh Parivar" (or the Sangh family) comprising the VHP and RSS together with all their affiliated groups is implicated in the spread of xenophobic conflict in India.[5] There is no doubt that BJP politicians have strong ties to the RSS. For example, Vajpayee himself was a RSS *pracharak* as was Narendra Modi, the BJP Chief Minister of Gujarat.[6] Therefore, it is reasonable to expect that a variation of the masculinized interpretation of nation emerges in its ideology.

BHARATIYA JANATA PARTY

Elsewhere I have argued that the demands of India's strained yet functioning democracy through a robust print and television journalism as well as a vital nongovernmental sector coupled with the BJP's desire to participate in a system of electoral democracy has ameliorated, until now, the totalitarian implications of its interpretation of cultural nationalism (Banerjee, 2002). Having said this, it must be accepted that unforeseen circumstances such as the BJP's acquiring a solid majority in the Indian parliament and/or the incidence of severe economic depression may create a situation wherein the BJP may choose to ignore the constitution of India and impose extreme cultural policing on Indian society. At this point, however, given the still existing diversity of opinion, public dialogue, and free elections, this does not seem likely.[7] Further, having chosen to participate in an electoral system, the centrifugal forces of party politics have to mute the strident colors of a militantly aggressive nationalism embodied by Savarkar's Hindu soldier. However, although muted, resolute masculine Hinduism does resonate in the BJP's ideology as illustrated by its choice of mythic and national heroes, cultural vocabulary, and political stance on conflicts.

The Nation and the BJP

Before moving on to the articulation of the BJP's brand of masculine Hinduism, a sketch of its interpretation of a cultural nationalism defined by Hinduism is necessary. Hindutva, according to the BJP, centers on the cultural (Hindu) oneness of India: "From the Himalaya to Kanya Kumari, this country has always been one. We have had many States, but we were always one people. We have always looked upon our country as Matribhoomi, Punyabhoomi [motherland and the land of purity, respectively]" (BJP, 1991, p. 1). Although, it is not explicitly stated that the unifying cultural principle is Hindu, it is clarified elsewhere. For example, Dr. Murli Manohar Joshi, former President of the BJP, locates the concept Hindu within the BJP's view of a homogenous India: "In my view, every citizen of the country is a Hindu . . . it is a geo-political concept, it is not a community, nor a sect. It is a way of life. . . . If Shahabuddin [important Muslim leader, resisting the BJP] goes to a foreign country, he is known as a 'Hindi' or a 'Hindu.' . . . We want to tell the people that term 'Hindu' is not an exclusive concept, but an inclusive one" (Joshi, 1996). However, this catholic interpretation of "Hindu" is frequently destabilized by other BJP ideologues who present a vision that can easily be interpreted as exclusionary: "Must we then persist with bogus slogan[s] of plurality? . . . Definitely not, because Bharat [Sanskrit name for India] is more than the plurality that has been forced upon us, it is more than the sophistry of a 'multinational construct': From Bharat stems the notion of Bharatiyata ['Bharatness' or 'Indianness'], the concept of nation, nationality and nationalism, of a resurgent Hindu India proud to proclaim its commitment to Hindutva. Bharat was, remains and shall continue to be a geographical location . . . whose people to quote Savarkar, 'are (Hindu) by blood, by race, by country, by God. Its name is Bharat and the people are Bharati. We, Hindus, are all one and a nation because chiefly of our common blood . . .'" (Gupta, 1995, p. 84).

Faced with such an unequivocal statement of the essential Hinduness of India, Muslims or indeed any group following other faiths in India may reasonably hesitate to identify themselves as Hindus in the geopolitical sense. L. K. Advani, a major BJP leader and past Home Minister of India, articulated similar sentiments, albeit in a less passionate form, when he delineated his idea of "Hindu-tinged" secularism: "The culture of any ancient country is bound to be composite. But in our country, emphasis on the composite character of Indian culture is generally an attempt to disown its essentially Hindu content" (Advani, 1990, p. 61). According to Advani, a national acceptance of the Hindu basis of India does not challenge tolerance and secularism. These values are an integral part of this philosophy symbolized by Hinduism's celebration of multiplicity since it believes that "all roads lead to God" (Advani, 1990, p. 60). The tension between Hinduism as an inclusive, catholic concept and an exclusionary cultural delineation becomes even more explicit in Advani's (1995) presidential address: "It is immaterial how you describe this concept of cultural nationalism—as Hindutva, or as Bharatiyata, or as Indianness. The content is the same. When the BJP struggles for the construction of a Rama Mandir in Ayodhya, it is with a view to strengthening these cultural foundations, the ultimate aim being to raise a magnificent Rashtra [national] Mandir [temple] of Bharat Mata. Hindutva, thus, is a unifying principle. It is a collective endeavour to protect and re-energise the soul of India" (pp. 4–5).

The worrisome implication of the BJP's view of the soul of India lies in the manner in which it chooses to delineate its vision with explicitly "Hindu" symbols, that is, with Ram who then is contrasted in opposition to an "other" located in the body of Mughal emperor Babar a foreign invader (the temple in Ayodhya of course is being built on the site of a mosque associated with him). Murli Manohor Joshi further explicates the Ram/Babar opposition in his presidential address: "Rama is worshipped by crores [one crore equals 10 million] of people. . . . His birth-place is a symbol of national glory. Babur was a foreign aggressor, on whose orders the temple standing at the birth-place was destroyed and replaced by a mosque structure which was a monument to our defeat and Babur's victory" (Joshi, 1991, p. 8). In the eyes of minorities who may seem themselves as being cast in the role of "other," the BJP's conflation of Ram and Rashtra (nation) may seem disingenuous and not really a call to join an inclusionary, tolerant Indian nation. To sum up, the BJP negotiates a ambivalent path through the terrain of cultural nationalism, on the one hand constructing "Hindu" to indicate a multicultural, inclusive model of citizenship (i.e., moving towards a version of civic nationalism), while on the other using "Hindu" to signify a rather exclusionary, uncompromising stance on group identity.

HINDU AWAKENING AND MANHOOD IN THE BJP

In face of this ambiguity, the BJP's passionate endorsement of Hindu awakening becomes rather ominous: "In the history of the world, the Hindu awakening of the late twentieth century will go down as one of the most monumental events in the history of the world. . . . During the era of Islamic invasions what Will Durant called the bloodiest period in the history of mankind, many Hindus gallantly resisted, knowing full well that defeat would mean a choice of . . . forced conversion or death" (BJP, Hindutva: The Great

Nationalist Ideology). The unleashing of a long-suppressed Hindu anger fuels this awakening: "The rage of Hinduism was suppressed during the entire freedom movement in order to get the compliance of Muslims and other minorities in the fight against the British. To assuage Muslim sentiment it became necessary to suppress every vestige of Hindu feeling and to call bodies such as the RSS 'communal.' . . . The RSS was crying for historic justice for Hindus. . . . It merely was a voice in the wilderness seeking the pre-eminence of Hinduism in the land of its birth" (Kamath, 1990, pp. 37–38). Finally, the official website of the BJP exultantly voices, "Hindus are at last free. They control their destiny now and there is no power that can control them. . . . The future of Bharat is set. Hindutva is here to stay" (BJP, Hindutva: The Great Nationalist Ideology). The themes circulating within Hindutva as imagined by the BJP include the suppression of the Hindu spirit by misguided politicians, a history of degradation and defeat at the hands of foreign (primarily Muslim) aggressors, and the need to resist.

Resistance, a reflection of Hindu militancy embodied by the figure of a Hindu soldier, forms a vital part of the BJP's configuration of the myth energizing Hindutva: "we must never, never forget our own history—both our proud martial tradition of defending ourselves against external aggression as also our sad tradition of excessive pacifism. . . . Indian sages and philosophers never suggested that cowards and weaklings, . . . can be the torch bearers of India's great tradition of suraksha [good defense]. . . . None but the valiant can achieve salvation" (Advani, 1997, p. 47). This text, an excerpt from Advani's speech to the party on the occasion of the fiftieth anniversary of India's independence, is located within a narrative glorifying past warriors including Rana Pratap and the Rani of Jhansi, as well as more recent militants such as Savarkar, Tilak, Aurobindo Ghosh, B. C. Chatterjee, and Madam Cama, men and women who according to Advani (1997) formed the "proud first chapter of India's freedom" (p. 16). Battles and wars pitting Hindus against both Muslim and British aggression also informed Advani's account of India's proud martial heritage. In the Election Manifesto released by the BJP for the 2002 Gujarat state assembly elections, promises to establish *shaktigrams* (literally, "villages of power") comprised of settlements of retired soldiers along the Pakistan border were emphatically iterated. The manifesto also pledged to provide specialized antiterrorist training to all young people attending colleges (BJP, Security). It was not clear whether both men and women would be trained. There is no doubt that the BJP can be situated within a discourse centered around notions of martial prowess and masculinized politics.

Mahatma Gandhi's path of nonviolence, though acknowledged, is not really celebrated, while the ideas of Dr. S. P. Mukherjee, the founder of the Jan Sangh, a party seen as the political predecessor of the BJP, are quoted at length: "If I have understood the history of my country aright, a pacifism that refuses to take up arms against injustice . . . does not represent the real teaching of India. . . . Let us not forget that valor was greatly esteemed by the sages and free rulers of India in olden times. . . . When the sword and the book of knowledge [were] kept together, justice, equity and liberty ruled the affairs of the state" (quoted in Advani, 1997, p. 46). As reflected by the above speech, the men, women, and events forming a part of Advani's vision of martial India do not merely represent raw physical aggression and martial prowess; rather, "sword and knowledge" should ideally go hand in hand. There seems to be reference to some sort of warrior honor centered on resisting injustice and perpetuating notions of spiritual wisdom. However, such ideals may not be adhered to when notions of militance and aggressive action devolve to the reality of political behavior on the ground.

The most provocative embodiment of this ethos of manhood defined as martial prowess is found in the changing iconography of Ram within the BJP's cultural vocabulary and the alleged involvement of its foot soldiers in 1992–1993 and 2002 Hindu-Muslim riots.

THE CHANGING ICONOGRAPHY OF RAM

The BJP's reconfiguration of Ram within its own message dramatically expresses political imagery based on masculine Hinduism. Artistically, most traditional Indian statuary of Ram is androgynous and unmuscled, displaying curves that could be considered feminine in terms of hegemonic masculinity: "It might be said that it is the Ramlila performances that have made Ram one of the most popular deities of Northern India . . . the deities are played by young boys. . . . It is a representation that is emphatically unmasculine, at least in comparison with the way we read off masculinity today as male, muscled and usually aggressive" (Kapur, 1993, p. 86). Since the author of this excerpt is Indian, her acceptance of a masculinity mirroring the ideas of hegemonic masculinity further emphasizes the influence of this ideal in India.

Recently, in BJP iconography, Ram has been transformed to reflect the ideals of masculine Hinduism. This Ram, the adult male, represents the strident militarism of a hyper hegemonic masculinity. In Hindutva posters covering the walls of Indian cities during the BJP's agitation for a Ram *mandir* in Ayodhya, the divine symbol's muscles ripple as he towers over a Hindu temple, protecting it against aggressors: "An apocalyptic leader is silhouetted against a purple sky, his torso and legs uncovered, his hair and loincloth flowing against a raging storm. This is Ram the disinherited, radiating a mood of elemental anger" (Basu et al., 1993, p. 62). The androgynous Ram has become a masculine warrior. This image of masculinity is emulated by BJP activists during moments of crisis, for example, during the destruction of the mosque in Ayodhya in 1992.

The mass agitation to locate a Ram mandir or temple on the site of the destroyed mosque signified both national resolution and unity for the BJP. The party does not merely interpret this as an act of construction but as "a mass movement to reaffirm the nation's cultural identity. It is the dynamo for a resurgent, resolute and modern India" (Advani, 1997, p.29). Further, in the BJP's discourse the temple symbolizes the unified Hindu consciousness of India: "The BJP is committed to the concept of one nation, one people, one culture. . . . On coming to power, the BJP government will facilitate the construction of a magnificent Shri Rama Mandir at Janmasthan in Ayodhya which will be a tribute to *Bharat Mata*. This dream moves millions of people in our land; the concept of Rama lies at the core of their consciousness" (BJP, 1996, p. 15). The political stance framing this interpretation of nationalism centered on the temple was bellicose, and although there were no explicit references to the aggressive Hindu manliness, the vocabulary and emotive tone emphasized the values of masculine Hinduism as expressed by the form of the Hindu warrior: "The demolition of the Babri structure [the avoidance of the word mosque is a deliberate attempt to deny the religious significance of this space for Muslims] was due to the pent-up feelings among the Hindus against continuous insult during the last 45 years. Now Hindu power will assert [itself] and the Hindu youth is not going to wait and tolerate any more this insult in their own land. Enough is enough. Bharat Mata ki Jai [Hail Mother India]" (Nayak, 1993, p. 8).

This belligerent perspective is further elaborated: "Rather than join forces and accept the rising tide, the oligarchy added fuel to the greatest movement in Indian history [this refers to the notion that the Hindus are finally awakening to seize their rightful preeminent, cultural position in India]. One that on December 6, 1992 [the date that the Babri mosque was destroyed] completely shattered the old and weak roots of Indian society and with it, the old political and intellectual structure. The destruction by the Kar Sevaks [activists converging on Ayodhya to express Hindu anger and pride] of the dilapidated symbol of foreign dominance was the last straw in a heightening of tensions by the government, and the comittant anger of more and more Hindus to rebuffs of their reasonable demands. . . . It is up to the Muslims whether they will be included in the new nationalistic spirit of Bharat" (BJP, Hindutva: The Great Nationalist Ideology). The above excerpt from the BJP's official website, uncompromising in tone, highlights a determination to seize and articulate Hindu strength and power in the terms of hegemonic masculinity while simultaneously warning Muslims that they must accept the "new" Hindu or face the consequences. In 1992, saffron clad *kar sevaks* from all Hindu nationalist organizations including the BJP, VHP, Bajrang Dal, Shiv Sena, arriving in Ayodhya, embodied this belligerent language by carrying weapons—tridents, swords, steel rods, wooden staffs—and shouting militant slogans—*Jo hum se takrayega, choor choor ho jayega* (He who takes us on will be crushed into smithereens) and *Hindu ka pahchaan, Trishul ka nishan* (Recognize Hindus by their tridents). These Hindu warriors, energized by the spirit of national unity, tore down "the dilapidated symbol of foreign dominance" to assert Hindu military might.

Further, Hindu-Muslim riots broke out all over India in the wake of the Ayodhya events wherein similar slogans and perspectives framed violence against Muslims. Some episodes of such sectarian violence in Mumbai were structured around a unique cultural ritual—*maha-arti*—constructed by the BJP with its electoral partner, the Shiv Sena. The *maha-artis* prompted a cultural venue for the performance of Hindu martial power. As reverent, floral tributes to the gods, artis are happenings that resonate deeply for the majority of Hindu India, who understand and participate in the rituals. Before the January riots, the Shiv Sena and BJP had organized and routed these events all around Mumbai's temples and open streets. Huge blackboards decorated with the snarling tiger emblem of the Shiv Sena and the lotus symbol of the Bharatiya Janata Party were displayed prominently. Food was brought in and distributed from huge pots as *prasad* (food that has been blessed by the gods). Gathered at the sites and interspersed among the throngs of devotees and spectators were the young men of the BJP and Shiv Sena displaying saffron—the sacred color of Hinduism on some part of their body—and brandishing tridents, symbols of Shiva's divine strength. As they shouted politico-religious slogans, the religious occasion degenerated into a scene of mob violence. Venting not only the frenzy of the moment but also the pent-up rage against the economic and social conditions in their lives as citizens of Mumbai's slums, the crowd moved on to wreak havoc in Muslim neighborhoods. The artis were religious spectacles the BJP and Shiv Sena choreographed for drawing Hindus together as a unified community and simultaneously separating them from the Muslims.

The BJP and Shiv Sena harnessed the *maha-artis* not only as symbols of Hindu pride and activism but also as methods to counter the conspicuous, so-called intrusive Muslim prayer practice of *namaaz* on Mumbai's streets:

> I will first tell you about the *maha-arti* episodes. On Fridays, Muslims offer namaaz in the afternoon. They offer it on the roads. Traffic is held up. Even on railway stations. . . . Now in some places restrictions were put on people [the government prohibited public assemblies and demonstrations in the interest of order]. So we said if you want to restrict other activities, why are you allowing these loudspeakers on the mosque? Actually, it started as a people's movement. If those loudspeakers are not stopped, we will also offer similar prayers on the road. Then that arti became *maha-arti*. (BJP MP, personal interview, Mumbai, India, April 7, 1993)

The Sena's artis performed by Hindu men in their role of warriors became a ritualistic challenge to Muslim holy practices.

Almost ten years after Ayodhya, the BJP's support for masculine Hinduism as represented by the figure of an Ayodhya kar sevak—saffron clad, angry, armed ready to perpetuate in violence—may not be so unequivocal. India's strained but functioning electoral democracy may have partially tamed its aggressive stance: "Ever since the BJP came back to power in October 1999, a conflict between it and the Hindu chauvinist wing of the Sangh parivar had been waiting to take place. . . . Today it is part of a 24 party coalition in which it holds only three-fifths of the seats. Its allies, with the exception of the Shiv Sena, are staunchly secular and pluralist. They made it absolutely clear to Vajpayee in December 1998 that they would continue to give the BJP their support only if Vajpayee kept the Hindu chauvinist fringe of the Sangh parivar under control. Vajpayee himself is a staunch champion of India's pluralistic culture and politics. He had made it clear as long back as during the 1990 confrontation over the Babri Masjid that he did not approve of the tactics of coercion that were being employed by the Vishwa Hindu Parishad" (Jha, 2002, p. 21). The BJP's ambivalence may have created tensions with the RSS: "The RSS and Vajpayee, at times, share an uneasy relationship. Despite his total commitment to the Sangh, he is not a run-of-the-mill *swayamsevak*. His liberal identity, ideological flexibility and aversion to militant Hinduism have become an asset as well as an embarrassment to the RSS" (Kanungo, 2002, p. 264).

Many observers remain skeptical of this fairly optimistic view of the BJP. In their view, this party remains a vocal advocate of xenophobic violence. They point to March 2002 when Hindu mobs—in the wake of a heinous attack by Islamic militants against Hindu families—targeted Muslim homes and businesses in the Indian state of Gujarat governed by a BJP chief minister, Narendra Modi. Again, as I have discussed above, the rioters embodied symbols of armed Hindu masculinity: weapons, saffron bandanas, and slogans expressing a militant anger. Muslim women's bodies were used to signify disrespect for and dishonor the Muslim community. Whatever the approach one adopts to read the BJP, it remains clear that a nationalism centered on martial and bellicose Hindu masculinity remains easily flammable within the Indian social landscape.

To sum up, through speeches, texts, religious/historic icons as well as websites, the BJP expresses a robust masculinized vision of nation best represented by Savarkar's Hindu soldier. There is some token acknowledgement of notions of wisdom and spiritual rigor as components of manhood, but in actual political behavior on the ground such a multifaceted vision is overshadowed by an exercise of unrestrained militant action. However, given its participation in electoral democracy and coalition politics, the BJP's unequivocal support for images of the Hindu soldier and the warrior-monk as representing a Hindu awakening may be wavering.

SHIV SENA

In contrast, the BJP's electoral partner in Maharashtra, the Shiv Sena still remains a vigorous advocate of a nationalism centered on the image of the Hindu soldier. The concept of reclaiming the pride of a martial spirit for a modern, aggressive, even violent Hindu resistance sparks the core identity of the Sena's political activities. Such messages become extremely attractive during times of acute political and economic anxieties.

HINDU SOLDIER IN THE SENA

Many walls around the streets of Mumbai are painted with the snarling tiger emblem of the Shiv Sena; statues and portraits of Shivaji rippling with muscles as he holds a bow and arrow are found in public squares; and in most Shiv Sena-sponsored religious processions, the young male participants carry tridents. The tiger, the bow and arrow, and the trident are a trinity of symbols that iconographically converge to eloquently configure a message of a nationalism based on the image of a Hindu warrior. The tiger represents anger and the readiness to attack; the bow and arrow and tridents are weapons wielded by ancient Hindu warriors and are also symbols of the divine. The trident, the weapon of Lord Shiva, has become a symbol of divine anger struck against Islam and the bow and arrow similarly represent anger as Lord Ram's weapon.

The Shiv Sena's activists are predominantly male as are the religious figures the Sena has chosen to emphasize, drawing on a tradition of Hinduism (created by Savarkar) and reconfigured to enhance Hindu manliness. The icons—the warrior Shivaji, the weapons, the aggressive tiger—all depict violence and militarism. The tiger symbol of the Sena provocatively provides a cultural reading in terms of masculine Hinduism. Bhavani, the traditional patron goddess of Shivaji, is usually associated with a tiger. In the Sena's lexicon, the goddess (a female representation of martial prowess) disappears, and the tiger stands alone. Not only does "sena" mean "army" but the Shiv Sena activists refer to themselves as *sainiks*, warriors. The cardboard facades of the local Shiv Sena offices imitate a traditional Maratha fortress. The *bhagwa dwaj* (saffron flag) of Hindu warriors flies from painted spires, proclaiming war on all enemies of Hindu warriors.

MASCULINITY AND THE SHAKHA

Young male followers of the Shiv Sena are introduced to this masculinized vision of the Hindu nation in the party's *shakhas*. The Shiv Sena mimics the RSS's use of *shakha* as the foundation for its organizational edifice. Although the Sena *shakha* is not organizationally or ideologically as disciplined as the RSS version, it does offer a place, a literal forum, for young men to find their voices, expressing both needs and aspirations and building affective ties that effectively lay the groundwork for organizing shared feelings into specific political action based on masculine Hinduism.

Much of the Shiv Sena's strength derives from its *shakhas*. Each *shakha* is a small one- or two-room office, sometimes fashioned with a cardboard facade made to look like an ancient Maratha fortress. The Hindu saffron flag flies from the roof. A picture of Shivaji and the Sena's tiger emblem frequently decorate office interiors. Since the *shakha pramukh* (local leader) tends to be away at work during the day, the *shakhas* come to life in the evenings. Inside, the atmosphere in the offices is not marked by any somber officiousness from being the headquarters of a political party. Rather it is relaxed and informal: people come and go, play board games, or read books from the lending libraries available in some.

The young men spend considerable time in the *shakhas*. Although not all sites offer libraries or board games, even the ones without these amenities still provide a space for social and political interactions. The offices are essentially fora where young men, under the tutelage of the *shakha pramukh*, discuss the strategies of a revival of Hindu pride and the need to protect Hinduism against an Islamic threat. Such informal interaction constructs communal solidarity. Besides offering an informal arena where ideas defining identity are worked out, the *shakhas* relay concepts of communal solidarity by sponsoring organized cultural festivals: Ganapati pooja (worship of the Hindu god Ganapati), Shiv Jayanti (commemorating Shivaji's birthday), and Janamashtami (celebration of Lord Krishna's birth). The events celebrate Hinduism and function as cultural markers separating Hindus from Muslims.

MANHOOD AND THE NATION TO BE DEFENDED

The Hindu community markers are simple in the Shiv Sena's vocabulary: respect for Hindu warrior heroes such as Shivaji and faith in the gods, such as Shiva and Ram, as well as in Hindu rituals, such as artis. Coupled with this vision of community is the desire to protect Hinduism. Interaction in the *shakhas* ground communal solidarity within relationships of direct contact and sharing. Physical unity facilitates the transformation of the *desire* to protect into aggressive *acts* in defense of the Hindu nation. Rituals and festivals symbolizing the Hindu nation stage the backdrop for this defense. In the 1970 Bhiwandi riots, young Sena activists attacked Muslim places of worship during *holi* (spring festival). Two months later, the Sena sponsored a Shiv Jayanti (Shivaji's birthday) celebration. A procession of young men carrying pictures of Shivaji provocatively wound its way through a small industrial town. As the procession entered Muslim areas, violence broke out.

In the Maharashtrian context, "Shiv" in the name "Shiv Sena" signified Shivaji, who is the great Maharashtrian hero. Shivaji fought many guerrilla battles against the mighty Moghul emperor Aurangzeb, defeating his great army with swift and brilliant strategies. The battle between Shivaji and Aurangzeb becomes a symbol in the language of conflict between Hindus and Muslims that the Sena's political vocabulary codifies; the Muslims are the enemy that Hindutva vows to resist. Political symbols centering on Shivaji also highlight fear of Islam's fanaticism and the danger Hinduism faces from it; in popular Hindu Indian historiography, Aurangzeb is seen as a fanatic Muslim, who was determined to wipe out Hinduism. The Sena constructs an intolerant Islam contrasted with a tolerant Hinduism that might become weak in the face of Islamic aggression. Hence, Hindus are called upon to arise.

The Shiv Sena does not equivocate; although it refrains from advocating violence as the only mode of political action, it does not hesitate to admit that aggression (martial might) may be an effective mode of expressing Hindu power. Bal Thackeray publicly explicates his theory of *thokshahi* or the rule of constructive violence (Purandare, 1999, p. 155). The Sena's involvement in the Durgadi Fort episode dramatically illustrated the intersection of thokshahi and the Hindu nation. In 1968, both Hindus and Muslims residing in the Maharashtrian town of Kalyan claimed a nearby fort as a sacred space. Hindus located a shrine—dedicated to the goddess Durga—within the fort while Muslims cleared a nearby area to perform namaaz. Such conflicting claims had created a communally tense situation, when the Shiv Sena decided to intervene. Thackeray's address to a large Hindu assembly within the confines of the fort emphasized the central location of armed masculinity within the Sena's discourse: "If you [i.e., Muslims] are loyal to the nation, nobody will dare touch you. But if you stay here and at the same time display inordinate pride and preach Islam, we won't hesitate to slash your limbs" (Purandare, 1999, p. 104).

The Hindu nation located within the Sena's narrative resembles the homogenous and united construct found in the BJP, VHP, and RSS discourses. In November 1986, Thackeray wrote, "The Flag of Hindu independence which Sant Ramdas [Shivaji's guru] placed on the shoulders of Shivaji now needs to be carried on our fighting shoulders in a triumphant march from Kashmir to Kanyakumari" (Purandare, 1999, p. 285), and "According to me, he who lives in Hindustan is a Hindu. And I have decided to bring all the Hindu organisations together and create a Hindu Rashtra Fauj [National Hindu Army]. . . . All Hindus should come under one flag to root out Muslim fanaticism" (p. 234). Thackeray narrates a martial Hindu nation pitted against a Muslim "other." Further, Hindustan, a continuous sovereign territory stretching from Kashmir in the north to Kanyakumari in the south, confirms the immutable presence of a monolithic Hindu nation. This ideological bias is nicely illustrated by the masthead on the Shiv Sena's official newspaper the *Saamna* or confrontation, "the only Marathi daily which advocates the cause of fiery militant Hindutva" (p. 325). Finally, the Hindu/Muslim dichotomy is cast as an adversarial relationship captured by the manichean Ram/Babar dichotomy; during the Ayodhya conflagration, Thackeray declared, "A sea of Ram bhakts has descended on Ayodhya, and now it's being joined by our brave Shiv Sainiks. . . . The time has come to decide if this country should be identified with . . . Ram or intruder-aggressor Babar. . . . Return as victors in the Ram Janmabhoomi struggle. This is my appeal to my staunch Hindu Shiv Sainik" (p. 362).

This potent fusion of armed masculinity and nation is articulated quite emphatically by Sena leaders other than Thackeray. When asked by a *Times of India* reporter to comment on the Sena/BJP government's refusal to publicize the findings of the Srikrishna commission that implicated Sena leaders in the 1992–1993 riots in Mumbai, Uddav Thackeray, a prominent Sena activist retorted, "We only retaliated so as to protect our people. We are not ashamed of defending our people. In fact, we will retaliate even harder if anybody tries to create trouble again. We are very clear about that" (*Times of India*, May 3, 1998, Mumbai edition). Other leaders echo this view:

> *Shiv Sena Politician:* Bhiwandi riots were there. That was 1984. That was the last riot. That was a major riot.
>
> *Author:* They blamed the Shiv Sena then too.
>
> *Shiv Sena Politician:* Of course. When the Hindus started getting a beating there, we had to take a stand. Bhiwandi is dominated by Muslims. Naturally when they started beating Hindus, our boys from outside started entering Bhiwandi. That is true. But that was their right. It was on a mass scale and organized. That you can call riots. That was the last riot. Thereafter no riot. Now the riots have stopped. Muslims have realized Shiv Sena will retaliate. So in [the] good old days they used to throw stones; now they are not doing so. In the old days they did not allow us to take our religious processions into their locality. Now they allow us. Muslims have realized that if they try to play any such mischief, their days will be numbered because of the Shiv Sena. (personal interview, Shiv Sena Politician, Mumbai, India, November 9, 1992)

The underlying theme in the Shiv Sena leader's above remarks declares how the Shiv Sena resists Muslim aggression and is the defender of the Hindu faith; its Shiv Sainiks are men protecting their way of life. The notion of a just war is represented by the leader's support of violence against Muslim actions:

Such a message was iterated in a more emphatic manner by another Shiv Sena leader:

> And Bala Saheb Thackeray says, Bala Saheb Thackeray, he is my political guru. He is not fighting only for Maharashtrians and Hindus. He is fighting

for all. He says India is our country; whoever is against India, Hindu or
Muslim, hang him. India and Pakistan play a cricket game. The Indian
team loses and Pakistan wins. Fire crackers go off in Bhendi Bazaar. Bhendi
Bazaar [is a] Muslim area. That means what? Their loyalty is not for India
but for Pakistan. They have no right to live in India . . . only a Muslim candidate can win there. No matter what party the candidate represents, he
has to be Muslim. No other candidate can be elected. Bala Saheb Thackeray says this country is Hindustan. It is Hindustan of the Hindus. What is
wrong with calling it Hindustan? Like Pakistan, which is a Muslim country. This is a country which belongs to Hindus. Communal riots will
increase in the future. (personal interview, Shiv Sena Politician, Mumbai,
India, October 5, 1992)

In his words, the leader initially adopted a view of nationalism that seemingly accepts both Hindus and Muslims. However, by emphasizing India as
Hindustan, land of the Hindus, and portraying Muslims as foreigners and
necessarily traitors to India—which is *Hindustan*—his bias is clearly indicated. The language of violence and aggression is conveyed implicitly
throughout his viewpoint. Further, in concluding that communal riots will
increase in the future, he warns Muslims that Shiv Sena activists are ready
for a violent confrontation.

Muslim intransigence becomes the explanation Hindutva offers to its
followers for the problems in their lives and provides an implicit reason for
the need for a confrontation: "All of us should be under the same law controlling religion. For example, if we want to do Satyanarayan Pooja or
Ganesh festival or Navratri festival we must get police permission. But we
hear the loudspeakers playing for 24 hours in the masjids [mosques]. . . . The
other thing is family planning laws are only for Hindus. Muslims do not follow them. They say our Koran forbids family planning. Does our *Mahabharat*
say we should have family planning?" (personal interview, Shiv Sena Politician, Mumbai, India, October 5, 1992). By interweaving notions of family
and religion in terms most ordinary folk will understand, the Sena leader
offers Hindutva as a simple but potent framework through which to visualize
life. He makes two claims: (1) Hindu religious festivals—Satyanarayan Pooja,
Ganesh, Navratri—were regulated by the government while Muslim religious
practice—namaaz in the mosque—was not; and (2) Hindu families were subject to family planning laws implemented by a government that exempted
Muslims from compliance. A discrimination against Hindus in areas vital to
community-building—biological and cultural reproduction—was laid bare.
The Muslims were the enemy who prevented Hindus from building a strong
community; consequently, Hindu men were called to defend their own, and
an acceptable manner of resisting the Muslims was the communal riot. In the
leaders' remarks above, no hesitation was evident in their advocating aggres-

sion as a political alternative. Such views are not unique to these particular Shiv Sena individuals but are widespread among all the leaders of the Sena and its followers.

The theme of masculinity and violence as well as the fear engendered by the Muslim male was most dramatically illustrated in the 1992–1993 Mumbai riots triggered by the destruction of the Babari mosque in Ayodhya. The Shiv Sena leaders and activists informed me of the prodigious sexual appetite of the Muslim male. That is why, they claimed, the Muslim birthrate was higher than the Hindu one and why the Koran allowed a man to marry four wives; presumably, four women were needed to satisfy a Muslim man. The other stereotype was that the Muslim male was a violent killer and rapist, with a predilection for blood. For evidence, they pointed to the jails: most prisoners committed for violent crimes were Muslim. These images typified Hindu fear of Muslim activity.[8] The Shiv Sena has drawn on these representations of Muslim men as individuals possessing uncontrolled appetites for violence and sex. Such imaginings both underline Hindu fear of Muslim virility and military prowess and provide the justification for Hindu men to assert their masculinity (through violence) against Muslim males.

A male Shiv Sena leader made the following comment: "At Radhabhai chawl they [Muslims] bolted the door from the outside and set it on fire. And all our [Hindu] children, families [died]. . . . [W]hen this hit the headlines the next day, even my wife told me, 'I should offer you bangles now. What are we? In our own country Hindus are being burnt'" (personal interview, Shiv Sena Politician, Mumbai, India, April 20, 1993).[9] In this quotation, the male Shiv Sena leader referenced Hindu weakness in the face of Muslim aggression with feminine images, that is, the bangles offered by his wife. In Indian culture, offering bangles or jewelry worn by women generally connotes an insult to Hindu men who have failed to protect their people. Equating weakness with the feminine and strength with the masculine places the Sena's interpretation of masculinity squarely within the parameters of hegemonic masculinity.

In the opinions of the Sena leaders, tolerant Hindus had failed in the mission to defend their property in face of Muslim aggression:

> Then every half hour we started getting reports that [the] riots are spreading, [the] riots are spreading. Bhendi Bazaar, Mahim, Bhendi Bazaar, Mahim.[10] This went on for three days; believe me, I'll not tell you a single lie. It went on for three days. It was very, very identical to December. Same pockets. Behrampada, Bhendi Bazaar, Dongri, Mahim. All Muslim pockets. Nothing was here. Nothing was in Dadar. Nothing was in Dadar, Lalbaug or Parel.[11] But one incident took place in Jogeshwari on [the] third night. At Radhabai chawl [tenement building], they [the Muslims] bolted the door from the outside and set it on fire and all our [Hindu] children, families were roasted.[12] (personal interview, Shiv Sena Politician, Mumbai, India, April 20, 1993)

Saamna, the Shiv Sena's official newspaper, seized upon the Radhabai chawl incident to call the Hindus of Mumbai to battle. On January 9, 1993, Bal Thackeray wrote within its pages an inflammatory editorial, "The Nation Must Be Kept Alive," which ended "The next few days will be ours." With these words, Hindu consciousness was awakened and the Shiv Sainiks literally roamed the streets of Mumbai, selectively targeting Muslim lives, businesses, and houses for destruction.

Shiv Sena corporators (or municipal council members) spoke openly of their desire to protect Hindus from Islam's encroachment:

> *Author:* Why do you think that only Muslims are responsible for . . . [the riots in Jogeshwari]?
>
> *Corporator:* Because I do not think builders were behind the riots in order to grab land. No one can build any special hotel on this land. The Hindus in Jogeshwari often complained to the police that the Muslims were threatening . . . and . . . preventing them from celebrating Hindu festivals. Hindus wanted to leave Jogeshwari because they are afraid of Muslim threats. But the government does not listen to these complaints. (personal interview, Shiv Sena Politician, Mumbai, India, March 6, 1993)

The actions of these leaders interweave the symbols of a national community with pragmatic strategies for living. The government failed to provide security, so the Hindu community led by the Shiv Sena was encouraged to rely on itself for protection. Such appeals could politically mobilize a Hindu nationalism purporting to defend the rights of a Hindu nation. Since the Jogeshwari arson incident demonized the assumed Muslim propensity for aggression and violence, Hindu residents willingly trusted the Sena's promises to protect them from this dangerous enemy. Such sentiments expressed by the previous corporators were echoed by others:

> *Author:* How about underworld involvement?
>
> *Corporator:* Maybe. But in the Radhabai chawl incident there is no question of underworld involvement. It is only nine kilometers from the municipal building and there are no illegal constructions there. The only underworld involvement [Muslim goons] I can think of is involvement in drug and liquor businesses. People working in these businesses wanted to have some fun.
>
> *Author:* Fun?
>
> *Corporator:* Now they say we were having some fun, but unfortunately this thing got out of hand.[13]
>
> *Author:* They were killing people for fun?
>
> *Corporator:* Yes. I don't say all Hindus are good and all Muslims are bad. But working in the community, I can say that Hindus are more tolerant

than Muslims. Shiv Sena has protected the people. If I don't protect my people, if I don't protect Hindus, then what is the use. We are staunch Hindus. India should be for all religions. But there is only [one] country that Hindus can call their own. India. Muslims can go to Arab countries but this is the only one for Hindus. So Hindus have to keep themselves strong. (personal interview, Shiv Sena Corporator, Mumbai, India, March 6, 1993)

The corporator seems to believe that India's geographical territory is coeval with a monolithic Hindu nation. But when it is politically expedient, the Sena has not hesitated to switch from Hindu nationalism to Maharash-trian regionalism. In the past, they have clashed with Hindu migrants from South India and Uttar Pradesh over access to jobs. But since 1984, because of an alliance with the more nationally based BJP, the Sena broadened its Maharashtrian Hindu vision to include a pan-Hindu focus. Thus, when the Sena leaders feel an occasion demands a pan-Hindu rather than a Maharash-trian emphasis, they have articulated the notion of India as culturally defined by a homogeneous Hindu state. This claim inherently contradicts India as being both a refuge for all religions as well as a Hindu homeland and would be resolvable only if the minority religions accept the Hindu cultural domi-nance the corporator hints at above, for example, by referring to India as the only country "Hindus can call their own," while Muslims "can go to Arab countries," which are seen as Islamic homelands. Additionally, both these interviews reflect a belief that Hindus need protection and that it is time for them to show their strength.

This vocabulary of Hindu anger flowing from this community's inability to assert its religious/communal dominance in its homeland continues on in a Shiv Sena *shakha pramukh*'s description of the riots concentrating on a defilement of Hindu scared sites:

In Shivajinagar Govandi, the riot took place on the 7th of December. [It was] initiated by Muslim youth attacking the Hindu temples. First of all, the mob of thousands of Muslims came to the streets and they attacked the Ganesh mandir. The mob of Muslims from Mohammed Raffi Nagar, armed with swords, knives, and other such dangerous weapons came out on the streets and set a BEST [Bombay Electric Supply and Transport] bus on fire. After that the mob attacked the Ganesh mandir in plot no. 3 and they threw away the image of Ganesh into the gutter. Then the same mob rushed to the plot no. 4 and broke 6 [foot] tall statues as well as some small statues which were all thrown into the gutter. The police immediately rushed to the site and the mob was scared. They ran way. Again the same mob rushed to plot no. 8 and demolished the Hanuman mandir, and the image of Hanu-man was broken; also, the mob looted the money boxes and other prayer things. (personal interview, Mumbai, India, April 28, 1993)

The ascetic warrior monk of Vivekananda's vision, that partially emerged in the RSS national imagining has completely vanished in the Sena's configuration of nation. The muscular Hindu soldier represents the nation as he responds to Savarkar's call to "Hinduise all politics and militarise Hinduism!"

CONCLUSION

The images of the Hindu soldier and the warrior-monk released by nationalist leaders Vivekananda and Savarkar into the Indian cultural milieu has been used by various modern organizations, both political and cultural, to configure a robust masculine nationalism. At times modern nationalists such as Golwalkar have drawn on the thoughts of Vivekananda and Savarkar without much modification at least textually. However, the discontinuity lies in the context as well as the manner in which activists actually live these ideal forms. The male figure—discplined and muscular—at the center of the RSS discourse relayed through its *shakhas* comes alive on the ground neither as the steadfast Hindu soldier ready to defend and conquer a Hindu empire animating Savarkar's view of the ideal national citizen nor as Vivekananda's physically strong yet spiritually vigorous warrior-monk poised to initiate India's grand spiritual conquest. Rather, he is an ordinary family man striving to bring social change through disciplined hard work with a determined patriotism. The two men working in the SEWA international office embody this vision. However, RSS *pracharaks* do attempt to live Vivekananda's idea of the warrior-monk. Whatever its interpretation at the grassroots, there is no doubt that the RSS notion of manhood moves beyond the exercise of raw power and violence to include ideas of patriotism such as service to the nation, discipline, frugality, hard work, and even moral fortitude.

In contrast, the vision of manliness animating the VHP, Bajrang Dal, and Shiv Sena seems to have moved away from this multifaceted interpretation of masculinity to a rather unidimensional view highlighting the exercise of uncompromising aggression reflected by their activists involvement in violent confrontation, for example, the 2002 riots in Gujarat and the 1992–1993 Mumbai riots. The BJP steers an ambiguous course through this masculinized terrain, at times valorizing muscular Hinduism unrestrained by morality or discipline while at others celebrating a muscular yet disciplined even ascetic male figure as the ideal expression of patriotism. The BJP's interpretation of masculine Hinduism also needs to be negotiated with the demands of electoral democracy wherein its coalition partners may not be enthusiastic in their support for any variation of Hindu manliness.

The intersection of gender and nation within modern Hindutva elaborates manhood as a fluid social construct, taking on myriad forms to express a range of political messages from national fortitude to raw anger. A similar state of flux defines images of womanhood stimulated by masculine Hinduism. Indeed as the next chapter will underline, it is the very flexibility (within certain limits) of gender that has enabled women to enter a very masculine view of nation.

FIVE

In the Crucible of Hindutva

Women and Masculine Hinduism

Let us unfurl the banner of unity
Forgetting the petty quarrels
Let feminine power bring,
Greater and higher laurels.

Shed O' my Hindu sisters
All the old and archaic shackles
Pledge our love, sacrifice and devotion
Do Sevika Samiti's work with utmost passion

—Chant attributed to Lakshmibai Kelkar,
Founder of the Rashtriya Sevika Samiti

PHRASES SUCH AS "maternal peace politics" (Ruddick, 1995) and images of mothers protesting violence in Argentina and Greenham Common (Kirk, 1989) highlight a tendency in some feminisms as well as in the popular imagination to link women's role as mother to a natural predilection for peace. Women's participation in Hindutva challenges this linkage in fundamental ways. As this chapter will underline, women in Hindu nationalism have not hesitated to validate violence and aggression as legitimate political expression. Furthermore, many feminist scholars have argued that women in the Hindutva movement do little to interrogate the patriarchal oppression inherent in the ideology they celebrate (Basu, 1999; Sarkar and Butalia, 1995). Thus, women in Hindutva reveal two issues about female political participation: one, women's alliance with hatred and violence, and two, female support for ideological movements that can be construed as antifeminist. Studying Hindutva women through a theoretical lens constructed with ideas of masculine Hinduism enables us to interrogate the location of violence and feminism within the ideological ties linking women and Hindu nationalism.

There is no doubt that Hindutva and masculine Hinduism fall squarely into the domain of right wing politics: "For us, if there is anything that actually distinguishes (both the center and far) right from other political tendencies, it is the right's reliance on some form of internal and external Other. Right wings differentially draw on, produce, and mobilize naturalized or culturalized self/Other criteria to reify or forge hierarchical differences" (Bacchetta and Power, 2002, p. 4). The previous three chapters have produced a genealogy of a self/other dichotomy defined by categories of gender as well as cultural identity (Hindu versus Muslim) within Hindu nationalism. Masculine Hinduism in the imaginings of the RSS, BJP, Shiv Sena, and VHP is not a flexible, inclusionary category but a certain rigid expression of a Hindu self defined in opposition to a Muslim "other" both outside and inside India's boundaries, as well as an effeminized Hindu "other" implicated in the degradation of Hindu national glory. Although the development of the following binaries are outside the scope of this book, the internal Hindu enemy may be conflated with caste (upper-caste men and women have the best potential for embodying masculine Hinduism as opposed to effeminate lower castes) or ethnicity and region (martial north Indian Rajputs and Punjabis are true manly Hindus as opposed to effeminate east Indian Bengalis or south Indian Tamils). Thus, we see a very exclusionary definition of Hindu identity opening up the potential for violence and hatred as rigidly drawn communal boundaries fail to accommodate negotiation and compromise.

So what are the implications and meanings of female activism within such an interpretation of politics and nation? My inquiry into female political participation in Hindutva is not guided by issues of intentionality. In other words, my primary research focus is not on why women support violence and antifeminism. Human intent is slippery and difficult to gauge. Rather, it seems to be more fruitful to investigate the manner in which Hindutva women construct social meaning by drawing on various interpretations of female identity and the implications of such constructions.

The first step of such an investigation would involve pointing out that most Hindutva women do not see themselves as antifeminist supporters of patriarchy. Indeed, in their celebration of feminine power through models such as heroic mother, chaste wife, and citizen warrior, they visualize themselves as strong proponents of female empowerment within a Hindu context. In their eyes, they are resisting forms of female oppression. Further, like many postcolonial women and racialized women in the West, they construct "feminism" as a label for a movement allied with Western imperialism (Bacchetta and Power 2002; Merrill 2001) and so they choose to reject it as a gesture of cultural resistance. Additionally, a part of their view of female identity involves accepting violence. Indeed, given some feminist demands for women's participation in military combat as an acceptance of their status as full and equal citizens, the Hindtuva women's actions may not seem that unusual.

However, with its exclusionary ideas of nation and links to riots as well as silence on certain crucial aspects of women's lives in the family—for example, domestic violence and incest—coupled with an overly harmonious view of the ideal Hindu family, Hindutva furthers a discourse about women in society that will not allow a comprehensive, national critique of women's lives in both the domestic and public sphere. The Rashtriya Sevika Samiti (allied with the RSS and hereafter referred to as Samiti) and the Sadhvi Shakti Parishad (associated with the VHP and hereafter referred to as Parishad) enable a female presence in the discourse of Hindu nationalism in multiple ways that cannot be dismissed as false consciousness or temporary activism: "Communalism [Hindutva] is also a deeply patriarchal ideology that seeks to draw women out of their homes in limited ways, to participate in riots and demonstrations, and then push them back into their designated spaces and roles" (Butalia, 2001, p. 102). Hindutva women, like men, do participate in extraordinary political episodes such as riots and demonstrations, but once the furor is over, women do not disappear completely from the public forum of political struggle. They remain active in disseminating the ideas of the Hindu nation. Indeed as a recent book on right women declares, "Right-wing women's political activities are as wide-ranging as elsewhere within the political spectrum" (Bacchetta and Power, 2002, p. 6). Further, I would argue that these activities are also quite complex in their imaginings of women, womanhood, and its relationship to masculinity.

Women in both these organizations explode any simplistic assumptions that they are submissive dupes who have internalized a passive view of their role within the nationalist discourse. They perform, interpret, and disseminate models of female activism in ways that are innovative and, at times, subversive to the normal, day-to-day functioning of patriarchy. However, this is not how Hindutva reads their actions. Rather such actions are visualized as reinvigorating the great Hindu tradition and family. It can be argued that both the Samiti and Parishad resist within tradition or transgress without radical critique. In other words, even as the Samiti and Parishad seem to reinstate traditional constructions of womanhood, they also seem to provide the possibility of an alternative reading of gender within the Hindu nation. Although in many ways women's roles are empowering in Hindu nationalism, in the end they remain incomplete. For example, it is remarkable that woman is never imagined as an active, sexual being within this discourse of nationalism. Consequently, the major problem associated with "woman" as a category in Hindutva is the deliberate silence on the structural violence of a woman's life within patriarchy, that is, its silence on domestic violence, rape, incest, and unwanted pregnancy as well as on positive aspects such as the role of love/desire in relationships and marriage. Frequent references to the need for modesty and chastity construct female sexuality as dangerous and as the basis for social anxiety.

Sadhvi Rithambhara and two other important female participants of the Hindu nationalist movement—Uma Bharati and Vijayraje Scindia—validate this interpretation of the intersection of masculine Hinduism and asexual female identity. All three of these women are celibate. Scindia (who died recently) was a widow, and Uma Bharati, like Rithambhara, is a *sadhvi*, a female renunciant (Basu, 1999). Widowhood implies celibacy because in certain interpretations of Hinduism, women who are widowed cannot marry again and since sexual relations are allowed only within the confines of matrimony, a widow is, by definition, celibate. All three women also wear/wore plain clothing with a minimum of makeup and jewelry.

Malathi de Alwis (1998) describes women warriors fighting for the liberation of the Tamil nation with the Liberation Tigers for Tamil Elam (or LTTE) as "masculinized virgin warriors." According to her analysis the LTTE woman soldiers have shed all external markers of femininity (no jewelry or makeup) while accepting a code of behavior that demands they be chaste and virginal (p. 266). Now one should not push this parallel too far. Obviously, none of the Hindtuva women are actually involved in armed combat (although as will be shown below they do participate in violent episodes), but a case can be made that they are indeed a part of a metaphorical battle for the Hindu nation. The activists and idealogues of the Samiti and Parishad insist that in the public sphere ideal Hindu nationalist women be pure, chaste, asexual mothers and/or wives.

This image of virgin warrior is potently expressed by the Parishad. All active members, dressed in saffron robes, are celibate female renunciants with modestly styled hair and no jewelry. Their activities include speaking in public about the need to protect the Hindu nation, organizing gatherings where young women are trained in martial arts and taught about the ideals of Indian womanhood, and coordinating the worship of Hindu mother goddesses in public spaces. In order to enter the masculinized reality of Hindu nationalism, *sadhvis* highlight their chaste and pure inner self by symbolically and practically shedding outer markers of their femininity.

A part of structural shifts in Indian society that shaped the declining legitimacy of Congress in the eighties and nineties along with the rise of the BJP and Shiv Sena involved transformations in gender construction and relations. As argued in the Introduction, female chastity can emerge as a form of resistance to an outside world seemingly defined by economic and political crises as well as a response to changing gender relations. It seems to me that the two processes can actually be closely intertwined within a context of general social anxiety. Amrita Chhachhi (1994) argues that as more and more middle- and lower-middle-class women enter the labor force, the traditional patriarchal norms of decision-making and breadwinning are breaking down. Social anxiety about the disruption of gender norms creates a desire to control women's labor, feritility, and sexuality in order to resist challenges to traditional structures. Chhachhi cites the Hindu nationalist celebration of Roop Kanwar's 1987 *sati* (ritualistic immolation by fire to indicate a woman's devotion to her dead husband) as a violent example of such regulation. The Samiti and Parishad's emphasis on ideas of chastity and modesty exemplifies a form of social control as does their discussion of the vulnerability of women within the public sphere as they go to work and school outside the confines of the family.

Women's vulnerability in a patriarchal world is feared by many Indian women, not necessarily just Hindutva women: "Indeed, the vulnerability of women was discussed by every single woman that I interviewed about this episode. This happened without exception—across classes, across generations, across communities. Draupadi embodied what seemed to be a crucial aspect of their understanding of what it meant to be a woman, an Indian woman, living in a man's world" (Mankekar, 2000, p. 241). Mankekar is referring to the broadcast of the Indian epic *Mahabharat* on Indian television. Of this serial broadcast, a particular episode focused on the disrobing of Draupadi. Her husband, of the Pandava lineage, had just lost her in a game of chance to his enemy, the Kaurava family. In an attempt to humiliate him, the Kauravas sent for Draupadi. Since a man's honor is symbolized by his protection of his women, the public harassment of Draupadi would shame her husband. The Kauravas attempted to disrobe Draupadi as her husbands (she had five) looked on mutely. If Lord Krishna, in answer to her entreaties, had not intervened to protect her, Draupadi would have stood naked before the entire royal court. During her public disrobing, Draupadi was scathing in her vocal contempt for her husband Yudhishtir, a gambling addict, who saw her as his property to be wagered and furthermore did not have the capacity to protect her honor. Although the *Mahabharat* is not necessarily a text consciously appropriated by Hindutva ideology, the disrobing of Draupadi dramatically highlights several social themes regarding the vulnerability of a woman constructed in the discourse of Hindutva—women embodying a man's (and a nation's) honor, the inability of many men to protect their women, and the consequent necessity for women to be chaste, pure, and at times martial in their own defense.

Given that many Samiti and Parishad activists and idealogues work outside the home, these organizations cannot ignore women's vulnerability in the public sphere. Consequently, as the following sections will demonstrate, there is discussion of sexual harassment in the workplace as well as the incidence of assault. [It is important to remember that lower-caste and lower-class women have always worked outside the home and have been vulnerable in the public sphere. But Hindutva and other political ideologies have tended to ignore them because of their middle-class and upper-caste bias.]. But this discussion is always juxtaposed with a parallel discourse of chastity, purity, motherhood, and wifehood, which leads to solutions—the evermore vigilant attention paid to the control of female sexuality and the protection of the harmonious Hindu family—that ultimately retreat from examining certain aspects of women's lives. For example, power relations within the family are not excavated and the possibility of women's exposure to violence and inequity within the family—illustrated by the inaction of Draupadi's husbands and the humiliation she suffered because of her status as her husbands's property—is quietly ignored since such an examination would destabilize the notion of the spiritual, nonconfrontational Hindu family underlying the nationalist narrative. Furthermore, this retreat is necessary if one is to maintain an arena of control against crises and decay. If the family disappears as a space of control and calm within a national context defined by political and economic frustration, then seemingly, in the terms of Hindutva, chaos has won and resistance becomes futile. It is against this context that the Samiti's and Parishad's celebration of woman as heroic mother, chaste wife, and citizen warrior should be read. Interviews conducted in New Delhi and Mumbai over the last decade as well as publications of these organizations form the basis of the following analysis.

RASHTRIYA SEVIKA SAMITI

In April 1998, I attended a large meeting of the Samiti in Mumbai, India. The Mumbai meeting took place in a local school. At the back of the room where we met, a large poster depicted a beautiful woman projected onto the map of India. This was the Devi Ashtabhuja or the eight-armed goddess, embodying the Indian nation. Later, a *pracharika* (or celibate activist) of the Samiti explained the icons held aloft by each arm: the fire symbolizing purity; the *japmala* (a Hindu prayer necklace), national responsibility; the sword, martial resistance to the enemy; the upraised hand, a blessing; the saffron flag, Hindu culture; the Gita, knowledge; the bell, a call to an awareness of the purity of life; and the lotus, the burgeoning purity of the new Hindu nation among the filth of cultural decline. The lion by her side represented control and martial power (personal interview, New Delhi, India, February 15, 2002).[1] I watched young girls brandish wooden daggers and practice martial arts. The juxtaposition of India imagined as a warrior-goddess and young Indian women performing martial arts eloquently illustrated the female representation of the citizen-warrior. It must be noted that these young women were not really practiced in martial arts; rather their moves were stylized, almost a dance, symbolizing the Samiti's emphasis on the need for Hindu women to cultivate their ability to protect themselves and their nation.

The immediate reason given for a woman's need to protect herself is the fear of rape by unknown assailants in the public realm. The Samiti's official publications (Rai, 1996, p. 23) emphasize this rationale by retelling a well-known story about founder Lakshmibai Kelkar. It seems that just after the founding of the Samiti, she was horrified to hear of a Hindu woman who was raped in public while her husband and other men stood by. Given the Samiti's link to the narrative of Hindu nationalism and their depiction of nation as woman, I assumed that the rapists were to be demonized as "the other," the enemy of the Hindu nation, that is, as Muslims who dared to pollute Indian womanhood (and hence nation as woman) while cowardly Hindu men looked on. The publication does not mention the religion of the assailants but the Samiti members in response to my question claimed that they were actually Hindu. So the Samiti claims that women must embody traits of hegemonic masculinity—martial prowess and physical hardiness—not only to protect Mother India but also to prevent the Hindu sons of Mother India from attacking her daughters. If Samiti members are then questioned as to whether this means women occupy a rather ambiguous position within a masculinized Hindu nationalism, they provide evasive answers and are not willing to address this potentially contentious issue. This, it seems to me, is an indication of the tensions that may arise when women claim to take on masculine traits and step outside the confines of the family within the context of a militaristic Hindu nationalism that is ultimately conservative and suspicious of women who begin to emulate the powerful warrior-goddess Durga too successfully.

This gendered tension is maintained throughout the Samiti's actions and thoughts. Nowhere is this tension more evident than in the Samiti's origin story, which is usually narrated through the life of its founder, Lakshmibai Kelkar. In 1936 Lakshmibai Kelkar persuaded Dr. Hedgewar, the founder of the RSS, that women needed to be a part of nation-building because "Men and women are both wings of the society. Unless both were strong, the society will not progress properly" (Rai, 1996, p. 24). Thus the Samiti was established as the women's wing of the Sangh. Kelkar's original demand had been for women to join the RSS, but in the face of Hedgewar's refusal, she came up with the equal but complementary compromise illustrated by the creation of the Samiti (Menon, 2001). In the origin story, although women are seen as strong and active agents, a gender dichotomy is always assumed and at times Kelkar's life seems to transgress these boundaries. For example, "Kamal [Lakshmibai's real name. Her name was changed to Lakshmi when she was married] was always in the company of her brothers and behaved like a tomboy, playing all the boyish games. . . . Kamal enjoyed playing with the doll [sic] as much as she enjoyed boyish games" (Rai, 1996, p. 4). In the above passage, any potential of Kamal being seen as aberrant or challenging to conventional ideas of womanhood is contained with the statement that she liked

dolls as well as "boyish games." But note that the Samiti also deemed it necessary to describe Kamal as a "tomboy," signaling her extraordinary role in
Hindu nationalism. Thus, we see the beginnings of an incipient transgression
without radical critique as gender boundaries are quietly challenged.

The Samiti's narration of Lakshmibai's life follows a trajectory that may
dislocate rigid patriarchal views of Hindu womanhood, but there is always a
conceptual retreat before complete disruption of gendered categories is initiated. Lakshmibai's unconventional behavior continued after her marriage into
a family where "it was believed that the women should remain within the confines of her home, and the world outside belonged to men. The women need
only to be seen (that too only by the family members, within home) and not
heard" (p. 10). Lakshmibai rebelled against such seclusion, challenged her
husband on many occasions, and circumvented the rules of gender governing
extended family life. For example, in 1924, she attended a patriotic rally with
her younger sister-in-law and gave away her jewelry. Since the jewelry was not
necessarily hers but her husband's property, this was a grave violation of
extended family rules: "In those days when women could not take any decision on their own, this was indeed a very bold step" (p. 15). Ultimately, in the
Samiti's narrative Kelkar's behavior, unconventional though it was, did not
pose a threat to the Hindu family because she remained a chaste wife, under-
took all her household duties, and was an ideal daughter-in-law.

Following the death of her husband, she became involved in financial
matters: "Thus, Lakshmi managed to bring what were supposedly affairs of
'male domain,' firmly under her control. . . . She realized that the horizon of
a woman was much wider than being bound to the domestic duties. It was
important for her to acquire as many talents as possible, to develop her personality into a multidimensional one. Hence, she encouraged the girls to
learn skills like swimming and cycling" (pp. 17–19). As Laksmibai ventured
into the male realm, she became aware of women's vulnerability. However,
this vulnerability was never cast in terms of power inequities in the family or
seen as rooted in ideas of Hindu womanhood. Rather, the vulnerability was
explained by the presence of menacing strangers, the Muslim "other" and/or
weak Hindu men unable to protect their women. The following story of the
women in the orange market underlines this view well. According to the
Samiti's account, in a market near Kelkar's hometown, Hindu male vendors
bought fruit on credit and sometimes the debt could not be paid. The money
lenders were Muslim and when the vendors defaulted on their debt, the Muslim men took this as permission to molest the daughters and daughters-in-law
of the vendors. After being exposed to such abuse, the women were in turn
rejected by their own families because they were seen as contaminated. Thus,
Hindu men fell short on many counts: failing to support their families without debt, reneging on their duty to protect female honor, and not having the
courage to stand up for their women.

This story within the Samiti's narrative uncovers a hidden anxiety about women's dependent and precarious social status. But rather than embarking on a trenchant social critique of the Hindu family and associated ideas of female purity, Lakshmibai looked for a solution within Hinduism and seized upon female icons to frame a resolution that did not deviate radically from so-called Hindu norms: "If Sita managed to protect her honour, it was only due to self-confidence and moral strength, neither her husband, nor Lakshman nor the vast army was of any help to her. Hence, it was most important that women should be motivated to increase their spiritual strength" (p. 21). Kelkar's words implied that since Hindu men were weak, women needed to inspire them with their spirituality while simultaneously drawing on inner strength to endure hardship. It did not occur to Laksmibai or the Samiti to challenge or reveal gendered power inequities within the family; rather, the responsibility for action was shifted onto women as they were expected to sacrifice for and be inspiring symbols of national honor. By providing rigorous training, the Samiti would create disciplined *sevikas* (literally, female workers dedicated to the service of the nation) ready to endure and sacrifice for the nation. It is possible that *sevikas* were held personally liable, if after their experience with the Samiti, they failed to uphold these spiritual and moral standards. *Sevikas* would never interfere with nor were they similar to the workers of the Sangh: "Although, the ideological principles which guided the working of the Samiti were the same as those of Sangh (male workers of the RSS), yet the Samiti evolved its own independent internal structure and working pattern suitable for women" (p. 30).

The Samiti is very aware that its program for the *sevikas*—comprised of physical training, long periods of absence from home, and discussions aimed at creating able decision-makers—may be perceived as disrupting norms within the Hindu family. The radical implications of these ideas is contained by a familiar model of female behavior—nonthreatening to the landscape of masculine Hinduism—motherhood:

> Even though the *Sevikas* were not after power, if the occasion demanded, they must have the capacity to become able administrators. It is mother, who can train the children to shoulder any responsibility in life. Hence, she herself had to be an able administrator as she is the commander of her home. Hence, Mausiji [auntie, an affectionate term for Kelkar] put the ideals of motherhood, efficiency and leadership before the *sevikas*. The basis on which a mother can lead her family is her sense of duty. . . . The term 'Motherhood' has vast dimensions, it extends beyond the family to town, society, country, nation, and the entire universe. Hence, the personality of a woman is all pervading. Samiti had to strive to develop the personalities of the *Sevikas* on the ideals of Rani Lakshmibai (Leadership), Ahilyabai (Efficiency) and Jijabai (Motherhood)." (p. 45)

Clearly in the Samiti's vision mothers are perfectly justified in reaching beyond the confines of the family to participate in local, national, even international affairs. This is a mother who is heroic, strong, efficient, and even muscular. The Samiti defines its mission to be the creation of heroic, Hindu mothers: "Her [Kelkar's] whole life and work was dedicated to the restoration of women's status through energizing their physique by routine exercises and yoga, to rejuvenate the mind by chanalising [sic] the thoughts through discourses on epics like Ramayan and Mahabharat. Her efforts were to organize the young women and bring them together and imbibe in them the value of our ancient glorious culture, increase their self-confidence and love towards the nation and pride for 'Hindutva'" (p. 65).

This interpretation of motherhood was not constructed in a social vacuum. Under Kelkar's leadership, the Samiti acknowledged that social and economic forces were changing the Indian landscape and women's roles within it:

> Vanadaniya Mausiji [literally, respected aunt, a term of affection for Lakshmibai] wanted to prepare young women to face the changing socio-economic environment which had emerged after independence. The joint family system was fast disappearing . . . women should be able, enlightened and efficient housewives, because on them will depend the future of the society and nation. . . . Mausiji always tried to bring in new ideas regarding the programme work of Samiti so that the *sevikas* could ably meet the *challenges and increase awareness of economic independence*. (p. 66; emphasis added)

Clearly, the Samiti was becoming aware that whether by choice or because of economic need, middle-class women were leaving the home to earn a living and this movement brought with it a new set of social considerations. The Samiti orders and disseminates its vision of female participation in Hindutva against a changing socioeconomic context through the skillful use of historic female figures.

JIJABAI, AHALYABAI, AND LAXMIBAI: MYTHIC ICONS OF THE SAMITI

Radhaji, the main *pracharika* (ascetic activist) of the Samiti's Delhi office, explained the central location of Jijabai, Ahaliyabai, and Laxmibai in the Samiti's story: Jijabai symbolizes motherhood; Ahaliyabai, efficient administration; and Laxmibai, the Rani (Queen) of Jhansi, martial prowess (personal interview, New Delhi, India, February 15, 2002). Conversations with various Samiti activists and readings of the various publications of the Samiti including *Empowerment Pragmatic* (hereafter *EP*) shore up her claim. None of these feminine figures provide an one-dimensional interpretation of womanhood; they are complex, powerful women. However, all have this in common: the men in their lives either fail them or die or both. In their lives, the Muslim is cast as the "other," a threat to Hindu glory and simultaneously Hinduism's valorous imperial past is lauded in an attempt to provide inspiration for contemporary political behavior.

JIJABAI. The Jijabai of the Samiti's narrative was mortified by her husband's subordination to a Muslim ruler and in addition she decried the declining martial prowess and pride of Hindus: "It is said that a Maratha youth marries a sword first, then a bride. Gone were those courageous youths. She realized that the need of the hour was a courageous visionary Hindu leadership" (*EP*, p. 3). She prayed to the goddess Bhavani for a son who would fulfill Hindu India's need for leadership. Bhavani answered her prayer. Thus, we have two feminine images, the goddess and Jijabai, the mother, molding the perfect Hindu warrior, Shivaji, ready to defend communal honor. Shivaji's father, Shahaji, according to the Samiti's narrative, had no influence on Shivaji's education; indeed, it seems to be implied that as Jijabai was contemptuous of Shahaji's capitulation to the Islamic rulers, she moved Shivaji away from his father so that he could be exposed to good Hindu training including "writing, archery, horse-riding, sword fighting along with the Vedas, Astrology, and the other shastras" (p. 4). Thus, according to the Samiti's reading, Shivaji's patriotism, martial ability, and administrative skills derived from his mother's, not his father's, training. However, the Samiti's Jijabai never disrespected her husband nor did she deviate from the roles of dutiful daughter-in-law or ideal wife. The section on Jijabai ends with the following claim: "One has to pay reverential salutations to Jijabai before Shivaji. . . . Rashtra Sevika Samiti looks upon her as an ideal for Matrutva—that is motherhood" (p. 11).

This privileging of Jijabai over Shivaji is quite interesting and is shored up by Menon's (2001) comparison of the RSS and Samiti's competing interpretations of Shivaji. In the former's accounts, Jijabai disappears while Shivaji appears as the strong representation of masculine Hinduism. Further, this erasure of the feminine presence is also illustrated in Hindutva iconography. For example, the Shiv Sena molds its ideas of manhood on the masculine Hindu warrior image of Shivaji. It is commonly believed that the goddess Bhavani—for reasons stated above—was Shivaji's patron goddess. However, in the Sena's narrative, the goddess has disappeared, while her animal familiar—the tiger—stands alone. In the BJP's posters the muscular Ram representing masculine Hinduism stands alone. Usually Ram and his consort Sita are depicted as a couple; rarely does one come across illustrations of one without the other. In contrast, the Samiti's version "portrays Shivaji almost as a pawn in Jijabai's strategic victory over the Muslims. Men in general are portrayed as weak, immoral or fickle. . . . Shivaji is represented as vacillating in his commitment to fight for the Hindu nation. And in the many 'moments of trial' it is Jijabai, not Shivaji, who preserves those vulnerable incipient 'coals of self rule' through her cunning strategy and exemplary commitment" (Menon, 2001, p. 32).

AHALYABAI. The gendered choice of various icons used as cultural referents in Hindutva illustrates the tensions created by a female presence within a masculinized vision of nation. In the male interpretations (RSS, BJP, Shiv Sena), women and womanhood retreat to the background, while in female accounts (Samiti, Parishad), men (not masculinity) are often constructed as weak and unable to effectively express masculine Hinduism. Indeed, it is the heroines of the Samiti's stories who represent masculine Hinduism effectively and with honor. *Empowerment Pragmatic* begins the tale of Ahalyabai as follows: "Marriage in a way shattered her dreams of [sic] happy life" (*EP*, pp. 12–13). Her husband, Khanderao, was weak and addicted to "material and sensual pleasures" (p. 12). Disappointed in his incompetent and cowardly son, her father-in-law trained her in the administrative and martial duties of governing. Ahalyabai had a son, but, unlike Shivaji, he disappointed his mother because he failed to live up to the exacting standards of Hindu nationalist behavior. Indeed, she imprisoned him for breaking the law and he died behind prison walls. Ahalyabai lost all her family: husband, son, daughter, son-in-law, father, and mother-in-law in rapid succession. She was left alone to govern the kingdom of Indore. A powerful queen without male protection may pose a challenge to the Hindu family, since she stood alone, ready to govern, control, and most importantly, protect her own honor. Further, if she could not be defined as mother or wife, who is she? The Samiti legitimizes her entry into the public sphere by drawing on the image of celibate warrior and emphasizing her modesty, chastity, and devotion to Hindu gods and rituals.

According to the Samiti's narrative, Ahalyabai transgressed gender boundaries in yet another way: she trained an all-women battalion that she used strategically. For example, when faced with the prospect of an invasion, she supposedly wrote to the (male) aggressor: "My ancestors got Indore after a lot of hard work. I will not give it up easily. My women battalion is ready for war. Winning battle [sic] against women is no big deal for a person of your stature. On the other hand, if you lose—you will be dragged to shame. Before deciding on a battle, please think of the pros and cons" (p. 15). The above statement is a subversive reading of gender stereotypes within masculine Hinduism in two ways. One, women have taken on traits of masculine Hinduism through their presence as warriors and administrators. Two, Ahalyabai cleverly uses the tensions between masculinity and femininity within the discourse of masculine Hinduism (how can true masculine Hindus be defeated by women!) to avert war. Ahalyabai's tactics within its discourse indicate that the Samiti is quite aware of masculine Hinduism's suspicion of women's presence in the public, national sphere. In other words, women may take on masculine traits in honorable and effective ways, but they can never be true "men!" Finally, in its tale of Ahalyabai, the Samiti does not overtly cast the Muslim as the other of Hinduism; however, there is much emphasis on Ahalyabai's protection of sacred Hindu spaces and her glorious reconstruction of Hindu temples destroyed by foreign (Islamic) invaders.

RANI LAXMIBAI OF JHANSI. One of the incidents woven into the Samiti's account of the Rani's childhood is her encounter with Nanasaheb, a hero of the 1857 war. When they were children together, Nanasaheb lost his balance and fell off his horse. As he cried, Laxmibai laughed at him. When they met later in the day, Nanasaheb demanded a reason for her laughter. The Samiti's tale describes her response as follows: "She replied by saying that she would have had such a command on the horse that she would have never fallen, but if such an incident did occur she would not have cried but would have taken it bravely" (p. 24). Again the contours of transgressing without radical critique are visible. Nana is mocked by Laxmibai for not being "man" enough while she becomes a better "man" than he. Manliness in this instance being measured by the ability to ride a horse, a skill necessary to lead troops into battle. Yet once again having introduced this confusion of gender traits, the Samiti backs away from any radical critique, choosing instead to interpret the Rani as a heroic mother, drawing on Savarkar's view of her as modest, chaste, and asexual.

After her husband's death, when the British proposed to annex Jhansi, Laxmibai refused to give up without a fight. Like Ahalyabai, she too had formed an all-woman battalion who were her trusted companions. It is interesting to note that in the Samiti's reading, both Ahalyabai and Laxmaibai, as rulers, felt the necessity to train and organize all-women armies. This provides avenues of subversive gender readings. Did the queens not trust their male armies as much? Were the women warriors there to provide a safe zone for a woman who may have felt alone in a job seen as masculine? All these interpretations are a possibility and form the basis for creating spaces of resistance within a conventional Hindu nationalist interpretation of history.

It is clear that the British were the enemy of the Hindu nation in the Samiti's story. But again we find—as in the RSS texts—an ambivalence towards British aggression in the Samiti's account. There is a reluctant admiration of British commanders whose respect for the Indian martial spirit is eagerly repeated. However, the Muslim enemy manages to intrude into the Samiti's account even though Laxmibai lived during the 1857 war against the British. The Rani is constructed as a compassionate woman, who, although fighting British soldiers, gave shelter to the women and children of her enemy. As her mercy is eloquently described, a rather incongruous statement is inserted into the text: "This [meaning Laxmibai's compassionate treatment of the women and children] is the true Hindu spirit—enmity should be with oppressive tendencies but not with the weaker sections. We have experienced the fanaticism of other religions who did not spare women or children,

Kashmir and Bangladesh are glaring examples" (p. 26). The phrase "fanaticisms of other religions" refers clearly to Islam. Even in the celebration of Hindu resistance to the British, somehow Islamic perfidy intrudes, while the British are seen as a noble and worthy adversary. The Rani's tale ends with her defeat but British admiration for her courage in battle—"Sir Hugh Rose (the commander Laxmibai faced) has described her as the bravest and greatest . . . commander of her time" (p. 30)—is emphasized.

In conclusion, the Samiti's role models are complex and multi-faceted imaginings of the female spirit. Women as heroic mother, chaste wife, and celibate warrior intersect the landscape of the Hindu nation, tracing a very delicate balance between creating a space for female activism and initiating a radical critique of women and ideas of womanhood in the Hindu family.

SITA. Another mythic icon which emphasizes this dynamic interpretation of womanhood within Hindutva is the figure of Sita. The Samiti does not claim Sita as an official role model within its literature, but Sita, as the heroine of the epic *Ramayana* and the consort of Ram, who occupies a central position in Hindu nationalist mythology, remains a meaningful model for ideas of femininity.

On one hand, Sita is seen as the ideal *pativrata* (devoted wife) who accepts her husband's decisions without any protest. She followed Ram into an exile of fourteen years. Further, she remained faithful to Ram during her long years of imprisonment succeeding her abduction by the Lord Ravana. Sita's abduction precipitated the epic battle forming the basis of the *Ramayana*. However, when she was rescued, Ram refused to accept her as his wife as she was seen as unchaste because of her abduction and unprotected exposure to enemy males. Thus, a pregnant Sita was exiled. This, too, she accepted without complaint. However, this submissive image is only one interpretation of Sita.

Madhu Kishwar (1997) argues for the existence of a more rebellious Sita in folklore. In her research of folklore in north India, Kishwar finds a Sita who does protest. For example, she refers to a folk story that narrates Sita's reaction to Ram's repentance. When Ram finds out that his exiled wife has given birth to sons, he sends his brother to bring her back. But Sita refuses to return. When a sage who has sheltered her during her exile chastises her, a traditional folk song attributes these rebellious words to Sita: "Guru, you who know what I went through . . . ask me this question / As though you know nothing / The Ram who put me in the fire [Ram insisted that Sita walk through fire to indicate her chastity, she passed this test, yet Ram still exiled her] / Who threw me out of the house, Guru, how shall I see his face? / But I will never in my life see the face of the heartless Ram again" (p. 24). Furthermore, "Sita, in her rejection of Ram, goes to the extent of giving her sons a matrilineal heritage. . . . And when Ram comes repentantly to take her back, this is how the folk songs deal with Sita's reaction: Sita looked at him one moment, her eyes filled with anger / Sita descended into the earth, she spoke not a word" (Kishwar, 1997, p. 24).[2]

I am not arguing that Samiti activists are entirely cognizant of such an interpretation of Sita; however, the presence of such a folkloric image in their social milieu does dovetail effectively with their multifaceted interpretation of Jijabai, Ahalyabai, and Laxmibai. Consequently, this hidden core of resistance in the image of Sita may well be accepted. The lives of many Samiti women actually replicate this "resistance within tradition" or "transgressing without radical critique."

WOMEN OF THE RASHTRIYA SEVIKA SAMITI

The Samiti women I have met over the years have been articulate women who cleverly negotiate their way in a patriarchal society (although they may not describe their society as such). For example, Mitaji—a lawyer and active member of the Samiti—assured me that her work outside the home did not detract from her duties as wife or mother. Indeed she insisted that the commitment and ability to juggle these multiple roles defined women in Hindu society (personal interview, New Delhi, India, March 5, 2002). Lataji, who is a retired school teacher and has spent forty years as an active Samiti member, also reiterated these ideas. Her daughters, one a college professor and the other a computer programmer, also voiced their support for the Samiti's emphasis on a woman's need to prioritize her maternal responsibilities over all others (personal interview, New Delhi, India, February. 22, 2002).

The *pracharika* of the Delhi office lives by herself, actively organizing and coordinating the work of the Samiti. In India, a woman alone, without male protection, remains suspect in the eyes of society. However, Radhaji has transcended these social barriers by explicitly rejecting her sexual nature. She welcomed me into the Samiti's headquarters in New Delhi, which consists of two rooms in a gated compound with a temple (note: the presence of the temple also tames any social fear of a young woman's sexuality and legitimizes Radha's presence).[3] According to Radhaji, weekly *shakhas* or meetings along with the annual camps form the foundation of the Samiti's work among young women. In these arenas young women participate in physical exercise, learn about Hindu myths, and join in group discussions. When I asked her about the topics of discussion, she looked at me and asked, "What do Canadian women speak of?" I answered, "They discuss juggling home and work, being mothers and workers." "Then Canadian women," answered Radha, "are not so different from us" (personal interview, New Delhi, India, February, 15, 2002). It became clear that negotiating home and work within the boundaries of traditional Hindu ideas of wifehood and motherhood forms a vital part of the Samiti's discourse. Jijabai,

Ahalyabai, Laxmibai, and Sita provide imaginative, multifaceted female models that help Samiti women deal with the stresses of juggling multiple roles within a social landscape in transition. Radhaji had a temporary room-mate who was a member of the Samiti and was studying for her Chartered Accountancy exams. She admitted that she was attracted to the Samiti because of its emphasis on discipline and self-confidence.

However, not all women of the Samiti work outside the home. I met women like Neetaji who were stay-at-home wives and mothers. She avidly read all the major Indian daily newspapers, disseminated her ideas through letters to the editors, and led weekly Samiti *shakhas* or meetings. She made it clear that she chose to stay at home because according to the Hindu tradi-tion, being a good wife and mother are the highest ideals for a woman. Her political interest and activity highlight that she looked to Jijabai as her model of motherhood rather than any stereotypical vision of a submissive maternal figure confined, mentally and physically, within the four walls of a house (personal interview, New Delhi, India, February 16, 2002).

Such models of Samiti activism were replicated in Mumbai. My visit to a Samiti *shakha* in April 1998 was coordinated by Kamalatai, Hematai, and Sheelatai, three older women who had been involved in the Samiti for many years.[4] Sheelatai, a retired school teacher, had written a monograph discussing the life of Lakshmibai Kelkar. All three were strong and articu-late middle-class women dedicated to the Samiti. They brought me to a school where I saw young girls perform physical exercises and play games. The girls ranged in age from eleven to twenty-two. All were in school, ambitious, and self-confident. I spoke to a young married woman who had just begun a master's program in education. She informed me that all was going well because her husband and in-laws approved of her decision to study, and furthermore, she made sure that her household duties were not neglected. A group of young girls, gathered around us to listen. They, too, referred to the necessity of privileging the roles of wife and mother over all other roles a middle-class woman can choose to play in contemporary Indian society. In speaking with these girls and women, it was unclear whether they were really inspired by the ideology of maternal glory dissem-inated by the Samiti or if they had shrewdly grasped the circulation of power relations in middle-class Hindu families, where women can only win the right to education or a career by not disrupting gender stereotypes too radically. Put another way, are they really convinced of the Samiti's ideol-ogy of heroic mother in the Hindu nation or do they accept that getting up early to cook meals and wash clothes before they go to work or university is the price they pay for their choice—for some it may not be a choice but an economic compulsion—to join a changing modern India? Indeed, it does not matter. The Samiti provides them with a language to order and accom-modate gendered social change.

In order to contain the radical potential of woman in her guise as mother, wife, or warrior, the RSS and the Samiti erase female sexuality. For example, romantic love and desire has no place in the lives of Samiti icons or activists. The figures of Jijabai, Ahalyabai, and Laxmibai in the Samiti discourse are remarkably chaste. The former two were married to men they rejected as husbands and the latter was the young second wife of an older man who died quite early in the marriage. All three are celebrated as modest, with no desire for feminine adornment and a contempt for frivolity or sensual pleasure. Full time *pracharikas* have to take on a vow of celibacy. The figure of the asexual woman is linked to a harmonious, idealized view of the Hindu family to counteract any apprehension that an active female presence in Hindu nationalism will dilute masculine Hinduism and/or seduce men away from their duty. This idealized family is used adroitly to both explain and resist charges of male dominance in Indian society. For example, a Samiti publication titled *Awakening Among Women and RSS* (hereafter, *Awakening*) claims, "It is true that Indian society, like many other societies of the world, has not been having [sic] a healthy view towards women. . . . Whether in past or present, one can easily feel the unfair and partial treatment meted out to the female folks in every walk of life" (p. 4). This inequality is attributed to foreign invasions and the degradation of the Bharateeya (Hindu) family. A Samiti pamphlet—*Happy World through the Bharateeya Family*—claims that it was the British ideas of materialism and secularism that destroyed the extended Hindu family and its fundamental assumptions of gender equality and respect for women. After the British left, the rulers of Bharat still emulated Western lifestyles and this has led to the decline of the Indian family. In this context some misguided women (that is, feminists) pushed their demands for equality too far and destroyed the Indian family (p. 8). Alongside the feminists who demanded too much change too fast was the materialistic media, blindly emulating the Western craze for immodest clothing, beauty shows, and fashion models. This view of feminists and the corrupt Westernized media as the impetus for the decline of the Hindu family is echoed again and again by Samiti members as well as women in the VHP and BJP.

The pamphlet then goes on to provide a more gender-segregated idea of family than hitherto discussed:

> Generally the earning is done by the males and the house management, religious purificatory rites, and other household works are looked after by the females. . . . The ladies of the house without compromising with [sic] their household work, many times render help in the family trade in their available time, doing works requiring less labor . . . they work together with pleasure and make themselves merry by singing folk songs and dancing together. . . . (pp. 40–42)

Such an idyllic view of family life flies in the face of the tensions defining the multiple feminine roles traced by the lives of the Samiti and their
icons. It seems that the existence of such a traditional, uncomplicated view
of family alongside the more complex and dynamic view of women and their
roles in the family within the Samiti discourse highlights its reluctance to
deal with social complications arising from focusing too closely on the multiplicity of women's lives and their roles in the family.[5]

In conclusion, the Rashtriya Sevika Samiti is centered around a rather
complex and multifaceted idea of womanhood. The *sevika* may be a heroic
mother or chaste wife or even celibate warrior furthering the Hindutva cause.
For many Samiti women these roles are not abstract concepts. Rather, they
provide a way of ordering their lived experiences as they attempt to juggle the
duties of wife and mother in a rapidly changing socioeconomic context.
Indeed, these roles may actually assist *sevikas* in making sense of or at least
being comfortable with women's role in the public and the family. The radical
implications of these models are circumscribed by the simultaneous valorization of traditional, gender-hierarchal families and asexual, chaste women,
whether they be warrior, wife, mother, administrator, or leader. These ideals
are echoed in the narratives of the VHP's Sadhvi Shakti Parishad.

SADHVI: A CELIBATE WARRIOR IN HINDU NATIONALISM?

Sadhvi Rithambhara, a prominent female proponent of Hindu nationalism
associated with the VHP's Durga Vahini [the title literally means a battalion of
Durgas (the warrior goddess)], provides another model of female participation,
not a foot soldier in direct combat, but an eloquent speaker, celebrating the
idea of masculine Hinduism. Although she does not take up arms or embody
martial prowess, she can by no means be dismissed as a "cheerleader" for the
"real" male warriors. The power of the sadhvi's words equals that of a Hindu
warrior's weapons. The prefix "sadhvi" is the feminization of the masculine
"sadhu," who, in the Hindu worldview, has renounced a worldly life to search
for personal salvation and enlightenment. The sadhvi's message to Hindus is
not one of tolerance and nonviolence. Rather, it focuses on lamenting that
Hindu passivity has enabled Muslims to enjoy special privileges at the expense
of Hindus and eloquently arguing that the time has now come for Hindu warriors to demand their rights and protect their nation: "I mean to say that the
long-suffering Hindu is being called a religious zealot today. . . . The Muslims
got their Pakistan. Even in a mutilated India, they have special rights. . . . What
do we have? An India with its arms cut off. An India where restrictions are
placed on our festivals, where our processions are always in danger of attack"
(cited in Kakar, 1995, p. 207). It is interesting to note that even though she
does not use a nation-as-woman metaphor to explicitly describe India, she very
clearly embodies the nation by invoking ideas of mutilation as she refers to the

partition of India by the British (supposedly in response to Muslim demands). Embodying the nation enables masculine Hindu warriors to more effectively imagine a defense of the Hindu nation because what they are protecting is no longer abstract or lifeless but rather becomes alive. She warns the Muslims, "Live among us like the son of a human being and we will respectfully call you 'uncle.' But if you want to behave like the son of Babar [the founder of the Mughal empire in India; the Mughals were Muslim] then the Hindu youth will deal with you as Rana Pratap and Chatrapati Shivaji did with your forefathers [Rana Pratap, like Shivaji, is a Hindu warrior celebrated by Hindu nationalists as a popular symbol of Hindu resistance]" (p. 205). Her speeches continue in this vein skillfully invoking Ram, Shivaji, ideas of a glorious Hindu nation, casting Muslim/Islam as the "other" of this nation, and calling upon masculine Hindu warriors to defend their nation. This is the model of female activism embedded within the Sadhvi Shakti Parishad.

SADHVI SHAKTI PARISHAD

On a cool winter's day in February, I met Sadhvi Uma. She lives in a modestly furnished room in the VHP's sizeable compound in New Delhi. Dressed in saffron robes, her salt and pepper hair tied back, and devoid of any jewelry, she welcomed me warmly. Once I had been given tea, I asked her about the Sadhvi Shakti Parishad (literally, the Association of Sadhvi Power). She spoke at length about the Parishad and its goals. This association was formed in 1998 under the aegis of the VHP and at the moment has one thousand members. According to the Sadhvi, women *sadhvis* or *sants* (ascetics) who have taken a vow of celibacy and eschewed a householder's life to preach Hindu values form the basis of this group. The *sadhvis* know the basics of Ayurveda, practice meditation, and are well versed in various Hindu rituals. They reach out to young women and impress upon them the importance of self-reliance, independence, resistance to Westernization, and the necessity for celebrating woman as mother (personal interview, New Delhi, India, February 8, 2002). I asked her about the saffron robes. She answered, "The saffron robes of the *sadhvis* emphasize detachment. Celibacy is necessary as family detracts from following the truth path of nation-building. We must focus on social activism. *Sadhvis* should not just pray but be active in society" (personal interview, New Delhi, India, February 8, 2002). Then she went on to emphasize that a woman should be modest, be ready to sacrifice, and be ready to take on the mantle of a dutiful wife because a woman's husband forms the core of her strength. The Sadhvi's latter words sketched a stark contrast with her own life: she was not a dutiful wife and yet she was strong. Thus, perhaps, a woman's strength need not necessarily flow from her husband. Further, her celibate life challenged her insistence on a woman's social role being defined by wifehood and motherhood.

A young law student sat quietly by us. When I queried about the reasons behind her decision to be in Delhi, she told me that she was in the audience when the Sadhvi delivered a speech in her hometown; the eloquence of her words and emphasis on a woman's need to be self-reliant and confident inspired her so much that she came to serve the Sadhvi and the Hindu nation.

Sadhivs, like the *sevikas*, are traversing a delicate path between accepting the ideals of traditional gender hierarchy in a vision of a Hindu family and creating pockets of strong female activism. Many *sevikas* tame the radical potential found in the presence of women in the discourse of masculine Hinduism by emphasizing woman as heroic mother and/or chaste wife, while the *sadhvis* legitimize their presence within the VHP's masculinized nationalism by propagating a similar discourse and simultaneously shedding any outer physical markers of female sexuality and remaining celibate. Both organizations assume a multifaceted image of woman, using motherhood and family values to support woman's public speaking, political mobilization, discussions of tensions between home and work, and analyses of women's vulnerability in the public sphere. This creation of transgression within tradition is even more clearly reflected in a Sadhvi Shakti Parishad publication titled *The Power of Motherhood* celebrating its second anniversary. The collection of essays in this monograph, mostly penned by important Parishad activists and idealogues, outlines the manner in which *sadhvis* are intersecting the landscape of Hindutva.

"The Sadhvi Shakti Parishad: An Introduction," authored by Sadhvi Kamlesh Bharati, outlines some ideological trajectories that are pursued and elaborated in other essays found in the volume to create a space for female activism that at times threatens to destabilize the Parishad's blithe assumption of a harmonious Hindu family as the basis of Hindutva.[6] In this essay Sadhvi Bharati claims, "Therefore, woman in the form of Prakriti [nature] is the main foundation of society" (p. 11). However, "As time passed, men created institutions that have destroyed this image of women. . . . They have limited her greatness . . . if we make her only a mother or a wife, then her personality's most important part does not blossom. . . . After independence when educated women resisted, they joined a so-called Westernized women's liberation movement that killed the Indian family" (p. 11). Alongside, this misguided Westernized women's movement, Indian leaders bedazzled by Western materialism focused on economic growth, ignoring the country's spiritual evolution. Remember, argues the Sadhvi, "A country's strength lies not in sky scrapers, roads, big schemes, nice clothes but in their citizen's character, especially their women's decency, their cultures" (p. 11). Simultaneously, because of this neglect of Indian (Hindu) spiritual development, "crores [one crore equals 10 milllion] of rejected Hindus became Christians and Mussalman and we . . . Hindus stayed dreaming in our ashrams. As a result, hundreds of Hindus were killed in Kashmir, and the numbers of Hindus declined in Assam, Manipur, Kerala, Mizoram, Bengal, Bihar" (p. 11). Given this national situation, "The Sadhvi Shakti Parishad was created to reinvigorate the traditional power/respect of Indian women" (p. 11). Finally, Sadhvi Kamlesh Bharati ends her chapter by enumerating the following goals of the Parishad: to unite Indians around a single national interest; to make *vanavashis* [literally, forest dwellers, a reference here to the extremely marginalized scheduled tribes of India] self-reliant through education, to disseminate Indian culture; to help poor, homeless, widowed women; to facilitate devotional events around the country; to encourage women to participate in Hindu devotion; to preach Hinduism among vanavashis, *girijans*, [literally hill dwellers, a reference to marginalized hill tribes of India], and harijans [literally children of god, a use of the term Gandhi coined to refer to the untouchable castes of India]; to increase character-building curriculums in schools; to resist dowry, child marriage, and the tradition of *devadasis* [literally, female servants of the gods, usually girls who have been dedicated to temple service, but have become outcast and sexual prey of the priests], and to establish Sadhvi Ashrams around the country (p. 12).[7]

The essay clearly links a woman's body (modesty) and her role as cultural (and biological) reproducer to the health of a nation. If women do not perform their cultural role in a proper manner, then the family, and by extension the nation, suffers. Feminism, an alien Westernized construct is demonized as the enemy of the Hindu family. Sexism in Indian society is not denied, but is linked to the degradation of Hindu culture just as Golwalkar, and before him Savarkar, linked Hindu martial defeat to the decline through effeminization of Hindu society. Golwalkar was clear that Islamic invasion, internal enemies, and British perfidy were responsible for such devolution. The Sadhvi does not clarify where the forces responsible for the degradation of Hindu culture lie, but it is possible to infer the following chain of reasoning from her observations: exposure to Western ideals lead many Indians to privilege materialism, and consequently women become wanton, retreating from their role as mother (as cultural and biological reproducer), causing the Hindu family and the nation to falter. Thus, by reinvigorating Hindu womanhood, the Parishad will resist this decline. It is also interesting to note that she argues that a woman will not blossom if she is seen "only as mother and wife." Presumably, given the title of the monograph and the Parishad's focus on motherhood, the Sadhvi is not rejecting women's role as wife and mother but rather proposing the models of heroic mother (e.g., Jijabai) and/or chaste but powerful wife (later essays mention Savitri who snatches her husband from the clutches of Yama, lord of death, because of her devotion) as the ideals to be emulated. Therefore, it is possible to deviate from these models and be a bad mother and wife. The reasons for such deviation may either lie in the influence of Westernization or the failure of Hindu society to train women in the values expressed by the lives of Jijabai, Savitri, and/or Sita.

Women's failure to undertake their cultural duty is also linked to the decline of the Hindu nation measured by conversion and death at the hands of Islamic miltants (e.g., Kashmir). It is made clear that such conversions occurred solely because Hindus were not proactively reaching out to each other and consequently Christians and Muslims lured the poor away with material benefits. Thus, "religious conversion" as a theme underlies the Parishad's goals. The Parishad (like the VHP) emphasizes "homecoming," that is, a movement to bring converts to Christianity and Islam, especially the poor and lower castes, back into the Hindu fold through the spread of Hindu culture centered around the rejuvenation of traditional Hindu feminine power.

The later essays build on these themes in multiple ways. For example, some stress the existence of a glorious Hindu, Vedic age where women scholars like Gargi and Apala debated important philosophical issues (Vedic, 2000, pp. 18–21). Heroic mothers such as Jijabai and Rana Pratap's mother are lauded. Following the Samiti's characterization of men as fickle and weak, the Parishad casts both Shivaji and Pratap's father as nonmartial, cowardly, and unpatriotic men. For example, Rana Pratap's father is described as "not very courageous"; his lack of courage led him to lose his fort at Chittor and hide in the Aravalli mountains. In contrast, Pratap's mother was a courageous woman who never bowed her head before anyone; she taught her son never to surrender, to be brave, patriotic, and self-reliant. As a result, "Pratap was willing to eat grass rather than live under Emperor Akbar's rule" (Giri, 2000, p. 26). Jijabai is celebrated in ways similar to the Samiti.

Through tales of conquest, harassment of women, and drunken debauchery, the Parishad's writing clearly constructs Islam as the enemy of a glorious Hindu nation. Westernization in the form of immodest clothing for women and a celebration of brazen physical sexuality is also cast as a threat to the rejuvenation of Hindtuva. One article—"Tulsidasa's Wife: The Great Sadhvi Ratnavali" (Mishra, 2000, pp. 34–39)—suggests a method for resisting Westernization: proper education for women. In outlining this method, the author actually brings to the foreground a woman poet—Ratnavali—who has been overshadowed by her famous husband, Tulsidas the author of the *Ramcharit Manas*. The article begins by rebuking Hindi literature for forgetting Sadhvi Ratnavali, who was a poet in her own right. Once again the Parishad balances tradition and resistance. On one hand, the author resurrects a woman poet forgotten by a patriarchal society but on the other tames her by constructing her as a sadhvi and downplaying the fact that Tulsidas actually abandoned his wife. In the Parishad's version, Ratnavali did not berate or condemn her husband. Realizing that Tulsidas needed to leave his householder status to find enlightenment, she herself began to live the life of an ascetic sage. She wrote 209 couplets before she died. Ratnavali's poetry, on one hand, depicts a brave woman bewildered by the loss of her husband and, on the other, impresses with the tenderness and generosity expressed by her words. The article describes her as an accomplished, devoted, and educated wife learned in Sanskrit language and literature. Ratnavali's poetry, argues the author, should be taught in schools to form the basis of cultural resistance to contemporary society's moral decline. Sadhvi Ratnavali's poetry will help create ideal heroic mothers and wives because she celebrates the *pativrata* [devoted wife] and the mother. Lamenting social degradation, the author claims that an evil like AIDS only haunts society when motherhood fails. Instead of taking on the roles of heroic mother and chaste wives, women are becoming seductresses failing to properly perform their roles as cultural and biological producers of citizens for the nation. Teaching Ratnavali's poetry will be the first step towards challenging such degradation. This article shifts the entire responsibility for the Hindu nation's moral and spiritual fortitude onto women. Consequently, a woman's chastity and maternal nature become the barometer for a nation's moral climate.

Finally, there are articles that analyze sexual harassment, assault, and women's legal rights: "Contemporary Women's Problems and their Solutions" (Sharma, 2000); "Protection of Women's Rights" (Bajaj, 2000); and "The Oppression of Women and Some Ways to Resist" (Khanna, 2000). The second essay is actually written by a woman lawyer who provides a devastating critique of the Indian legal and judicial system's inept handling of sexual assault.

However, lest such views be construed as too radical or confrontational, women's problems including sexism and dowry deaths are blamed by one author on women themselves and the demon of Westernization: "However, all the evils that women face in society is their own creation: mothers are the ones that discriminate against girl children, they are the ones that demand dowry, and women do not rush to the aid of other women being ill-treated by men. Further, in a blind imitation of Western mores they have become too selfish and independent, breaking up the extended family and all the harmonious kinship relations within it" (Sharma, 2000, p. 63). Further, they are several essays extolling the virtues of *pativrata* (literally, women devoted to their husbands): "Woman as wife has only one goal: serving her husband. . . . A woman who serves her husband assiduously and well can gain the same kind of boons and knowledge as rishis who have been immersed in meditation. . . . Devotion to her husband is the greatest trait a woman can have" (Giri, 2000, p. 31). This piece, titled "The Glory of *Pativrata* Women," ends with a mythic account of the great *pativrata* Anusuya advising Sita about the nature of devotion: "Oh princess, all our relatives wish us well but there is always a limit to their good wishes, but our husbands can give us unlimited happiness. A wife who does not serve her husband is a sinner. . . . Patience, Duty, Friendship, and Woman are all tested during crisis. Old, sick, foolish, poor, blind, angry, even such a husband, should not be insulted by a wife" (p. 33).

Further, these rather conservative ideas of woman are validated by boxed sayings—proverbs outlined by bolded borders—inserted after essays and photographs in this monograph. For example, "It does not look good for women from respectable families to daily sit out on the balcony, look at unknown men through windows, and to laugh without any reason" (p. 13). The ideology of *pativrata* coupled with admonishments against perceived "uncontrolled" behavior capable of enflaming male passions provide an effective counterfoil to any social anxiety stemming from fear of the radical disruption of gender roles—marked by articles on sexual harassment, sexual assault, as well as the entrance of women onto the political stage—within the VHP's vision of the Hindu nation. Other boxed sayings include, "A sati (an extreme *pativrata*) can rescue humanity with her power. . . . The husband of a sati can be freed from all sins" (p. 63) and "Women are like oil and men like fire. So if one separates oil and fire to prevent a conflagration, then men and women should be separated for similar reasons" (p. 65).

In conclusion, the Sadhvi Shakti Parishad draws on the image of a celibate masculinized warrior to define women's participation in the ideological work of masculine Hinduism. The *sadhvis* are strong women who travel alone across India, speak out in public (sometimes using slang and swear words), lead devotional meetings, and teach women the need for self-reliance and confidence. The Parishad also addresses some aspects of women's vulnerability as they enter (either by necessity or choice) the public sphere by discussing issues of sexual harassment in the workplace or sexual assault in public spaces (there is silence on issues of sexual violence within the family). However, the potential challenge to masculinized Hindu nation by both types of female participation is tamed by the celebration of *pativrata* and the need to strictly regulate women's sexual nature.

In addition to the fact that the resistance within tradition or transgressing without radical critique tactics of the Samiti and Parishad do not facilitate a comprehensive discussion of the entire spectrum of women's lives, (for example, they are silent on female sexuality and women's vulnerability within the family), their celebration of a masculinized warrior has important implications for the role of violence in female nationalist activism.

FEMINIZATION OF VIOLENCE

The BJP, claiming to represent the voices of Hindu nationalism, demanded that a mosque allegedly built on the ruins of an ancient temple celebrating the birthplace of Lord Ram and occupying sacred Hindu ground should be torn down to make way for a new Hindu temple. It had been agitating around this issue throughout the eighties and in December 1992, its political agitation culminated in the destruction of this building. This event unleashed a wave of violence that swept throughout the country, as Hindus clashed with Muslims.

The city of Mumbai—a stronghold of the Shiv Sena—was one of the most violent conflict zones. During this period of turmoil, a feminist activist commented in a daily newspaper on the feminization of violence: "A very, very disturbing aspect of these killings was that women were some of the most aggressive participants in the riots. . . . There were cases of women assaulting other women" (*The Telegraph*, April 5, 1993). Other scholars agreed with this assessment: "large numbers of women have been extremely active and visible, not only in the rallies and campaigns but even in the actual episodes of violent attacks against Muslims" (Sarkar, 1995, pp. 189–91). Given the nature of such participation, it becomes reasonable to conjecture that certain women, in a specific situation, have indeed taken on traits of masculine Hinduism to enter into the fray as citizen-warriors protecting the Hindu nation. However, this interpretation of masculinity taken on by the women tends to be exemplified as raw power. For example, "In October 1990 in the western Uttar Pradesh town of Bijnor, Hindu women led a procession through a Muslim neighborhood with . . . (swords) in hand, shouting bigoted, inflammatory slogans" (Basu, 1999, p. 105).

However, women as active agents expressing and advocating violence only capture a partial view of women within masculinized nationalism. More commonly, women's bodies express the intersection of violence and nationalism in passive ways: "On 14 August, 1947, the day before the country was partitioned and became a 'nation,' the front page of a Hindu right wing weekly, the *Organiser* [the RSS paper], carried a map of India on which lay a woman. Her right limb (which mapped Pakistan) had been severed, with Jawaharlal Nehru, India's first Prime Minister, leaning over her holding in his hand a bloody knife" (Butalia, 1996). This imagining of India as a woman's body of course fits into my discourse of nation as woman, which in turn links with ideas of national honor being expressed by female bodies. Sadhvi Rithambhara uses similar imagery to call citizen-warriors to defend Bharat Mata. Further, in a more horrific articulation of this conceit, the rape of women becomes a weapon to dishonor the enemy. Generally, there are three explanations for rape of women during war. One, women's bodies are seen as the "loot" needed to confirm the victor's conquest. Two, as mentioned above, rape of women is meant to convey humiliation to men, the message being relayed man to man that the conquered has failed a test of "manhood" by failing to protect his women (Cockburn, 2001, p. 22). Three, rape is sometimes encouraged by officers to build camaraderie among men (Cockburn, 2001; Enloe, 1998). All three explanations revolve around the women's body being property and/or a symbol of male honor. Widescale rape of the enemy's women is a common feature of nationalist conflict in India.

Butalia (1995) noted such a cultural interpretation of rape in the partition riots, and this narrative framing rape in sectarian violence has continued on in modern India, the most recent manifestation being the 2002 violence in Gujarat. Following the death of fifty-eight Hindus (of which twenty-six were women) in the Godhra attack by Islamic militants, rumors spread (aided by reports in certain vernacular newspapers) that before being burnt to death, Hindu women had been raped and violated by Muslim "thugs."[8] This "violation of our women" narrative became an important component of the moral framework of the violence unleashed by various Hindu militant organizations in the city of Ahmedabad. It worked as an effective cultural metaphor because such an interpretation of honor is understood by both communities. A prominent Muslim editor in Gujarat claimed, "When someone is murdered, you are hurt. But a man can bear it quietly; it is when your mothers and daughters are violated, then [sic] he definitely responds, takes revenge" (Hameed et al., 2002, p. 11). And Hindu men did take revenge as, in retaliation for supposed communal dishonor, they raped and brutalized Muslim women and girls as young as nine (Hameed et al., 2002, pp. 11–20). Further, if Hindu men were perceived to be hesitant in their defense of honor, that is, reluctant to participate in violence against Muslim lives and property, VHP and Bajrang Dal activists sent bangles wrapped in red cloth to their homes to signify the effeminacy of the male residents (p. 34).

Hindutva women have also accepted this reading of honor, and when this understanding is juxtaposed with the feminization of violence, a provocative view of female empowerment comes to the fore. Put another way, women as celibate, masculinized warriors protect their bodies from being violated by the enemy while simultaneously deeming it legitimate to facilitate the violation of enemy women as an act exemplifying public shaming of the "other." These modern-day Draupadis have accepted the parameters shaping communal honor (women's bodies and associated ideas of modesty); instead of calling on divine intervention, they choose to resist through aggressive action and do not hesitate to urge the use of violence against enemy women. Resisting violation actively rather than passively entreating (as Draupadi did) implies a kind of empowerment, and such an approach dovetails with the Hindutva predilection for transgressing without radical critique. Uncompromising radical social critique would entail challenging the equation of a chaste female body and national honor or even more fundamentally the implications and meaning of denying female sexuality within a nationalist discourse.

CONCLUSION

Masculine Hindusim has enabled a complex trajectory of female participation within nationalist politics. The strong and articulate women of the Parishad and Samiti trace a delicate compromise between upholding ideals of womanhood that celebrate a simplistic vision of a "happy" Hindu family underlying a morally strong and virile Hindu nation and destabilizing this vision by speaking of woman's vulnerability in the public sphere and the need for strong female activism within nation-building. I have interpreted this negotiation as resistance within tradition or transgression without radical critique.

Such a strategy is necessitated by the fact that economic and social changes have increased women's participation in higher education, professional schools, and the labor force, changes which have, in turn, transformed the contours of the public sphere as well as decision-making and norms in traditional families. So even the most sheltered Hindutva woman has to acknowledge these demographic transformations. Further, these changes in gendered norms are unfolding in an India beset by political and economic crises. However, the radical implications of these changes is contained by a stress on chastity, a fear and denial of female sexuality, a blame that holds women responsible for their vulnerability, and a celebration of violence as a tool for creating a pure Hindu space free of any threats to a women's person or honor.

The implications of such a strategy within a nation are multiple. One, a vision of nation emerges wherein women's desire and sexuality are not celebrated, but instead women are taught to ignore a vital part of their nature. Two, if women's sexuality is seen as dangerous and shame-inducing, acts of domestic violence, rape, incest, and marital abuse are either blamed on wanton female behavior or shrouded in silence. Three, women (and men) participate in violent acts energized by visualizing women as the repository of honor and, hence, further a nationalist discourse wherein violence against women is justified in the name of dishonoring the enemy nation. Four, if women are seen as the cultural and biological reproducers of the nation, then they are held responsible for population as well as cultural decline. Such implications shape the tension between women within Hindutva and the Indian feminist movement explored in the next chapter.

SIX

Heroic Mothers, Chaste Wives, and Celibate Warriors

Feminist or Feminine Nationalism in India?

I don't understand what you mean by this nation business. What does it have to do with me? All I'm concerned with about is my family and where their next meal is coming from. Why should I feel any concern for this thing you call a nation? After all, no-one asked me how I felt when it was being made.
—Ramrati, Indian woman laborer

"Our country," she will say, "throughout the greater part of history has treated me as a slave; it has denied me education or any share in its possessions. . . . Therefore, if you insist upon fighting to protect me or 'our' country, let it be understood, soberly and rationally between us, that you are fighting to gratify a sex instinct which I cannot share; to procure benefits which I have not shared and probably will not share; but not to gratify my instincts, or to protect either myself or my country . . . in fact as a woman I have no country."
—Virginia Woolf, *Three Guineas*

RAMRATI AND VIRGINIA—two women separated by time, culture, class, language, and access to education, but voicing remarkably similar sentiments. However, the similarity of their sentiments must not be seen as implying a sense of universal sisterhood stemming from a common marginalization in the nation. As Pierson (2000) points out about Woolf, "who but a woman with a secure place within a nation can speak high-mindedly about not wanting a country" (p. 53)? It is possible that under different circumstances Woolf would not be as sanguine about her security or privilege in the British nation, but indeed her class, education, and implication in the Empire give her a

139

stake in Britain that differs from Ramrati's complete marginalization within
the Indian nation. However, for the purposes of this analysis I am interested
in the theme of homelessness, of not belonging, infusing their words. Indeed,
the location of nation and nationalism within women's lives is remarkably
contested. If, historically, women did not have a right to property, political
power, and education, what stake do they indeed have in the idea of an imagined community created by others?[1] Yet the desire to belong naturally arises
because very few women (and men) would like to exist as permanent outsiders. Therefore, when new nations like India are forged, there is excitement
within some marginalized groups that perhaps they may participate in the
imagining of this new community.

Women forge a nation in myriad ways, as wives, mothers, politicians, soldiers, and nurses. Some may choose to begin a critique of gender and patriarchy, others may remain silent. The history of women in the Indian nationalist movement illustrates that although some elite women actively agitated
to include their voices in the construction of the concept of India, ultimately
the task was dominated by a group of elite men (Chakravarti 1998; Kumar
1993; Sangari and Vaid 1989). Further, as Chatterjee (1999) points out, the
nationalist elite made a distinction between the "inner" and "outer" worlds
of the nation. The "outer" world was coeval with the public sphere where the
negotiation with colonial authorities over economic and political power took
place. In contrast, the "inner" world referred to the domestic realm—beyond
the reach of colonial rule—occupied by women who represented the spiritual
superiority of India. One implication of such a stance is that women's bodies
become the arena where cultural conflicts are played out. According to this
mode of thought, Indian women as pure, chaste figures threw into relief the
West's crass materialism embodied by the so-called immodest behavior of
Western women. As chapter 3 pointed out chaste wives and mothers in
Vivekananda's texts represented India's spiritual fortitude and superiority. But
it is clear that these virtuous female figures were middle class. Indeed, in this
discourse of female chastity representing Indian spiritual superiority, "A
woman's right over her body and control over her sexuality is conflated with
her *virtue*. So powerful does this characterization become that only the middle class woman has a right to purity. In other words, only *she* is entitled to
the name of woman in this society" (Tharu and Niranjana, 1999, p. 505;
emphasis in original).

WOMEN, VIRTUE, AND NATIONALIST ACTIVISM

We see this discourse shaping female participation within Hindutva, as the
figures of heroic mother, chaste wife, and celibate warrior are grounded in the
notion of virtue being the precondition of women's entry into the public
sphere of nation-building. As I have argued, to an extent, this is linked to

social anxiety stemming from disruptions of gender norms as educated women enter the labor force, coupled with structural changes in the Indian polity and economy. Not only do women in the public sphere represent change but also a heightened awareness of their vulnerability. This vulnerability, as the previous chapter argued, is very much linked to the danger posed by adult female sexuality. A discourse centered on middle-class virtue neutralizes and denies this sexuality while simultaneously casting the "other," whether it be Muslim men, women, or lower-caste women, as the enemy who embodies uncontrolled sexuality and threatens Hindu female virtue. Thus virtuous women situated within a harmonious Hindu family ultimately become a representation of resistance to social fear and anxiety.

Another implication of this emphasis on virtue is the threat of female sexuality to the male expression of masculine Hinduism. The separation of women's organizations from the main political groups, such as creating the Samiti for women rather than allowing women to join the RSS to work side by side with the men and boys in the *shakhas*, indicates this fear. Although women can indeed take on the traits of masculine Hinduism and become heroic mothers and celibate warriors, a residual fear of their sexuality remains. In other words, it is feared that women through their sexual nature will seduce men away from their true dedication to nation-building. The Parishad most clearly articulated this view with its boxed warnings about the dangerous consequences of unchaperoned meetings between men and women.[2] The underlying perspective informing such fears assumes that men remain helpless in face of female sexuality, which is what must be curbed. This is, of course, not a stance unique to Hindutva or even India.[3] For example, Gandhi's views on celibacy and sexuality reflected this assumption: "No woman who was not 'chaste in thought, word and deed' was to be allowed *into his movement.* When in 1925, the Bengal Congress Committee organized some women prostitutes under its banner, Gandhi was almost hysterical with rage" (Kumar, 1993, p. 83). The body of the adult prostitute of course symbolized sexuality, the opposite of chastity, and therefore posed a threat to dedicated nation-building.

Masculinized interpretations of nation in India, whether they be infused by Hindu ideology or not, also express this ambiguity towards female sexuality: "This episode of *Param Veer Chakra*, a series shown on Doordarshan [Indian national television] from July to October 1990, vividly dramatized the central problematic of the melodrama series: the construction of nationalist zeal and the depiction and naturalization of female sexuality as a threat to masculine valor" (Mankekar, 2000, 259). This television serial focused on narrating the lives of Indian soldiers who had received the *Param Veer Chakra* (literally, the circle symbolizing the greatest act of valor), a high military honor in India. In contrast to Hindutva discourse, in which female sexuality has been completely erased, this cultural depiction of militaristic nationalism—because it was based on true stories—is forced to deal with female sexuality in the form of wives who fail to provide unambiguous support for their husband's participation in war, highlighting the presence of sexual love and desire, albeit within the parameters of marriage. Mankekar argues that ultimately the serial condemns female sexuality and celebrates the figure of the heroic mother encouraging her son to war. Indeed, Mankekar relates an interesting incident in which an Indian Air Force representative would not allow the series director to depict a mother weeping when her son, an Air Force officer, died. The representative preferred and okayed the scene as it was shown on television: "The episode's last scene shows the weeping figures of the soldier's widow, his father, and his brother. But his mother stands dry-eyed, a picture of grim dignity" (p. 283). This indeed is cultural homage to heroic motherhood echoing back to a Spartan mother's mythic admonishment to her son, "Return with your shield or on it."

Hindutva women, in a desire to be a part of the nationalist project, have intersected it by accepting the ideas of masculine Hinduism and the associated ideas of female virtue underlying models of heroic mother, chaste wife, and celibate warrior. Such an intersection is of course only one interpretation of female political participation within a particular idea of nation. Other women have rejected their politics as right-wing and antifeminist and ultimately harmful for women's well-being.

FEMINISM AND HINDUTVA

The relationship between feminism and Hindutva is complicated and centers around multiple issues including the location of multiplicity, diversity, and hierarchy in society; the role of female sexuality in society; and the concept of belonging. A first step towards interrogating this complex relation is to focus on some historical and contemporary models for insight. Galucci (2002) in her analysis of Margherita Sarfatti, Mussolini's mistress, introduces the concept of "Fascist Feminism." She argues "that even in works in which Sarfatti is more closely aligned with Fascist ideology, these writings may also contain feminist impulses. . . . Sarfatti . . . drew . . . positive portraits of women. . . . In Dux, Sarfatti attempted to reconcile feminism to Fascism by presenting women not only as lovers and mothers, but also as influential, intellectual women. . . . Sarfatti showed how Fascist gender ideology disempowered women in many of her writings of this middle period" (pp. 23–24). However, Fascism's ultimate fear of empowered women forced Sarfatti to make inconsistent claims in its name. For example, she interpreted Fascism as providing opportunities for women, despite the fact that "Fascist laws were introduced to force women out of schools and teaching positions" (p. 25). Gallucci (2002) ends her article by claiming that "Sarfatti challenges us to rethink critical categories and . . . to redefine contemporary notions of feminism" (p. 27). Her conclusion is quite timely given my analysis of Hindutva women. Although Fascism is a specific cultural and historical movement, scholars have named the Hindutva movement such (Sarkar, 1995; Vanaik and Brass, 2002). At this point, I do not argue whether Hindutva and Fascism are comparable, but given scholarly tendencies to equate the two, it is fruitful to see if certain feminine models within Fascism can provide insights. Although Sarfatti and Fascist feminism may not be completely applicable to the Hindutva women, it is interesting to note two things for the purposes of our discussion. One is the tension between Sarfatti's support for feminism and her celebration of a government that passed laws limiting women's access to education. The BJP and the Shiv Sena, whatever their ideological inclinations, have not yet rolled back women's legal rights in India. The need for them to participate in ideologically diverse coalitions to remain in government as well as the presence of a lively watchdog press seems to check, barring the explosion of some political catastrophe, any tendency of these parties to roll back existing laws (however inadequate) protecting women's rights (Banerjee, 2002). Despite this fact, it would be a conceptual stretch to view these parties as unambiguously woman-friendly, let alone feminist. Consequently, like Sarfatti, the Hindutva women have to reconcile their enthusiasm for critiquing and celebrating women's lives with the explicit masculinity of Hindtuva. This reconciliation is of course fraught with tension. As this chapter will show, "Hindutva feminism" may be an inherently contradictory and/or problematic concept.

Two, as my discussion of "transgressing without radical social critique" has shown, no Hindutva woman—unlike Sarfatti—has really challenged the location of chaste woman and harmonious family in Hindu nationalist ideology regardless of their celebration of heroic, muscular, even scholarly women. The troubled relationship between feminism and antifeminism in the Hindutva (and Sarfatti) model may begin with the problems inherent in constructing a model of female freedom and feminist justice within a blatantly racist political ideology founded in a very unnuanced "us versus them" view of the nation. Further, any discussion of women's lives, obstacles faced by women, and female vulnerability has to be conducted in a nationalist context privileging women as wives and mothers within a cult of domesticity.

Another interesting political model is provided by Australian politician Pauline Hanson (Winter, 2002), a strong, articulate woman who founded the One Nation Party. Using Hanson as a model, Winter argues that an empowered woman is not necessarily a feminist: "Empowerment, however, is not synonymous with feminism, even if it can be seen as one component of feminism. . . . In fact feminism is not primarily 'about women' and it is certainly not about different ways of being a woman or of being empowered as a woman" (p. 203). Winter concludes that Hanson is not a feminist because she is racist, disseminates a cult of domesticity, is against affirmative action for women, and supports capitalist individualism, which is "decidedly *anti-*feminist" (p. 208). Both Hanson and Sarfatti underline that feminism does not center on female activism or even empowerment but on the context of nationalist meaning within which this activism is situated. It is the Fascist ideological background in which Sarfatti's ideas of female empowerment were embedded as well as the racist and antiwelfare content of Hanson's activism that ultimately complicate their relationship to feminism. Similarly, an Indian feminist scholar points out that the Hindu nationalist context of their actions implicate Hindutva women in "fascist intolerance and violence, toward the creation of an authoritarian, anti-democratic social and political order" and, hence, "No feminist can possibly argue that the movement can contribute anything to the broad rights of women" (Sarkar, 1995, p. 210).

I offer a final perspective on feminism and nationalism: "What makes these movements and the analysis of them different is that women are (re)constructing the meanings of both nationalism and feminism from a women-centered viewpoint, what some feminists call women's or feminist 'standpoint theory.' This theory begins with women's viewpoints where we reside in our everyday lives" (West, 1997, p. xiii). These viewpoints, according to Lori West, are multiple, diverse, and eclectic. But they are united in that they resist women's victimization and fight to create a nation with justice for all, not just women. The difference between the views of Hindutva women and West lies not so much in a "woman-centered viewpoint," as the former can argue that they are indeed providing a feminine stance based on women's everyday lives, but in the latter's emphasis on multiplicity and diversity. As will be shown below, Hindutva provides a remarkably monolithic view of women's lived experiences that does ultimately hinder the creation of a nation with comprehensive ideas of justice for women. The above discussions of nationalism, feminism, and right-wing politics open up a space wherein the relationship between Hindutva women and feminism can be located. It is not so much a question of whether Hindutva women support women's education and right to work outside the home (which they do) or offer some realization of women's vulnerability in the public sphere (which they do) or agitate for women's legal rights, but whether the female identity and ideology they see as forming the basis of their nation can accommodate a comprehensive critique of the multiplicity of women's lives.

Hindutva women support the creation of a monolithic Hindu nation centered on ideas of a masculine Hinduism that draws on a mythic, glorious imperial Hindu past. Masculine Hinduism celebrates notions of a martial self ready to aggressively protect and fight for cultural dominance defined in opposition to an effeminized Muslim or Hindu "other." This implacable self/other construct offers no room for negotiation, compromise, diversity, or multiplicity. Further, an implication of such a stance is that violence can be used against the other in the interest of protecting or creating this nation.

Note I am aware this such constructions are not unique to Hindutva nor even to cultural nationalism; however, I would argue that whenever in the invention of a nation, ideas of negotiation, compromise, diversity, or multiplicity are pushed to the background, the danger of creating a rigid and intolerant society emerges. Further, the use of violence (as various national liberation guerilla movements demonstrate) is not unique to Hindutva, but again within this context, violence as political tool acquires a meaning—cultural targetting—as seen in the 1992–1993 Hindu-Muslim riots in Mumbai as well as the 2002 Sabarmati Express tragedy and the violence that followed it in Gujarat. In both these incidents Hindu mobs targeted and either injured or killed Muslim citizens constructed as the enemy of the Hindu nation. Not only are Hindutva women accepting this construction and meaning of nation, but they are disseminating a female identity that does not capture the full spectrum of women's lives and their diversity.

Feminist analyses acknowledge that identity is a slippery notion and do not claim that "woman" is easy to locate. A debate still rages in feminist theory about the exact definition of "woman." Who is the "woman" who forms the basis of feminist or feminine activism? Morgan (1970) in *Sisterhood is Powerful* chooses to construct "woman" by drawing upon what she perceives as shared universal experiences of male domination. Her definition is challenged by Third World and minority feminists (hooks, 1981; Mohanty, 1991) who see Morgan's global sisterhood as erasing diversity among women. They argue that there is no single "woman" but a variety of women shaped by differences in class, race, culture, and sexual orientation. The woman that underlies many early feminist analyses is not universal woman but a white, middle-class woman privileged over all others. More recently, feminist theory has become fragmented as voices of many women struggle to be heard and "woman" is constructed in a myriad ways. Some welcome this fragmentation and flux (Butler, 1991; Harraway, 1989) while others deplore the recognition of excessive diversity as being paralyzing (Bordo, 1989).

Extending this analysis to Hindutva, my discussion clarifies that the "woman" underlying Hindutva female activism is a Hindu, middle-class, middle- to upper-caste, fairly well-educated woman. Integral to this identity are notions of virtue and chastity linked to an idealized vision of a harmonious Hindu family. This is the essentialized female identity Hindutva women draw on as they enter the discourse of masculine Hinduism as heroic mother, chaste wife, and celibate warrior. Whether or not the reality of their lived experiences expresses this identity, it remains an ideal worthy of emulation.

Such a view of Indian womanhood even within a monolithic Hindu nation is problematic. Caste and class hierarchies along with regional (Nagaland versus Tamil Nadu) and linguistic (Bengali versus Kannada) variations in the interpretation of Hinduism and women's position in Hinduism are denied. Even the idea of female virtue or chastity has different interpretations within different contexts. For example, Vaishanavas (followers of sixteenth-century saint Sri Chaitanya) will construct ideas of female virtue in ways that differ from a Tamil Brahmin's perspective. Obviously, the perspectives of poor Dalit women and middle-class Brahmin women on virtue, chastity, and the protection provided by family differ radically as does their view on the types of obstacles women face in the public sphere. Marginalized Dalit women who usually take on manual labor (for example, as construction workers or domestic servants), vulnerable to the sexual preying of middle-class employers, have concerns that differ from middle-class, educated, upper-caste women facing discrimination as professors or doctors. Further, when one moves beyond Hindu India to include the various religions [Christianity, Islam, Jainism, Buddhism, and Judaism as well as certain animistic practices of the indigenous people of India (a.k.a. scheduled tribes)], the limited perspective offered by the Hindutva view of female identity becomes even more prominent.

In addition to the idea of a monolithic Hindu nation erasing the diversity found in India, the conflation of womanhood and chastity within marriage coupled with the privileging of the Hindu family distorts the articulation of women's sexuality within society. Jyoti Puri's (2002) study of the role of sexuality in middle-class north Indian women's lives provides some insight into this distortion. She argues, "What is to be challenged as well are the ways in which awareness of the female body is heightened in the experiences of women on a daily basis. . . . Through menarche, continued menstruation, and experiences of sexual aggression women contend with the ramifications of their sexed bodies. Their lives are framed in terms of femininity and sexual responsibilities, and their bodies, genders, and sexualities are social effects of a system the requires self-surveillance and internalization of responsibility" (202). Note that Puri is not discussing just Hindutva women, but women from a range of backgrounds. Her book emphasizes the shame and discomfort many Indian women feel with their sexualized body (pp. 75–101). Any inappropriate attention is constructed by the women Puri interviewed as being their fault for not following a proper form of sexual respectability. Of course, instead of going against the grain and freeing women of this shame, Hindutva's view of the chaste and virtuous woman further shores up this reading of womanhood.

Feminists in India (Kumar, 1993; Viswanathan, 1997) have begun to challenge and resist this reading of female sexuality. One implication of such a reading is that when women become the target of sexual aggression ranging from "eve-teasing" (getting pinched, poked, and/or verbally harrassed) to rape, women and society feel that it is inappropriate female behavior or clothing that provoked such aggression. The Samiti's and Parishad's cautionary advice to women to be modest, to not laugh around strange men, and to avoid eye contact with strangers confirms these ideas of sexual respectability focused on blaming women for attracting sexual aggression, whatever its form.

Further, in this context, rape becomes a crime of lust. However, it is clear that rape in India is more than that. It is about power: "all women are potential rape victims, irrespective of age, manner of dressing or conduct" (Agnes, as cited in Vishwanathan, 1997, p. 322). Rape is not usually a spontaneous outburst of male lust provoked by women's immodesty or the lack of male protection (as Hindutva would encourage us to read it). It can be and often is an attempt to intimidate or demonstrate social power over women: upper-caste men raping Dalit women; soldiers raping the women of the conquered nation; men of the "enemy" community raping innocent Muslim or Hindu women during partition and post-independence communal riots; or husbands raping wives who have refused them sexual access. Further, the discourse of shame around female sexuality prevents women from resisting these types of aggression. The Hindutva women's heroic mother or celibate warrior would never prove effective in erasing women's shame and/or removing the responsibility women feel when subjected to sexual violence. The notion of virtue underlying these models make women behave in ways—not laughing freely, walking with lowered eyes, stifling creative fashion to preserve modesty, remaining ever vigilant that one's physical demeanor is not provocative— that limit women rather than encouraging a social critique aimed at celebrating their freedom of movement and expression. Additionally, the discourse of middle-class virtue obscures the fact that lower-caste and poor women along with sex workers have absolutely no recourse to any kind of redress in Indian society (Kumar, 1993) and will continue to have no protection in a Hindu nation defined by ideas of chastity and virtue because their lower social status defines them as inherently "unchaste": "The freedom of tribal women is a threat to diku [tribal word for nontribal people] morality be it Hindu, Muslim, or Christian. Unlike diku women, Santhali women are not ashamed of being women or afraid of their sexuality. The dikus hate this freedom and say that they are 'loose women.' They rape Santhal women to force them into fear, shame and subjugation. They rape to show their hatred and contempt for tribal society" (report by Stri Sangharsh—an Indian women's group—as cited in Kumar, 1993, p. 140). While this report refers specifically to tribal women, lower-caste and poor women are also, in the eyes of the purveyors of Hindutva middle-class, upper-caste morality, suspect until their actions decisively prove that they have accepted notions of modesty and sexual respectability.

The idea of the harmonious Hindu family tied to the construct of woman as chaste and virtuous has a twofold implication. One, power relations within the patriarchal family are not discussed. Two, there is a silence about sexual aggression within families. The sexual aggressor in both the Samiti and Parishad discourse is always the "other" or outsider. There is no acknowledgement that women can experience aggression from close family members. For example, the Hindutva discourse cannot adequately analyze the sexual aggression described in the following account: "The worst is cousins. Parents think they are very nice, everyone thinks they are very nice, and you get to share so much—share rooms, bed also. You wake up in the middle of the night [and feel] that somebody is watching you, reach[ing] out and touch[ing] you. It's such a horrible, dirty feeling I can't tell you" (Puri, 2002, p. 82). If the Samiti and Parishad even chose to address such an issue, they would offer the following analyses: one, the young girl behaved in an immodest manner; two, the family environment itself was "Westernized" and culturally degraded, failing to follow proper Hindu morality; and three, young girls were not properly protected and trained in this family. All three interpretations, rather than providing an excavation of the power relations enabling such aggression, actually enhance a woman's feeling of shame and responsibility for provoking aggressive behavior. Finally, the Hindutva discourse falters if the "horrible, dirty feeling" is provoked by a brother, father, father-in-law, uncle, or even mother or sister.

Many aspects of Indian feminism challenge the Hindutva discourse surrounding the role of women and the family. Before embarking on a scrutiny of this challenge, the concept of the "Indian women's movement" must be clarified, as this term embraces a wide range of women's groups including those affiliated with national political parties and academic institutions as well as autonomous organizations which refuse to ally with political parties or universities. Not surprisingly such organizational diversity also gives rise to considerable ideological dissension. I would argue that most groups comprising this diverse movement would be united in being suspicious of the Hindutva notion of female empowerment for the reasons I will discuss below. But, I realize that what I define as the "Indian women's movement" would be most closely aligned with those autonomous women's groups which have emerged since the 1970s to protest violence against women, communalism, and the role of women in the Hindu family.

One of the major contributions made by Indian feminism to the lived experiences of women in the nation has been an organized resistance to female shame and responsibility for being subjected to sexual aggression. The Indian women's movement has also agitated for lower class/caste rape victims to receive redress and to have the social taboos preventing the discussion of incest removed. They have also resisted, in certain cities, the incidence of eve-teasing. In conjunction with this resistance, feminist activism in India and elsewhere has attempted to encourage women to enjoy or at least discuss their sexuality.

However, the feminist movement has not been able to come to grips with two associated issues integral to women's lives: a need to belong and the location of family. The Samiti and Parishad, like various women's organizations, encourage women to come out into the public sphere and emphasize women's activism within the construction of nation. But as I have argued above, the female identity that forms the basis of their activism denies multiplicity in India as well as fails to provide a comprehensive analysis of women's lives, that is, of the role of female sexuality. The dilemma for feminist activists can be located in the fact that so many Indian women resonate to this female identity disseminated by the Samiti and Parishad.

Their success turns on the multiplicity of meaning hidden within the various models of female activism they have chosen to emphasize. The multifaceted identity of Hindu womanhood—heroic mother, chaste wife, celibate warrior—that these organizations have constructed is based on folklore, historic icons, and mythology that reinforce a sense of comfort and belonging in a hostile world by drawing on the strengths of everyday life. As yet feminist organizers have not been able to provide an alternative identity that can woo women away in large numbers from the appeal of the Samiti and Parishad.

In a way, this may be an impossible task, given the discourse Indian feminists are circulating. Within feminism the construction of woman requires an acceptance of diversity as well as a rebellion against the idea of harmonious Hindu family and critique of faith. Indian women's groups are asking women to defy traditional faith and family structures. Such defiance is alienating and requires an abundance of strength and determination. Further, given the lack of women's shelters, job-training programs, state-funded child support payments, and welfare, the cost of defiance is quite high in India. Feminist organizers are aware of this. A organizer of a Mumbai group, *Majlis*, which provides a forum to promote awareness of female oppression in the family through cultural devices such as plays and films as well as providing some legal aid, commented on the location of identity and a sense of belonging in feminist organizing:

> So when a woman comes to me, she may get enriched or she might not get enriched but she definitely does not belong. She realizes she does not belong. Though she talks of her rights . . . at the very same time it attacks the concept of family . . . the Shiv Sena does not take away that comfort from them. A lot of women come here for their maintenance rights or divorce rights—but they do not belong to us. But it [the Shiv Sena] gives them a different kind of belonging. Now our [feminist] weakness is we did not realize this desire to belong. We thought of need, of rights [but not of the desire to belong]. . . . Rebellion does not make a movement, does not make a craze. Rebellion remains an alienating, isolating factor. It may give a moral boost to a lot of people but that does not make a movement. (personal interview, Mumbai, India, March 21, 1993)

The organizer is speaking of women in the Shiv Sena, but I would argue her point can be extrapolated to the actions of the Samiti and Parishad, which, being more organized and focused than the Sena's women's wing, have been more effective in creating a sense of belonging within a nation.

This interpretation is confirmed by other feminist scholars: "The family is the source of continuing emotional and material support to which women's groups have been unable to provide an alternative, for women in struggle. This is where Hindu right-wing organizations have been successful, because they have politicized women without disturbing the family system" (Menon, 1999, p. 12). Indian feminists are attacking the fundamental expression of the harmonious Hindu family. The very assumption of the feminist movement is that women do not belong, should not want to belong to the family or the nation in its present form. This tension is found in Indian feminist Urvashi Butalia's words as she queries, "So why do I as a woman feel so uncomfortable about my relationship with the nation-state? Tanika Sarkar, an Indian, historian enlightens me: 'Women will always be incomplete national subjects. This is because a nation is a territorial concept. Land is central. Yet women, often, and most women in India certainly, have no right to land. These two things, home and land, will never belong to them'" (Butalia, Mother India). But the nation is not just about land. Belonging to the nation is shaped by access to political ideas, economic benefits, resonance with cultural myths; as the quotes at the beginning of this chapter indicate, many women feel marginalized to this entire process. The Samiti and Parishad have provided women access to the nation by shoring up and manipulating traditional ideas of family and womanhood. Thus women feel a sense of belonging, a stake in the nation, without actually challenging many of the fundamental assumptions of the family. Resistance within tradition offers the thrill of nationalist activism without the accompanying loneliness accruing to radical social critics who stand on the margins of the nation as they defy the foundations of the imagined community.

CONCLUSION

Hindutva provides a comfortable shield against the alienation and dispossession articulated by Virginia Woolf and Ramrati at the beginning of this chapter. Further, this shield also protects against the political and economic anxiety sketched in the Introduction. But protection comes at a cost; the construction of this comfort and belonging erases power imbalances in the family, oversimplifies the multiplicity of Indian women's lives, and exacerbates aggression within society. An India where Ramrati is not prey to sexual advances from her employers, where she knows that her family will be fed, where all women work and walk confidently in public, will not be built by armed masculinity and its associated ideas of female activism as they are presently configured within Hindutva. It may be understandable, given the social uncertainty discussed in the Introduction, why some women and men search for meaning and comfort with models of masculinity and femininity that signify resolution and tradition embedded in Hindu nationalist discourse, but as this chapter has shown, these models have disturbing implications for women's lives. Further, the inflexible self/other dichotomy underlying masculine Hinduism will not easily be amenable to negotiation and compromise. Armed masculinity in such a context always contains the potential for violence. The Indian women's movement will have to accept that Hindutva women may never join them. However, as long as women's groups endeavor to expose the multiplicity of women's lives in India, the sexual aggression within and outside of the family, the ways in which shame hinders women's spontaneity, and the dangerous implications of masculine Hinduism, their resistance remains a visible symbol of the limitations of the female identity underlying Hindutva politics.

SEVEN

Summary

ARMED HINDU MASCULINITY narrates a potent story about nationalism in India. Men and women both respond to the call of a nationalist narrative glorifying aggressive fortitude embodied by young men with an uncompromising resolve to defend their nation. While some may find this resolve admirable, this book has shown that it is not innocent. This is so because the internal logic of masculine Hinduism requires both the images of armed masculinity and nation as woman. The latter concept animates cultural metaphors that conflate women's bodies and communal honor while celebrating chastity as a major indicator of female value. Indeed the constructs of the Hindu soldier, warrior-monk, heroic mother, chaste wife, and celibate, masculinized warrior come into focus as a cultural narrative only when a lens created by the logic of masculine Hinduism is trained on them. Further, the constructions of femininity included in the rubric of a masculinized Hindu nation are linked to a vision of a harmonious family built on the global notion of women's virtue as a prerequisite for maintaining national and family honor. If one fuses this focus on feminine chastity with beliefs that locate honor in women's bodies and then situate them in a nationalism defined by rigid self/other views, it becomes clear how rape can become the expression of rage between men. The national "self" (in our case male Hindu soldiers) expresses its anger at the "other" (Muslim men) by dishonoring "their" women violently through rape. Women, in this scenario, are the canvas on which anger between men is drawn.

However, as this work has shown, women in nationalisms defined by ideas of armed masculinity do not necessarily have to be passive objects. The Samiti and Parishad women emphasize that transgression without radical critique can enable some forms of feminine subjecthood and empowerment embodied by Samiti founder Lakshmibai Kelkar. But this subjecthood and empowerment is unidimensional, locked within the stranglehold of

middle-class ideas of chastity and the myth of the monolithic, harmonious
Hindu family. Fear of deviating from norms of virtue will inhibit women
within the constructs of masculine Hinduism from protesting the trajectory
of power as it circulates within the family. The constant vigilance required
to maintain norms of virtue will necessarily inhibit women's confidence
and freedom as well as creating depths of shame and fear if these norms are
violated. Finally these norms are class, caste, and religion specific. Under
the gaze of masculine Hinduism, lower-class, Dalit, scheduled tribe women
as well as all women belonging to other religions are by nature promiscuous. Consequently, the constructs of femininity within the logic of masculine Hinduism become constraining, if not dangerous, for certain Hindu
and all non-Hindu women.

As I argued in the Introduction, masculine Hinduism with its attendant
images of masculinity and femininity is a specific cultural interpretation of a
greater narrative unfolding in the world today. As I finish up this book, the
United States has engaged in a war against Iraq. The rhetoric employed by
both George W. Bush and Saddam Hussein fall squarely within the parameters
of hegemonic masculinity: uncompromising, aggressive, and infused with martial and religious metaphors. There is no doubt that muscular male bodies radiating martial prowess, strength, anger, and resolute confrontation lie at the
center of their speeches. As we saw the United States and the Royal Marines
juxtaposed with images of Mr. Hussein's Republican Guard, this masculinized
discourse became vividly illustrated. Additionally these ideas of manhood are
embedded within a nationalism founded on a simplistic self/other view of the
world. Mr. Bush's reference to Iraq as the axis of evil as well as Mr. Hussein's
(and other Islamic leaders') aggressive anti-Americanism accept the script of
an uncomplicated dichotomous "us versus them" view of nation. Both perspectives have erased diversity and differences in the two nations. It is simplistic to project the views held by Bush and his coterie of advisors or Saddam
Hussein and his inner circle onto nations divided along ethnic, class, gender,
ideological lines. Although it is true, Mr. Bush, in his speeches, attempts to
separate "the Iraqi people" from Mr. Hussein's government, certain traits are
implied as being inherent to citizens of Arab countries—ultra-religiosity, irrationality, fanaticism—that deny the immense diversity of the people residing
in Iraq. More importantly, as the constant debate on the war unfolds in our
print media, radio, and television, we see that women and ideas of womanhood are largely absent from public discussion. Male leaders, experts, and soldiers disseminate an international politics based on hegemonic masculinity.

Women and womanhood entered this discussion during the early stages,
when the world's eyes were focused on Afghanistan. The veiled Afghani
woman under the Taliban regime intersected international debate as many
Western leaders justified their aggression against the Taliban and
Afghanistan as an attempt to liberate Afghani women from a brutal patriar-

chal system. Some Western feminists agreed. Many Islamic men and women responded by pointing to the veil as a symbol of cultural resistance to Western imperialism and claiming that the presence of the veil does not necessarily reveal brutal patriarchy. It is important to note that both sides of the debate accept women's bodies as the canvas on which nation is drawn. In the Western discourse, the veiled woman represents a backward, underdeveloped, traditional nation, while in the Islamic response the covering of women's bodies implying proper female modesty represents national honor and an oppositional identity. Further, one central construct of the anti-Americanism unfolding in many contexts is the image of the promiscuous and lewd American woman. Indeed, masculine Hinduism has also resorted to this strategy. Echoes of Vivekananda's violent condemnation of immodest Western women who are bad wives and mothers are found in the beliefs of many VHP and RSS men I interviewed. (The construct of the monolithic American woman has erased the diversity of women's lives created by racial, class, religious, and other differences). Thus, American honor is violated by the disrespect shown its women. The celebration of the rescue of Jessica Lynch can also be read in this context. The American nation can brook no dishonor to its women (even if she is a soldier). This book has revealed the implications for women's lives, when their bodies become the symbol for nation and nationalism.

Now that women are a part of the Anglo-American forces, how will this presence play into the idea of the protection of the "traditional Islamic" women? Can women as warriors liberate other women? Women soldiers have taken on masculine traits, their female sexual nature has been completely erased. Indeed, they are celibate, masculinized warriors. As casualties mount on both sides, women will enter the international stage as chaste wives and heroic mothers, lamenting the loss of husbands and sons. Sometimes they will transform their laments into calls for vengeance against the enemy. Finally, the most poignant image of women in this conflict will be the mothers and children, stateless, nationless, displaced by a confrontation they most probably did not create nor will benefit from. Indeed, life in a refugee camp, forgotten by the world, without the protection of a nation or a state, poignantly represents the grave consequences of not belonging, of being homeless. Perhaps many women (like those of the Samiti and Parishad) accept nations without too much radical critique because they fear this desperate form of homelessness.

The logic of masculine Hinduism as it unfolds is not innocent. The images of the Hindu soldier and the warrior-monk are implicated in a rigid self/other dichotomy tied to uncompromising action that becomes implicated in violence and intolerance. Additionally, the corresponding feminine images of heroic mother, chaste wife, and celibate masculinized warrior both shore up this rigid dichotomy as well as disseminating a narrative that constricts women's lives by imposing certain norms of modesty and virtue. Masculine Hinduism is not a unique expression; it draws on a more general narrative of nation that is found in many cultural contexts. If the implications of this narrative is to be resisted, the logic of hegemonic masculinity, armed manhood, and nation need to be excavated in diverse contexts.

Notes

CHAPTER ONE
INTRODUCTION: CONSTRUCTS OF NATION AND GENDER

1. Interviewees have requested anonymity and will be designated descriptively, either by affiliations and/or titles. Interviews were conducted by the author during various research trips to India, spanning the past decade (1992–2002).

CHAPTER TWO
EMPIRE: CHRISTIAN MANLINESS AND THE BRITISH GAZE

1. The first Indian troops of British India were the guards of the East India Company, who protected the trading stations. These then evolved into the three armies of the presidencies: Bombay, Calcutta, and Madras. After 1857, the Company's troops were transferred to the Crown and the number of British officers per battalion was reduced. Over time, the British Indian Army underwent various changes. For example, in 1902 Lord Kitchener abolished the presidency armies. All troops then belonged to one corps: the Indian Army. In the 1930s, an attempt to "Indianize" the Officer Corps began (Jackson 1940).

2. Letter of Arthur Joseph Reginald Pepper, Calcutta trader, June 1857, #MSS Eur C 488, British Library's India Office Collection, original texts, London. Note here and subsequently, document identification, letters and numbers, are indexed to the British Library's manuscript cataloging system.

3. Original texts written by British administrators in India, Document L/MIL/17/6/74, 2, British Library's India Office Collection.

4. Document L/MIL/17/72, 1884, 91.

5. Memo, Colonel Chesney, 1885, L/MIL/17/6/76.

6. Document L/MIL/17/5/56, 3.

7. Anonymous, Document L/MIL/17/6/72, 1884, 5.

8. His book figured significantly in British discourses about Indian resistance.

CHAPTER THREE
NATIONALISM: MASCULINE HINDUISM
AND RESISTING THE BRITISH GAZE

1. The poem's full version runs as follows:

Away! Away to the battlefield!
Sing your loudest songs of triumph:
Guard your faith imperiled!" Mother India cries.
Will you consider but your lives
When peril threatens mothers, wives?
Put on your war dress, all of you,
Hark the trumpet sounds unceasing!
March on! To pour our lives in battle.
Praise to Mother India, praise to Mother Kali!
Does it fit the god of terror
To sit and take his ease!
Neither it behooves you to be in the embrace of your sweetheart
When your breast has been wounded by the trampling of the
English!
Will the shiny sword rest in its sheath
When the Indian is offended?
We shall wheel about in the fight, so as not to show the back.
We shall never be taken captives by the enemy.
We know no fear, whatever may be in store for us,
We will not make any truce with Sin,
There must be an end to our servility to the Feringhi.
Victory or death! We have to make a selection in a face-to-face
Battle.
Rush to war! Rush to war!
We shall disperse the troops of the enemy. There will be left no
Traces of the foe in old and sacred Aryavarta.
We shall make our ablutions in the blood of the enemy.
And, with it, we shall tint Hindustan red!

2. Let me at the outset state that Indian resistance to British colonial authority took multiple forms. Gender as a salient part of one particular discourse, centered on masculinity, forms the basis of the present study. Such a focus does not, of course, deny the existence of other types of resistance. Further, gender was not a static category, and masculinity and femininity as well as male and female bodies intersected the nationalist discourse in varied and unique ways.

3. Author interviews, Mumbai, India, March 1993, June 1996, June 1998; and New Delhi, India, February 7–March 16, 2002.

4. Although outside the scope of this study, Nivedita's representation of Indian women is problematic. Feminist scholars (Neogi, 2000; Roy, 1998) have begun to question her presumptions both to speak for and describe Indian women and in the process deny Indian women agency.

5. Sarala Debi co-edited the journal with her sister from 1895 to 1897; by herself from 1899–1907 and again from 1924–1926. I refer to such articles as "Bangaleer Pitridhan" (loosely translated, "The Paternal Heritage of Bengalis"), *Bharati*, Jaishtha, 1310 (Bengali month and year according to which the issues of *Bharati* are organized. 1310 is 1903.), pp. 188–95; and "Bilati Ghusi Banam Desi Keel" (loosely translated "English Blows versus Indian Hits"), Asadh, 1310, pp. 216–26.

6. See Sister Nivedita, *Hints on Education*, Calcutta, India: Brahmachari Ganen-dranath, 1913 and *Studies from an Eastern Home*, London: Longmans, Green and Co., 1913.

CHAPTER FOUR
CULTURAL NATIONALISM, MASCULINE HINDUISM, AND CONTEMPORARY HINDUTVA

1. It is the goal of this chapter to provide a discussion of the history, structure, and politics of these organizations, only as they shape the manner in which ideals of masculinity have unfolded in the RSS, VHP, BJP, and Shiv Sena. For a more com-prehensive discussion of history, structure, organization, and mobilization for the RSS, see Anderson and Damle, 1997, and Basu, Datta, Sarkar, Sarkar, and Sen, 1993, as well as the RSS's own publication, Bajpai and Barthawal, 2001; for the VHP see Basu et al., 1993; for the BJP see Malik and Singh, 1994; and for the Shiv Sena see Baner-jee, 2000, and Gupta, 1982. Two frequently cited scholarly works on India's Hindu nationalist movement are C. Jaffrelot (1996), *The Hindu Nationalist Movement* (New York: Columbia University Press) and T. Hansen (1999), *The Saffron Wave: Democ-racy and Hindu Nationalism in Modern India* (Princeton: Princeton University Press). However, none of the above works deal with the significant gender dimension of Hindu nationalism in great detail.

2. An excellent discussion of the relevance of Fascism as an analytic descriptor for Hindutva is found in Vanaik and Brass, 2002, pp.13–17.

3. This organization should not be confused with the women's trade union SEWA, or Self-Employed Women's Association, in Ahmedabad, Gujarat.

4. Much of the textual material I use to illustrate my argument is drawn from the VHP website. The internet has offered Hindutva groups an effective way of dissemi-nating its message globally. However, the fusion of electronic media and Hindu nationalism is beyond the scope of this work. The texts on the VHP websites are drawn from various sources but mostly from editorials in various Indian newspapers that the organization perceives as illustrating its arguments. The words of Francois Gautier a French journalist who has resided in India for more than twenty years appear frequently on this website. Gautier, a follower of Sri Aurobindo, sees himself (one assumes) as a Hindu, and the VHP's frequent use of his ideas and words seem to indicate its acceptance of such self-identification. The words of David Frawley, an American who also identifies himself as Hindu, are also found on the VHP (and at the times the RSS) websites as well as in their publications. The RSS, VHP, and BJP also endorses ISKCON (or the International Society for Krishna Consciousness) founded in New York City by a Bengali Hindu. However, most of the devotees,

though not Indian, view themselves as Hindu. If this acceptance of non-Indians as Hindus is authentic, then it seems to me that the VHP (and perhaps the RSS and BJP) does believe that one can become as well as be born a Hindu. The prominence of a non-Indian journalist in the articulation of Hindutva raises interesting questions about representation both in the sense of speaking for and speaking of. I quote Gautier often as his ideas clearly illustrate the notions of masculinity under study in this book. It seems to me that if the VHP chooses to use Gautier's words to represent their ideology, then I can also accept his words as such.

5. For example, Hindu attacks against Muslim property and lives in the Ahmedabad in March 2002 is constructed as a BJP-sponsored progrom. Since Ahmedabad is in the state of Gujarat, governed by a BJP Chief Minister, this point of view may not be unreasonable.

6. The precise relationship between the RSS and BJP as well as the RSS's professed disdain for politics is problematic.

7. After the 2004 general elections held in April/May the BJP and its allies no longer govern India. A new ruling coalition led by Congress is now in place.

8. The origin of these stereotypes is hard to pin down; they form part of the inter-subjective cultural context in which most Hindus participate.

9. Radhabai Chawl was a slum building allegedly burnt down by Muslims seeking to intimidate Hindus. A small girl was among the victims. This incident occupied an important position in the Shiv Sena's narrative of the Hindu need to resist Muslim aggression.

10. Traditionally Muslim-dominated, the areas are sometimes referred to as a "mini" Pakistan by Hindu politicians.

11. These are traditionally Hindu-dominated areas.

12. Readers should note the Shiv Sena leader's clear differentiation between "us" (Hindus) and "them" (Muslims).

13. Clearly, "they" signifies Muslims.

CHAPTER FIVE
IN THE CRUCIBLE OF HINDUTVA:
WOMEN AND MASCULINE HINDUISM

1. I have changed the names of all the women I interviewed in the interest of privacy.

2. According to folklore, Sita was the daughter of Mother Earth. Her father, the King Janak, found her in a furrow dug in a field. Thus, in her moment of disgust with the mortal realm she returns to her mother.

3. The Samiti headquarters are considerably smaller than the RSS compound.

4. I have changed their names in the interest of privacy.

5. It might be worth mentioning that the author of the above extract was a man.

6. This monograph was written in Hindi and I translated it.

7. See chapter 4 for a discussion of the BJP/RSS/VHP's attitude towards these groups in the nation.

8. It should be emphasized that human rights activists could not find any evidence of such rape (Hammed et al., 2002, pp. 10–11).   .

CHAPTER SIX
HEROIC MOTHERS, CHASTE WIVES,
AND CELIBATE WARRIORS:
FEMINIST OR FEMININE NATIONALISM IN INDIA?

1. I realize groups excluded from nation-building because of race, ethnicity, class, or caste also will have similar ambiguities about nations and nationalism. But my story is about women. Further, despite the similarity of Woolf and Ramrati's words, differences among women (as shown by the Hindutva movement) certainly shape women's perspectives on and relationships to the nation. I am quite aware that the leading proponents of Hindutva and leaders of Indian feminism are educated, middle-class women.

2. See chapter 5.

3. For example, such fears were articulated when women participated in the French Revolution. The presence of female sexuality presumably threatened the life of the revolution and the purity of the new French nation (Tomalin, 1977, pp. 190–209).

Bibliography

Advani, L. K. 1990. Hindu Tinged Secularism. In *Expanding horizons: The BJP's first decade* (pp. 59–61). New Delhi: Bharatiya Janata Party.

———. 1995. *Presidential address*. New Delhi: Bharatiya Janata Party.

———. 1997. *Swarna Jayanti Rath Yatra: To commemorate the golden jubilee of India's independence*. New Delhi: Bharatiya Janata Party.

Afshar, H. 1987. *Women, state and ideology*. London: Macmillan.

Agarwal, P. 1995. Surat, Savarkar, and Draupadi: Legitimising rape as a political weapon. In T. Sarkar and U. Butalia (eds.), *Women and the Hindu right* (pp. 29–57). New Delhi: Kali for Women.

Aiyar, V. S. 2002. Losing faith. *India Today* (18 March): 31–39.

Alderson, D. 1998. *Mansex fine: Religion, manliness, and imperialism in nineteenth century British culture*. Manchester: Manchester University Press.

Alter, J. 1994. Celibacy, sexuality, and the transformation of gender into nationalism in north India. *Journal of Asian Studies* 53 (1): 45–63.

Anderson, B. 1991. *Imagined communities*. London: Verso.

Anderson, J. 1913. *The peoples of India*. Cambridge: Cambridge University Press.

Anderson, W., and D. S. Damle. 1987. *Brotherhood in saffron: The Rashtriya Swayam-sevak Sangh and Hindu revivalism*. New Delhi: Vishtaar Publications.

Atkinson, C. 1888. *Christian manliness: A sermon preached to the Third Lancashire artillery volunteers*. Bolton: Law Printing.

Bacchetta, P., and M. Power. 2002. Introduction. In P. Bacchetta and M. Power (eds.), *Right wing women* (pp. 1–18). New York and London: Routledge.

Bajpai, S. C., and H. C. Barthawal. 2001. *RSS at a glance*. New Delhi: Suruchi Prakashan.

Bajaj, S. 2000. Protection of women's rights. In *The power of motherhood* (pp. 64–65). New Delhi: Vishwa Hindu Parishad.

Banerjee, S. 2000. *Warriors in politics: Hindu nationalism, violence, and the Shiv Sena in India*. Boulder: Westview.

————. 2002. Civic and cultural nationalism. In A. Vanaik and P. Brass (eds.), *Competing nationalisms in South Asia* (pp. 50–84). New Delhi: Orient Longman.

Basu A. 1998. Appropriating gender. In P. Jeffrey and A. Basu (eds.), *Appropriating gender: Women's activism and politicized religion in South Asia* (pp. 3–15). New York: Routledge.

————. 1999. Women's activism and the vicissitudes of Hindu nationalism. *Journal of Women's History* 10 (4): 104–24.

Basu, S. P., and S. B. Ghosh (eds.). 1969. *Vivekananda in Indian newspapers 1893–1902*. Calcutta: Basu Bhattacharyya.

Basu, T., P. Datta, S. Sarkar, T. Sarkar, and S. Sen. 1993. *Khaki shorts and saffron flags: A critique of the Hindu right*. New Delhi: Orient Longman.

Beatson, S. 1903. *A history of the imperial service troops of the native states*. Calcutta: Office of the Superintendent of the Government Printing, India.

Bharatiya Janata Party. (n.d.). Hindutva: The great nationalist ideology. Retrieved July 23, 2002 from <http://www.bjp.org/history/htvintro-mm-1.html>.

————. (n.d.). Security. Retrieved July 23, 2002 from <http://www.bjpguj.org/manifestro/m3.html>.

————. 1991. *Towards Ramrajya. Mid term poll to Lok Sabha, May 1991: Our commitments*. New Delhi: Bharatiya Janata Party.

————. 1992. *Humanistic approach to economic development (A Swadeshi alternative)*. New Delhi: Bharatiya Janata Party.

————. 1996. *For a strong and prosperous India: Election manifesto 1996*. New Delhi: Bharatiya Janata Party.

Bhusan, R. 2002. Thy hand, great anarch. *Outlook* (18 March): 28.

Blee, K., and F. W. Twine. 2001. Introduction. Feminist antiracist maps: Transnational contours. In F. W. Twine and K. Blee (eds.), *Feminism and antiracism: International struggles for justice* (pp. 1–16). New York: New York University Press.

Blom, I., C. Hall, and K. Hagemann (eds.). 2000. *Gendered Nation: Nationalism and gendered order in the nineteenth century*. New York: New York University Press.

Bordo, S. 1989. Feminism, post-modernism, and gender skepticism. In L. Nicholson (ed.), *Feminism and postmodernism* (pp. 133–56). New York and London: Routledge.

Brookes, J. 186–?. *Manliness: Hints to young men*. London: James Blackwood.

Bruce, G. 1969. *Six battles for India: The Anglo-Sikh wars 1845–6, 1848–9*. London: Arthur Banker.

Butalia, U. 1995. Muslims and Hindus, men and women: Communal stereotypes and partition of India. In T. Sarkar and U. Butalia (eds.), *Women and the Hindu right* (pp. 58–81). New Delhi: Kali for Women.

———. 1996. Mother India. Retrieved July 23, 2002 from <http://www.newint.org/issue277/mother.html>.

———. 2001. Women and communal conflict: New challenges for the women's movement in India. In C. O. N. Moser and F. C. Clark (eds.), *The gendered dynamics of armed conflict and political violence* (pp. 99–114). New Delhi: Kali for Women.

Butler. J. 1991. *Gender trouble: Feminism and the subversion of identity.* New York: Routledge.

Caird, J. 1871. *Christian manliness: A sermon.* Glasgow: James Maclehouse.

Cama. (n.d.). Retrieved May 15, 2002 from <http://www.kamat.com/kalranga/itihas/cama.html>.

Caplan, L. 1991. "Bravest of the brave": Representations of 'The Gurkha' in British military writings." *Modern Asian Studies* 25 (3): 571–97.

Chakravarti, U. 1998. *Rewriting history: The life and times of Pandita Ramabai.* New Delhi: Kali for Women.

Chatterjee, B. C. 2002. *Anandamath.* New Delhi: Orient Paperbacks.

Chatterjee, P. 1992. History and the nationalization of Hinduism. *Social Research* 59 (1): 111–49.

———. 1999. The nationalist resolution of the women's question. In K. Sangari and S. Vaid (eds.), *Recasting women: Essays in Indian colonial history* (pp. 233–53). New Brunswick: Rutgers University Press.

Chhachhi, A. 1994. Identity politics, secularism, and women: A South Asian perspective. In Z. Hasan (ed.), *Forging identities: Gender, communities, and the state in India* (pp. 74–95). Boulder: Westview.

Chirol, V. 1910. *Indian unrest.* London: Macmillan.

Chowdhury, I. 2001. *The fragile hero and virile history: Gender and politics of culture in colonial Bengal.* New Delhi: Oxford University Press.

Cockburn, C. 2001. The gendered dynamics of armed conflict and political violence. In C. O. N. Moser and F. C. Clark (eds.), *The gendered dynamics of armed conflict and political violence* (pp. 13–29). New Delhi: Kali for Women.

Connell, R. W. 1995. *Masculinities.* Berkeley: University of California Press.

D'Monte, D. 1993. A grisly second round. In D. Padgaonkar (ed.), *When Bombay burned: Reportage and comments on the riots and blasts from the Times of India* (pp. 129–72). Mumbai: UBS.

De Alwis, M. 1998. Moral mothers and stalwart sons: Reading binaries in a time of war. In L. A. Lorentzen and J. Turpin (eds.), *The woman and war reader* (pp. 254–71). New York: New York University Press.

Derne, S. 2000. Men's sexuality and women's subordination in Indian nationalisms. In T. Mayer (ed.), *Gender ironies of nationalism: Sexing the nation* (pp. 237–60). New York: Routledge.

Diwanji, A. (n.d.). Christians cannot face Islamic anger. They consider Hindus a soft
    target. Retrieved May 14, 2002 from <http://www.vhp.org/englishsite/g.Chal-
    lenges/dConversion%20to%20Chri../rediff_interviewdr%20surrinderjain.html>.

Duff, A. 1858. *The Indian rebellion: Its causes and results*. London: James Nisbet.

———. 18—?. *India and Indian missions including sketches of the gigantic system of Hin-
    duism*. Edinburgh: John Johnstone.

Empire Annual for Boys. (n.d.). London: Boy's Own Paper Office.

Enloe, C. 1989. *Bananas, beaches, and bases: Making feminist sense of international poli-
    tics*. Berkeley: University of California Press.

———. 1998. All the men are in the militia, all the women are victims: The politics
    of masculinity and femininity in nationalist wars. In L. A. Lorentzen and J.
    Turpin (eds.), *The woman and war reader* (pp. 50–62). New York: New York Uni-
    versity Press.

———. 2000. *Maneuvers: The international politics of militarizing women's lives*. Berke-
    ley: University of California Press.

Evolution of the Indian Flag. (n.d.). Retrieved July 23, 2002 from <www.tiranga.
    net/evolution.html>.

Fane, H. E. 1862. *Five years in India*. London: Henry Colburn.

Faludi, S. 1999. *Stiffed: The betrayal of American men*. New York: William Morrow.

Faulker, D. 1994. The confidence man: Empire and the deconstruction of muscular
    Christianity in *The Mystery of Edwin Drood*. In D. Hall (ed.), *Muscular Christian-
    ity: Embodying the Victorian Age* (pp. 175–93). Cambridge: Cambridge University
    Press.

Gallucci, C. C. 2002. She loved Mussolini: Margherita Sarfatti and Italian Facism. In
    P. Bacchetta and M. Power (eds.), *Right wing women* (pp. 19–28). New York and
    London: Routledge.

Gardiner, J. K. (ed.). 2002. *Masculinity studies and feminist theory*. New York: Colum-
    bia University Press.

Gautier, F. (n.d.). Import of the bomb blasts. Retrieved July 23, 2002 from
    <http://www.vhp.org/englishsite/e.Special_Movements/dRanjanambhumi%20M
    uti/ayodhyaafterdec6.html>.

———. (n.d.). Indian Muslims: Babar or Ram. Retrieved July 23, 2002 from
    <http://www.vhp.org/englishsite/e.Special_Movements/dRanjanambhumi%20M
    uti/fg_indian_muslims__babar_or_ram_fg_.html>.

———. (n.d.). When war becomes Dharma. Retrieved July 23, 2002 from <http:
    //www.vhp.org/englishsite/hbharat/fg_when_war_becomes_dharma.html>.

———. (n.d.). Where is our Shivaji? Retrieved July 23, 2002 from <http://www.vhp.
    org/englishsite/hbharat/fg_where_is_our_shivaji.html>.

Gibbon, F. 1909. *The disputed V. C.: A tale of the Indian mutiny*. London: Blackie and
    Son.

Gilmore, D. D. 1990. *Manhood in the making*. New Haven: Yale University Press.

Giri, A. 2000. The glory of *pativrata* women. In *The power of motherhood* (pp. 31–33). New Delhi: Vishwa Hindu Parishad.

Giri, N. 2000a. Mothers are divine. In *The power of motherhood* (pp. 24–26). New Delhi: Vishwa Hindu Parishad.

Golwalker, M. S. 1981. *Bunch of thoughts*. Bangalore: Jagarana Prakashan.

———. 2000. *Bunch of thoughts*. Bangalore: Sahitya Sindhu Prakashana.

Gould, S. J. 1981. *The mismeasure of man*. New York: Norton.

Green, M. 1979. *Dreams of adventure, deeds of empire*. New York: Basic Books.

Greenberger, A. J. 1969. *The British image of India*. London: Oxford University Press.

Greenfeld, L. 1992. *Nationalism: Five roads to modernity*. Cambridge: Harvard University Press.

Grewal, I. 1996. *Home and harem: Nation, gender, empire, and the cultures of travel*. Durham: Duke University Press.

Grover, V. 1990. *Political thinkers of modern India: V. D. Savarkar*. New Delhi: Deep and Deep.

Gupta, C. 2001. *Sexuality, obscenity, community: Women, Muslims, and the Hindu public in colonial India*. New Delhi: Permanent Black.

Gupta, D. 1982. *Nativism in a metropolis: The Shiv Sena in Bombay*. New Delhi: Manohar.

Gupta, K. 1995. What is Bharatiyata? The concept of Hindu nationalism. In *Yugantar: A new era* (pp. 82–85). New Delhi: Bharatiya Janata Party.

Hall, D. 1994. Muscular Christianity: reading and writing the male social body. In D. Hall (ed.), *Muscular Christianity: Embodying the Victorian age* (pp. 3–16). Cambridge: Cambridge University Press.

Hameed, S., R. Manorama, M. Ghose, S. George, F. Naqvi, and M. Thekaekara. 2002. *How has the Gujarat massacre affected minority women? The survivors speak*. Ahmedabad, India: Citizen's Initiative.

Harraway, D. 1989. A manifesto for cyborgs: Science, technology, and socialist feminism in the 1980s. In L. J. Nicholson (ed.), *Feminism and postmodernism* (pp. 90–133). New York and London: Routledge.

Henty, G. A. 1894. *Through the Sikh war: A tale of the conquest of the Punjaub*. London: Blackie and Son.

———. 1896. *With Clive in India or the beginnings of an empire*. Glasgow: Blackie and Son.

———. 1902. *At the point of the bayonet: A tale of the Mahratta war*. London: Blackie and Son.

hooks, bell. 1981. *Ain't I a woman: Black women and feminism*. Boston: South End.

Hooper, C. 2001. *Manly states: Masculinities, international relations, and gender relations*. New York: Columbia University Press.

Hughes, T. 1879. *The manliness of Christ*. London: Macmillan.

Idate, D. 1997. *Global Hindutva in 21st century and Rashtriya Swayasevak Sangh*. Mumbai: Hindu Vivek Kendra.

Ignatieff, M. 1994. *Blood and belonging: Journeys into the new nationalism*. Toronto: Penguin.

Inden, R. 1990. *Imagining India*. London: Basil Blackwell.

Jackson, D. 1940. *India's army*. London: Sampson, Low, and Marston.

Jha, P. S. 2002. Soft saffron's litmus test. *Outlook* (11 March): 21.

Joshi, M. M. 1991. *Presidential address*. New Delhi: Bharatiya Janata Party.

———. 1996. Pamphlet. Interview with reporter from *The Afternoon Despatch and Courier*. Mumbai.

Jyotirmayananda (ed.). 1992. *Vivekananda: His gospel of man-making with a garland of tributes and a chronicle of his life and times with pictures*. Madras.

Kaifee, P. 2002. "200+ on the human Richter. *Outlook* (11 March): 22–28.

Kakar, S. 1978. *The inner world: A psycho-analytic study of childhood and society in India*. New Delhi: Oxford University Press.

———. 1995. *The colours of violence*. New Delhi: Viking.

Kamath, M. V. 1990. The importance of being Hindu. In *Expanding horizons: The BJP's first decade* (pp. 35–38). New Delhi: Bharatiya Janata Party.

Kamlesh Bharati. 2000. Sadhvi Shakti Parishad: An introduction. In *The power of motherhood* (pp. 11–13). New Delhi: Vishwa Hindu Parishad.

Kanungo, P. 2002. *RSS's tryst with politics: From Hedgewar to Sudarshan*. New Delhi: Manohar.

Kapur, A. 1993. Deity to Crusader: The changing iconography of Ram. In G. Pandey (ed.), *Hindus and others: The question of identity in India* (pp. 74–109). New Delhi: Oxford University Press.

Kapur, R., and B. Cossman. 1995. Communalising gender, engendering community: Women, legal discourse, and the saffron agenda. In T. Sarkar and U. Butalia (eds.), *Women and the Hindu Right* (pp. 82–120). New Delhi: Kali for Women.

Katzenstein, M. 1979. *Ethnicity and equality: The Shiv Sena and preferential policies in Bombay*. Ithaca: Cornell University Press.

Khanna, S. 2000. The oppression of women and some ways to resist. In *The power of motherhood* (pp. 66–72). New Delhi: Vishwa Hindu Parishad.

Kirk, G. 1989. Our Greenham Common: Not just a place but a movement. In A. Harris and Y. King (eds.), *Rocking the ship of state* (pp. 239–62). Boulder: Westview.

Kishwar, M. 1993. Safety is indivisible: The warning from the Bombay riots. *Manushi* 74–75: 2–8, 24–49.

———. 1997. The continuing popularity of Sita in India. *Manushi* 98: 20–32.

Kohli, A. 1991. *Democracy and discontent: India's growing crisis of governability*. Cambridge: Cambridge University Press.

Kumar, R. 1993. *The history of doing: An illustrated account of the movements for women's rights and feminism in India, 1800–1990*. New York and London: Verso.

Lake, M. 1992. Mission impossible: How men gave birth to the Australian nation— nationalism, gender, and other seminal acts. *Gender and History* 2: 304–21.

Lawrence, H. 1859. *Essays, military and political written in India*. London: William H. Allen.

Lord, J. (ed.). 1931. *Macaulay's essays on Lord Clive and Warren Hastings*. London: Ginn.

McClintock, A. 1993. Family feuds: Gender, nationalism and the family. *Feminist Review* 44: 61–80.

———. 1995. *Imperial leather: Race, gender, and sexuality in the colonial context*. New York: Routledge.

McClintock, A., A. Mufti, and E. Shohat (eds.). 1997. *Dangerous liaisons: Gender, nation, and postcolonial perspectives*. Minneapolis: University of Minnesota Press.

McDevitt, P. F. Muscular Catholicism: Nationalism, masculinity, and Gaelic team sports, 1884–1916. *Gender and History* 9: 262–84.

McDonald, I. 1999. 'Physiological patriots'? The politics of physical culture and Hindu nationalism in India. *International Review for the Sociology of Sport* 34 (4): 343–58.

MacDonald, R. H. 1993. *The frontier and the Boy Scout movement, 1890–1918*. Toronto: University of Toronto Press.

MacMunn, G. 1933. *The martial races of India*. London: Sampson, Low, Marston.

Macaulay, T. B. 1878. *Lord Macaulay and higher education in India: Being an address delivered at the Thirty-fifth Hare anniversary*. Calcutta: Stanhope.

Madan, T. N. 1993. Whither Indian Secularism. *Modern Asian Studies* 27: 667–97.

Mahurkar, U. 2002. Sins of Modi. *India Today* (18 March): 31–39.

Majumdar, R. C. 1963. Swami Vivekananda and man-making education. In R.C. Majumdar (ed.), *Swami Vivekananda centenary memorial volume* (pp. 488–504). Calcutta: Swami Vivekananda Centenary.

Malik, Y., and V. B. Singh. 1994. *Hindu nationalists in India: The rise of the BJP*. Boulder: Westview.

Mankekar, P. 2000. *Screening culture, viewing politics: Television, womanhood and nation in modern India*. New Delhi: Oxford University Press.

Massad, J. 1995. Conceiving the masculine: Gender and Palestinian nationalism. *Middle East Journal* 49 (3): 467–83.

Mayer, T. 2000. Gender ironies of nationalism: Setting the stage. In T. Mayer (ed.), *Gender ironies of nationalism: Sexing the nation* (pp. 1–24). New York: Routledge.

———. 2000a. From zero to hero: Masculinity in Jewish nationalism. In T. Mayer (ed.), *Gender ironies of nationalism: Sexing the Nation* (pp. 283–308). New York: Routledge.

Menon, K. 2001. Herstory. Symbolic power of Jijabai: Folklore of Hindu nationalist women in India. *Manushi* 109: 25–37.

Menon, N. 1999. Introduction. In N. Menon (ed.), *Gender and politics in India* (pp. 1–35). New Delhi: Oxford University Press.

Merrill, H. 2001. Making space for antiracist feminism in northern Italy. In F. W. Twine and K. Blee (eds.), *Feminism and antiracism: International struggles for justice* (pp. 17–37). New York: New York University Press.

Mohanty, C. 1991. Under western eyes: Feminist scholarship and colonial discourses. In C. Mohanty, A. Russo, and L. Torres (eds.), *Third world women and the politics of feminism* (pp. 51–77). Bloomington: Indiana University Press.

Morgan, R. 1970. *Sisterhood is global: An anthology of writings from the women's liberation movement.* New York: Random House.

Morison, T. 1899. *Imperial rule in India.* London: Archibald Constable.

Mosse, G. L. 1996. *The image of man: The creation of modern masculinity.* New York: Oxford University Press.

Mukherji, S. 1971. *The philosophy of man-making: A study in social and political ideas of Swami Vivekananda.* Calcutta: New Central Book Agency.

Nagel, J. 1998. Masculinity and nationalism: Gender and sexuality in the making of nations. *Ethnic and Racial Studies* 21 (2): 243–69.

Nayak, R. 1993. Pamphlet. From Somnath to Ayodhya: 45 Years of Insult to 75 Crore Hindus to Appease 8 Crore Muslim Vote-Bank by Psuedo-Secularists. Mumbai: Bharatiya Janata Party.

Neogi, C. 2000. "Sister Nivedita and the politics of gendered nationalism. In B. Ray (ed.), *Women and politics: France, India and Russia* (pp. 134–45). Calcutta: K. P. Bagchi.

Nivedita. 1960. *Aggressive Hinduism.* Madras, India: Natesan.

Pandey, G. 1993. *The construction of communalism in colonial north India.* New Delhi: Oxford University Press.

Patange, R. (n.d.). Pamphlet. *Manu, Sangh, and I.* Mumbai.

Peterson, V. S. 1998. Gendered nationalism: Reproducing "us" versus "them." In L. A. Lorentzen and J. Turpin (eds.), *The woman and war reader* (pp. 41–49). New York: New York University Press.

Pettgrew, J. 1996. "'The soldier's faith': Turn-of-the-century memory of the civil war and the emergence of modern American nationalism. *Journal of Contemporary History* 31 (1): 49–74.

Phillips, R. 1997. *Mapping men and empire.* London and New York: Routledge.

Pierson, R. R. 2000. Nations: Gendered, racialized, crossed with empire. In I. Blom, C. Hall, and K. Hagemann (eds.), *Gendered nation: Nationalism and gendered order in the nineteenth century* (pp. 41–61). New York: New York University Press.

Purandare, V. 1999. *The Sena story.* Mumbai, India: Business Publication.

Puri, J. 1999. *Woman, body, desire in post-colonial India*. New York: Routledge.

Rahbar, H. 1995. *Vivekananda: The warrior saint*. New Delhi: Farsight.

Rai, L. 1967. *A history of the Arya Samaj: An account of its origins, doctrines, and activities with a biographical sketch of its founder*. New Delhi: Orient Longman.

Rai, R. 1996. *Life sketch of vandaniya mausiji: Founder and chief of Rastra Sevika Samiti*. Nagpur: Sevika Prakashan.

Rashtriya Sevika Samiti. (n.d.). *Empowerment pragmatic*. Nagpur, India: Sevika Prakashan.

———. (n.d.). *Happy world through the Bharateeya family*. Hyderabad, India: Sevika Prakashan.

Rashtriya Swayamsevak Sangh. 2000. *Awakening among women and RSS*. New Delhi: Suruchi Prakashan.

———. 2000. *Hinduttva: A view and a way of life*. New Delhi: Suruchi Prakashan.

Ray, B. 1995. The freedom movement and feminist consciousness in Bengal 1905–1929. In B. Ray (ed.), *From the seams of history: Essays on Indian women* (pp. 174–218). New Delhi: Oxford University Press.

Religious Tract Society. 1866. *Christian manliness: A book of examples and principles for young men*. London: Religious Tract Society.

Risley, H. 1969. *The peoples of India*. New Delhi: Oriental Books.

Roper, M., and J. Tosh. 1991. *Manful assertions: Masculinities in Britain since 1800*. New York: Routledge.

Roy, P. 1998. *Indian traffic: Identities in question in colonial and post-colonial India*. Berkeley: University of California Press.

Ruddick, S. 1995. *Maternal thinking: Towards a politics of peace*. Boston: Beacon Press.

Rutherford, J. 1997. *Forever England: Reflections on race, masculinity, and empire*. London: Lawrence and Wishart.

Ryder, J. 1853. *Four years service in India*. Leicester, U.K.: W. H. Burton.

Said, E. 1978. *Orientalism*. New York: Pantheon.

Sangari, K., and S. Vaid (eds.). 1989. *Recasting women: Essays in Indian nationalist history*. New Delhi: Kali for Women.

Sarkar, T. 1995. Heroic women, mother goddesses: Family and organisation in Hindutva politics. In T. Sarkar and U. Butalia (eds.), *Women and the Hindu right* (pp. 181–215). New Delhi: Kali for Women.

Savarkar, V. D. 1942. *Hindu-Pad-Padashahi or a review of the Hindu empire of Maharashtra*. Pune, India: Manohar Granth Mala.

———. 1949. *Hindu Rashtra Darshan: A collection of speeches delivered from the Hindu Mahasabha platform*. Mumbai, India: Laxman Ganesh Khare.

———. 1949a. *Who is a Hindu: Hindutva*. Pune, India: S. P. P. Gokhale.

———. 1960. *The Indian war of independence*. Mumbai, India: Dhanvale Prakashan.

———. 1985. *Epochs of Indian history*. Mumbai, India: Savarkar Prakashan.

Seshadri, H. V. 2000. *RSS: A vision in action*. Bangalore, India: Sahitya Sindhu.

Sharma, M. 2000. Contemporary women's problems and their solutions. In *The Power of Motherhood* (pp. 61–63). New Delhi: Vishwa Hindu Parishad.

Sil, N. 1997. *Swami Vivekananda: A reassessment*. London and Mississauga, Ont.: Associated University Press.

Sinha, M. 1995. *Colonial masculinity: The 'manly Englishman' and the 'effeminate' Bengali in the late nineteenth century*. Manchester, U.K., and New York: Manchester University Press.

———. (ed.). 2000. Katherine Mayo's *Mother India*. Ann Arbor: University of Michigan Press.

Smiles, S. 1879. *Self-Help*. London: John Murray.

Snyder, C. R. 1999. *Citizen-soldiers and manly warriors*. London: Rowman and Littlefield.

Sofos, S. 1996. Inter-ethnic violence and gendered constructions of ethnicity in former Yugoslavia. *Social Identities* 2 (1): 73–91.

Srivastava, S. 1998. *Constructing post-colonial India: National character and the Doon school*. London and New York: Routledge.

Strachey, J. 1888. *India*. London: Kegan Paul, Trench.

Tharu, S., and T. Niranjana. 1999. Problems for a contemporary theory on gender. In N. Menon (ed.), *Gender and politics in India* (pp. 494–525). New Delhi: Oxford University Press.

Talbot, I. 2001. *India and Pakistan*. London: Arnold.

Thorn, W. 1818. *Memoir of the war in India*. London: T.E. Egerton.

Tickner, A. J. 1992. *Gender in international relations: Feminist perspectives on achieving global security*. New York: Columbia University Press.

Tomalin, C. 1977. *The life and death of Mary Wollstonecraft*. Middlesex, U.K.: Pelican Books.

Tone, W. H. 1818. *Illustrations of some institutions of the Mahratta people*. Calcutta: D Lankheet Times Press.

Vanaik, A., and P. R. Brass. 2002. Introduction. In A. Vanaik and P. R. Brass (eds.), *Competing nationalisms in South Asia* (pp. 1–20). New Delhi: Orient Longman.

Vance, N. 1985. *The sinews of the spirit: The ideal of Christian manliness in Victorian literature and religious thought*. Cambridge: Cambridge University Press.

Varshney, A. 1993. Contested meanings: India's national identity, Hindu nationalism, and the politics of anxiety. *Daedalus* 122: 227–61.

Vedic, V. 2000. The Vedic female ascetics. In *The power of motherhood* (pp. 18–23) New Delhi: Vishwa Hindu Parishad.

Vishwa Hindu Parishad. (n.d.). Aims and objects of Vishva Hindu Parishad. Retrieved May 14, 2002 from <http://www.vhp.org/englishsite/b-objectives/aim_object.html>.

———. (n.d.). Dimensions of VHP. Retrieved July 23, 2002 from <http://www.vhp.org/englishsite/d.Dimensions_of_VHP/myouth-wing/bajrand-dalsjain.html>.

———. (n.d.). Unifying Heritage. Retrieved July 23, 2002 from <http://www.vhp.org/englishsite/e.Special_Movements/dRanjanambhumi%20Muti/ayodhyaafter-dec6.html>.

Vishwanathan, K. 1997. Shame and control: Sexuality and power in feminist discourse in India. In M. Thapan (ed.), *Embodiment: Essays on gender and sexuality* (pp. 313–33). New Delhi: Oxford University Press.

Vivekananada. 1963. *To the youth of India*. Calcutta: Advaita Ashram.

———. 2000. *Our women*. Calcutta: Advaita Ashram.

Waring, E. S. 1810. *A history of the Mahrattas*. London: John Richardson.

Wee, C. J. W-L. 1994. Christian manliness and national identity: The problematic construction of a racially "pure" nation. In D. Hall (ed.), *Muscular Christianity: Embodying the Victorian Age* (pp. 66–90). Cambridge: Cambridge University Press.

West, L. 1997. Introduction: Feminism constructs nationalism. In L. West (ed.), *Feminist nationalism* (pp. xi–xxxvi). New York: Routledge.

Wilks, M. 1930 and 1932. *Historical sketches of the south of India*. Mysore, India: Government Branch Press.

Winter, B. 2002. Pauline and other perils: Women in Australian right wing politics. In P. Bacchetta and M. Power (eds.), *Right Wing Women* (pp. 197–210). New York and London: Routledge.

Wuhrgraft, L. D. 1983. *The imperial imagination*. Middletown, Conn.: Wesleyan University Press.

Yadav, B. R., and S. R. Bakshi. 1991. *Madam Bhikaji Cama*. New Delhi: Anmol Publications.

Yuval-Davis, N., and F. Anthias (eds.). 1989. *Woman-Nation-State*. London: Macmillan.

Index